The Experts on Mike Massey

Billiard Publications

"If you've ever hankered to try a trick shot for your own amusement, if you want to become a professional trick shot entertainer or belong anywhere in between, I couldn't recommend a book more highly that this one."
Tom Shaw – Pool & Billiard Magazine

"If you enjoy reading interesting stories about pool around the world, if you want to improve your pool game by improving the quality and quantity of your stroke, then get this book."
Mark Whiteside – Professor Q Ball

"Mike Massey's World of Trick Shots is a wonderfully entertaining, well-written manual that takes prospective trick shot artists under its wing and befriends them. It is beautifully easy to read and impossible to put down. For anyone who is attracted to the artistry of trick shots and how to master them, this book is for you."
Sally P. Timko – InsidePOOL Magazine

"Mike Massey has teamed up with prolific billiard author Phil Capelle to bring you everything you ever wanted to know about trick shots."
Sheri Richardson – Chalk & Cue Magazine

"Mike and Phil's latest effort is a real treat for trick shot enthusiasts."
John Cash – National Billiard News

"The looks of wide-eyed astonishment on my kid's faces as I performed the trick shots in the book conveyed to me that this book is indeed something extraordinary!"
John Evans – On the Wire

Champion Players & Trick Shot Artists

"Mike is definitely the best showman on the table."
Johnny Archer – 1990's Player of the Decade

"Mike is simply the best at what he does."
Allison Fisher – 4 time WPA World 9-Ball Champion

"I have seen Mike Massey doing his shows many times in Europe. He is the Efren Reyes of trick shot billiards."
Thorsten Hohman – 2003 World 9-Ball Champion

"I've seen Mike's show over 50 times and I always look forward to his next performance."
Gerda Hofstatter – WPA World 9-Ball Champion

"Without a doubt the greatest that I've ever seen."
Tony Robles – World Class 9-Ball Player

"When I was 18 I walked into a bar in Mobile, Alabama and there stood Mike Massey 10 feet from a bar table running and breaking one-handed. I sat and watched for a couple of hours at this man breaking and running out one handed. Then I quietly got up and left. I didn't want to see Massey shoot with two hands."

Mike and I have traveled together performing exhibitions in China, Europe, and America. He is undisputedly the greatest trick shot exhibition player of all times plus a really nice guy. He is my trick shot mentor."
Earl Strickland – 5 Times U.S Open Champion – 3 Times World 9-Ball Champion

"The first time I saw Mike Massey's show 20 something years ago I thought to myself, 'I can do all of those shots'. Now that I'm competing against him, I'm thinking 'How the hell did he do that'."
Charlie Darling – 2001 World Artistic Pool Championships

"A pool champion, teacher and statesman for the betterment of the sport for the ages. Mike Massey's new book is a must on anyone's reading list."
Dick Lane – World Class Straight Pool Player

"It stretches out the jaws to a new limit."
Neils Feijen – Runner-up, 2001 Tokyo 9-Ball

"The best stroke in the business belongs to Mike Massey. He is pool's finest statesman and showman."
Grady "The Professor" Mathews – Top All Round Player & Promoter

"For as long as I can remember, the name Mike Massey has been synonymous with trick shots. His shows are worth going out of your way for. I enjoy myself and learn something new every time."
Andy Segal – Runner-up, 2003 Trick Shot Magic

"The best player and showman in the history of pool."
Sebastian Giumelli –Twice 3rd - World Artistic Pool Championships

"Mike's book represents for any poolplayer such an irreplaceable source of knowledge. He's the only champion I can always learn something from. My wish is to see him inducted into the BCA Hall of Fame soon because he immensely deserves it for all of his accomplishments and his life long dedication to the sport."
Stefano Pelinga – 2nd Place - 2003 World Artistic Pool Championships

"Mike has been the premiere trick and fancy shot artist for as long as I can remember. His impact is felt in poolrooms all over the country every day."
Belinda Campos – WPBA Touring Professional

"Some of these shots alone are worth the price of the book and here you can find over a hundred of them."
Ralf Eckert – First Official EPBF Instructor & #1 European 9-Ball 2000

Industry Experts

"In addition to being a wonderful human being, Mike is so skilled that he rarely needs a second chance to make his most difficult trick shots."
Pat Fleming – Accu-Stats Video Productions

"Mike Massey on trick shots! I've been waiting years for this book."
Robert Byrne – Author of *Byrne's Complete Book of Pool Shots*

"Mike Massey is the world's master of trick shots, and performs magic on the green felt"
Matt & Bettiane Braun – Producer of Pool Events for ESPN

"Once in a lifetime a man comes around who is so special, we all sit and watch in awe. Mike Massey is the epitome of what every great trick shot artist aspires to be."
Chef Anton - 2-Time United States Trick Shot Champion

"Mike Massey is the best showman in the billiard business today. His talent and expertise is not even close to being equaled by anyone else."
Mike Zuglan – Joss Northeast 9-Ball Tour

"I've watched Mike perform exhibitions many times over the years and I never tire of his mastery of artistic pool and his ability to entertain. Teaming up with Phil Capelle makes *Mike Massey's World of Trick Shots* an instant classic. This book should be in every billiard library."
J.R. Calvert – Publisher, InsidePOOL Magazine

"Mike Massey is the most talented performer of his time. He has given more back to the game of pool than anyone else we know. He is also a great friend."
Bruce & Ann Barthelette – Second Largest APA League Operator

"How could you go wrong with a dream team like this. One of pool's best writers and one of the most talented trick and fancy shot artists of all time."
Martyne S. (Sue) Bachmen – Co-Author – *Blue Book of Cues*, 3rd Edition

"Mike Massey can do shots no other player attempts. An amazing player."
Bob Jewett – BCA Certified Instructor

"Mike Massey has the world's most powerful stroke, is a great entertainer and is extremely personable, making this book a 'have to read' in your billiard library."
Mark Kulungian – Pool Table Magic

"Today I run a ministry called Gospel Trick Shot Ministries Inc. and I can truly say that God used Mike to influence me to play the game of pool and share my faith."
Steve Lillis – Gospel Trick Shot Ministries

Mike Massey's
World of Trick Shots

Mike Massey
Philip Capelle

Illustrated by Dave Burton

First Edition
Billiards Press, Huntington Beach, CA

Mike Massey's
World of Trick Shots
By Mike Massey and Phil Capelle

Published by:
Billiards Press
P.O. Box 400
Midway City, CA 92655

Fifth Printing

Printed in the United Stated of America

10 9 8 7 6 5

ISBN   978-0-9649204-6-0

Library of Congress Catalog Card Number: 2003097808

Cover Photo by Phelston Jones
Cover Graphics by Janet Beal

Dedication

I dedicate this book to my wife Francine and Jesse Cue, our dog who passed away just before this book was finished.

Almost 18 years ago I was teaching pool at Buddie's Billiards in Jackson, Mississippi when Francine came in for a lesson. About three months later we were married by a minister who was a regular at the poolroom. I'm sure Francine didn't know what she was in for when we got married, but now she realizes that a poolplayer's life is a lot different than that of a person who works at a normal job.

They say love conquers all and we're definitely a testament to that. Our backgrounds are probably about as opposite as they could be, but although we're different, in a lot of ways were also a lot alike. The most important thing is we both love people and animals and have a deep love for each other. Francine has stuck with me when times were tough and gave me a lot of encouragement and support. Without her there is no telling where I would be or what shape I would be in. My nine world championship titles are just as much hers as they are mine. I couldn't have won them without her.

Jesse Cue has been with us since she was about six weeks old and has been like a child to us. We both have children from separate marriages, but they are grown up and haven't lived with us since we were married. Jesse Cue, who loved doing the Jesse Cue Shot, became quite popular all over the world. Anytime we showed up without her, the first thing people would ask is, "Where is Jesse Cue, are you doing her shot?" We will still be doing her shot with Xena or Star, but it will always be called the Jesse Cue Shot.

Acknowledgements

Mike Massey

I have been fortunate to have so many people come into my life who have meant so much to me in my life and career. Below is a list of family, friends and people in the world of billiards that I want to thank for their contributions to my life. I sincerely apologize to those who I may have overlooked.

Phil Capelle has become a part of our family. We love and respect him and this book would not have been possible without him. My son David and daughter Anna. Larry and Sheila Massey, Jack and Violet Massey, Granny, Wade and Melaine Hennessey, Graeme and Jenny Hennessey, Laura Lee Chmielewski, Rick and Carmen Rogers, Tom and Max Costello, Danny Scot, Bill Staton, Jimmy Caras, Jurgen Sandman, Hans Peter Schild, Jacob and Manfred Larch, Robert Helmand, Nick and Marsha Bell, Stan Haines, Tom and Dan Birkbeck and Family, Denny and Karen Lambo, Chet and Sarah Ito, Chuck Margolis, Herb Wilmott, Jim Chapman, David Wilson, Jody Hall, Billy Johnson and family, Phil Windham and Family, Bob and Linda Graves, Jay Thurman, Graham Earl, Wimpy Henry and Family, Dick Rule, Bruce and Ann Barthelette, Terry and Val Justice, Matt and Bettiane Braun, Bob Grudzinski, Gene Barkland, Doug and Becky Price, Merl and Boomer Humphreys, Paul Potier, Allison Fisher, Gerda Hofstatter, Alan and Dawn Hopkins, Dewey Boyd, Dave Burton, The Sardo Family, Martin Bachman, Renee Poehlman, Barry Hearn, Sharon Tokley, Steve Lillis, Rick and Judy Malm and all of the artistic pool players. I would also like to acknowledge all of the good old boys in Loudon and Lenoir City that I grew up playing with and that helped me become the player that I am.

Phil Capelle

It was a pleasure to work on this book with Mike and Francine Massey. We talked on the phone at least a hundred times and sent many packages to and fro. I especially enjoyed our time together at Danny K's, Pioneer Town, and in Las Vegas. We all got along amazingly well despite the heavy workload and impending deadline.

It was a real treat to work on this book with Janet Beal. Janet was responsible for the layout, graphics, advertisements and many other duties too numerous too mention. Janet proved to be a tireless worker. She handled all aspects of the production of the book in a highly professional manner, all the while maintaining her enthusiasm and cheerful disposition.

While in Las Vegas, Mike and I were lucky enough to receive a recommendation for a photographer. We spent an afternoon with Phelston Jones and his family at his studio. Phelston took the awesome photos that grace the front and back covers of the book.

Dave Burton is the man responsible for the capturing Mike at his best. His superb artwork appears throughout the book. Dave was incredibly cooperative and fast at getting his drawings finished and to us on a timely basis.

Mark Whiteside spent many hours next to Janet at the computer pouring over the diagrams and text. His many suggestions for improving the book and his work proof reading helped to improve the quality of the book.

Thanks also to Karen Beal who proofread the text and contributed to it's accuracy.

Forward by Rick Rogers

When I was working as an actor in Hollywood in the 1960s I went to see *The Hustler* starring Paul Newman and Jackie Gleason. That movie changed my life. It was an epiphany. I was so taken by the film that I watched it not once, but three times in one day. I was doing a lot of work at that time in 1960s shows like *Lawman, Cheyenne, Shannon, The Racers, Sugarfoot,* and others. When I wasn't working I was out aggressively seeking work which, in some ways, is harder than the actual work.

I would go to the pool hall every chance I had. I sent away for a Paradise Cue and a short time later I had my first cue. About 1962 or 1963 I saw a young, good looking Hispanic guy playing with the best looking cue I had ever seen. I asked him about the cue and he said he made it. I asked him if he would make me one and agreed to. That was my introduction to Ernie Gutierrez and Ginacue. To this day Ernie and I are friends and he is now a legendary cue maker.

Then I got the role of "Doc" in *Combat* and eased away from the game of pool for about 20 years. About 1980 I took up the game again. I played a respectable game of pool, but nothing to write home about. I did, however, start collecting cues again. My collection now numbers over 100, and I'm definitely a better collector than a player. This forward, however, isn't about me or my cue collection. It's about pool and how I met Mike Massey.

Seventeen years after I resumed playing, I saw an advertisement in *Pool & Billiard Magazine* for "Pool School in Paradise." The instructors were Allison Fisher, Gerda Hofstatter, Paul Potier, and Mike Massey – all players for whom I have a high regard. I knew I needed help; boy did I ever need help! So I signed up for class. On the first day this great big guy who looked like a cross between Davy Crockett and Daniel Boone challenged me to a race to five games in 9-Ball. Mike ran those racks so fast and effortlessly that it made my head spin. I really love to watch Mike play. He has one of the best pure strokes in pool. It's like watching a great surgeon without all of the blood. That first day at the school in the late 1990s we became good friends.

I've watched Mike compete in Las Vegas and at Hard Times in the Los Angeles area and have come to the conclusion that no one else can do the things with a cue ball that Mike can do – and with such consistency. There are a lot of very good artistic poolplayers, but Mike is indisputably the best in the world. I have been to a lot of seniors tournaments and through Mike have met a lot of great players whom I admire. Mike can play competitively with all of them. But how many of them can sing and write songs, play the guitar, write movie scripts, act in films and TV, play snooker, 3-cushion billiards pyramids (a Russian game) and artistic pool all really well? Maybe some, but at best, less than a handful.

I am truly honored to write this forward and to claim Mike as a true friend. I know a lot of talented people, coming from a show business background, and I can tell you Mike can hold his own with any of them, actors or poolplayers. He is the "Goodwill Ambassador of Pool" with a beautiful talent. And this book, a collaboration with Phil Capelle, the foremost writer of books on pool, is further proof of that talent. So enjoy the book.

Rick Rogers
September, 2003

Introduction

I have been traveling the world for almost 30 years giving clinics, competing in tournaments and entertaining audiences with the shots you will be studying in this book. During that time I've traveled over three million miles and visited over 35 countries. While I naturally love to make trick shots in front of a crowd, I also have seen the numerous expressions of glee from members of my audiences who have made them before friends and strangers. I know from personal experience how much joy these shots have provided to people of all nationalities.

I can't be everywhere at once playing these shots, so some time ago I got the idea that it would be neat to do a book on trick shots. This would enable people to shoot the shots I do anytime, any place where there is a pool table. I wanted to do a book that would teach aspiring trick shot artists everything they would need to know to make the shots. I have always felt that most people who apply themselves can master at least a fair percentage of the shots I shoot regularly. I also wanted a book that would teach readers how to put together a show their friends would truly enjoy.

Writing a book on trick shots was one of those things on my wish list that I'd never seemed able to get around to. My busy schedule traveling, giving exhibitions, and competing always seemed to get in the way. Then one day in October, 2001 I was practicing for *Trick Shot Magic* at Ace Billiards in Sunset City, which is near Salt Lake City, Utah. Phil Capelle had called Gerry Dickson, the owner of Ace Billiards, about placing an order for some of his books. Gerry was busy with a customer, so he asked Phil, "Would you like to talk to Mike Massey." Phil said, "Yes, of course."

During the course of our conversation the seeds were planted for this book. A couple of months later Francine and I were at Danny K's near Phil's home in Orange County, California. We met Phil for dinner in the lounge. At this point I still wasn't sure if he was the person I wanted to work with on this book. But Phil had brought me a copy of his *Play Your Best Nine Ball*. As I paged through the book, I became convinced that his work was of the highest quality. In fact, I read the book shortly thereafter on the plane to Japan and it inspired me to finish in a tie for 17th in a field of over 700 players in pool's richest tournament ever.

We began work in earnest at Danny K's in February 2002 with a three-day session going over about 40 shots for the book. We signed a formal agreement in May 2002 at Katy's Coffee Shop at the Riviera Hotel at the 2002 BCA Championships. Since then we have been in constant contact working to complete the book. It's been a real pleasure to work with Phil, and I know he likewise has enjoyed working with me to create this book.

Where Shots Come From

This is primarily an instructional book on trick shots. I have for the most part, chosen not to emphasize the history of these shots. Some of the shots in this book date back more than a hundred years. Tracing their origins and giving proper credit to the creator of those and other shots in the book would present a daunting research project. Even after an exhaustive search for the creators of these shots, it is possible that I could come up empty. Worse yet, I might give credit to the wrong person.

I have chosen to give credit to those who I know with reasonable surety have invented the shot. On other shots I have given credit to the first person who I saw perform the shot. It is quite possible they learned it from someone else who may have in turn been showed it by another player and so on.

On a majority of the shots in the book no person's name has been associated with the shot. Those were created by Mr. Anonymous or someone whose name may appear in another book on the history of pool or on trick shots. I want to express my sincere apologies to anyone who may feel the least bit slighted who feels that they are the creator of a shot.

The question of who is the creator has at least been solved on about 25% of the shots in the book because 44 of them are my creations.

How to Use the Book

I'm sure you are anxious to dive right into my collection of shots. Before you begin, I strongly advise that you take a few moments to read the sections that follow. They will teach you how to read the diagrams. You will learn what the abbreviations stand for and what the graphics mean. In the sections that follow are detailed explanations of throw, kicking, tangent lines and other assorted topics that will further your understanding of the shots in the book.

Once this assignment is complete, feel free to roam through the table of contents and the book. Pick out any shot or groups of shots that interest you and give it (them) a try. I hope that you will read the introduction to each chapter, but it is not mandatory in order to learn the shots in that chapter. Besides, you won't want to miss Dave Burton's art work that graces the first page of each chapter. I advise that you take the book to the table. Study each shot carefully. Then set up and execute the shots. Pay attention to your successes and learn from your failures.

In the Appendix you will find an extensive glossary of terms used throughout the book. So if you come across a word you are not sure of, you will likely find the definition in the glossary.

Chapters 1-16 - Selection for the Shots

The cost of printing books and common sense dictates that each shot be placed in only one chapter, although many of the shots in this book could easily be assigned to one or more additional chapters. Chapter 1, Hustler's Specials is a mere 15 shots. But you could theoretically wager on every shot in the book. I am not, of course, recommending that you do so.

You could hustle someone (Chapter 1) with a prop shot (Chapter 2) that is a real crowd pleaser (Chapter 4). The Silver Dollar Proposition Shot in Chapter 3 instantly comes to mind. The best solution was to place each shot in the chapter that most accurately expresses the dominant characteristic of that shot. The Silver Dollar Shot requires a prop (the silver dollar) so it goes into Chapter 3 on Prop Shots. The Bottle Shot is a jump shot with a prop that crowds just love. Since the bottle dominates the crowd's attention, it was placed in Chapter 3, Prop Shots.

Several of the masse shots are crowd pleasers, but they go into Chapter 13, which is devoted exclusively to masse shots. Shots where the cue ball is going to travel around the table are largely found in Multi-Rail Masterpieces. And most of the jump shots (but not all) are to be found in the chapter titled Jump Shots.

Chapter 17 - You're the Star

While this book is designed to be fun to read and study, my ultimate goal is to have you perfect a group of shots and create a show you can use to entertain your family, friends and relatives. In this chapter you will find numerous tips for giving a top-flight exhibition. In the second part of the chapter are three shows with 20 shots each.

Making the shots in this book can be very impressive all by themselves, but to be a great showman, you've also got to talk a great game. Learn the art of conversation and your value as an entertainer will skyrocket. You'll be the hit of any party. Since your ability to converse with the crowd is a big part of showmanship, I have provided you with some recommended lines you can use for every shot. Many are designed to get your audience into the act.

The Three Shows

You're the Star – For the aspiring trick shot artist.
The Greatest Pool Show on Earth – For the advanced trick shot artist.
Mike's Extreme Pool – For those who like the ultimate challenge.

Chapter 18 - Trick Shot Listmania

There are endless ways to group the shots. In this chapter you will find several lists that should be helpful in assembling a group of shots to master and to possibly include in your show. The lists are meant to be both fun and useful. Included is a list of nearly every shot in the book in ascending order of its Execution Rating. This list should help players of all levels to create a list of shots that's in accord with their current level of skill.

Chapter 19 - Mike's Poolography

Poolography is a new term I coined while writing this chapter. My poolography gives you a brief look at my life in pool. I've had many ups and downs as you will discover. Looking back, I have thoroughly enjoyed my life playing pool and traveling the world entertaining audiences while sharing my skills at the game we all love.

Reading the Diagrams

Pool diagrams are simple to read. Nevertheless, I strongly suggest that you take a few moments to review the items on the list below in conjunction with the diagrams on this and the following page. If you have any questions about the notation of a diagram while reading the book, refer back to these pages.

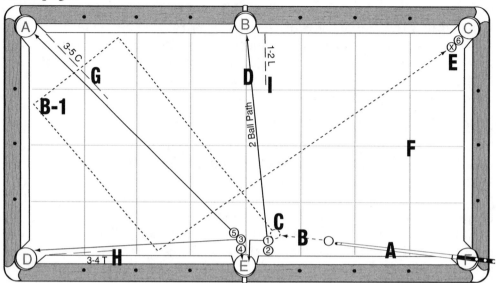

A Cue Stick - The cue shows the initial line of aim. When english is being applied, the cue will be positioned to either the left or right of center. You can gain the shooter's perspective by turning the book so you are looking straight down the cue stick, just as if you were playing the shot.

B Cue Ball Path - The dashed line shows the path of the cue ball to the object ball, as well as its path after contact.

B-1 The cue ball's path is shown by where the center of the cue ball is traveling. As a result, the line will never touch the rail.

C Contact Cue Ball - The dashed circle shows the cue ball's position at contact with the object ball. It does not appear on all shots due to space limitations.

D Object Ball Path - The solid line shows the path of the object ball.

E Cue Ball's Final Location – The cue ball with an X inside shows where the cue ball has come to rest. On straight in shots when the cue ball stops dead at the point of contact, the X cue ball is used to show both contact and the cue balls ending location.

F Grid Lines - It is important to place the balls precisely for a substantial percentage of the shots in the book. These lines should serve as a guide.

G Combination Line Up Lines - These will help you to set up combinations correctly. They reference the ball numbers in the combo.

H Tangent Line Up Lines - These lines show where the tangent line between two ball lines up with the rail or pocket. They reference the ball numbers that the tangent line runs between.

I Line Up Lines - These lines will help you set up a shot correctly. They reference the balls that must point in a certain direction.

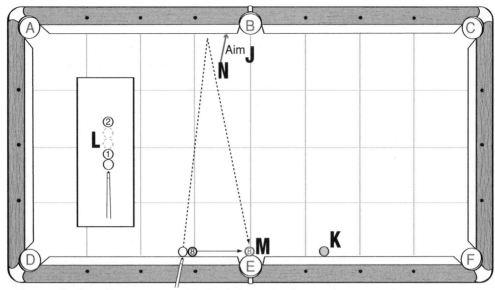

J Descriptive Text - You will find descriptive text on the diagrams where appropriate throughout the book.

K Gray Object Balls – When it doesn't matter which object ball you use you will often find one or more gray object balls.

L Ghost Balls – They are shaded versions of balls that are used primarily for setting up shots. They are removed when the set up is complete.

M Gray Numbered Object Balls – These show object balls that have come to rest at a different spot than their original location.

N Aiming Lines – These show where you should line up to shoot.

Using the Set Up and Execution Ratings

On the following page you will be introduced to my Set Up Ratings and Execution Ratings. While you are selecting a list of shots to work on, you should consider both ratings. Below are four basic combinations of the two ratings. The first is obviously the easiest combination. Combination 4 is certainly the toughest pair.

1 Set Up Easy / Execution Easy – These are a cinch even for novice players.

2 Set Up Difficult / Execution Easy – Novices will especially get a kick out of the response from setting these up correctly.

3 Set Up Easy / Execution Difficult – These are a challenge for anyone. They require precise aiming and/or an excellent stroke.

4 Set Up Difficult / Execution Difficult – These are a challenge even for me. The rewards for making them are well worth the effort.

Descriptive Material

Directly beneath most diagrams you will find a space with several descriptive items. There is much useful information on the shot's difficulty and how to play it correctly. On many shots you will also find some interesting items that do not affect playing the shot.

SUR: 2.5   MMS
EXR: 2.0   ESPN
MSR: 95%   AP
LMS   Video

SUR: Set Up Ratings

Set Up Ratings show how difficult it is to place the balls in the right positions on the table. On some shots there are ratings that appear quite high relative to the difficulty of executing the shot. This should tell you that even though the shot is easy to make, set up is critical. Conversely, some of the toughest shots to execute have some of the lowest Set up Ratings.

Set Up Ratings

1.0 - 2.0 Easy to set up. Execution is the key to the shot.
2.5 - 3.5 Some patience is required. These may take 2-3 tries to get right.
4.0 - 5.0 You must have the patience of a monk. These could easily take three or more tries to get right, especially while you are learning the set up. However, your patience will always be well rewarded.

EXR: Execution Ratings

This is the most critical of the three shot ratings. It measures what I feel is the shot's relative difficulty for the average player.

Execution Ratings

1.0 – Extremely easy. Your success is almost guaranteed.
1.5 – Very easy. Little if any practice is needed.
2.0 – Can be mastered with a little practice.
2.5 – Expect to make these regularly with sufficient practice.
3.0 – Just below average in difficulty. Skill and practice needed.
3.35 – is the average rating for all of the shots in the book.
3.5 – These start to separate average players from advanced players.
4.0 – Quite difficult. Lots of practice and some talent are required.
4.5 – Extremely challenging. Many hours of practice and talent needed.
5.0 – A big challenge even for Mike. They require lots of skill, practice and on some of them luck plays a big role.

MSR: Mike's Success Ratio

The final rating in the first column tells you how often I expect to make the shot. My execution ratings are not always in accord with those of the average player because of my experience and my level of skill at these shots.

LMS: Lefthanders Mirror Shot - (on some shots)

The majority of shots can be played as diagrammed whether you are right- or left-handed. On some shots, however, it will be awkward if not impossible for a left-handed person to play them as diagrammed. When this is the case, the shot is designated as a Lefthanders Mirror Shot (LMS). If you are left-handed, set up the shots exactly as diagrammed only on the opposite side of the table.

Items of Special Interest - (on some shots)

This group of abbreviations designates several items of special interest to fans of trick shots. It has nothing to do with the execution of the shots. This group of items appears after the shot ratings.

MMS: This indicates one of my creations.
ESPN: The shot has appeared on ESPN on Trick Shot Magic.
AP: The shot is part of the Artistic Pool program.
Video: I demonstrated the shot on one of my videos.

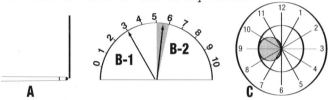

Cue Angle (A)

Most of the shots require that you hold your cue as level as possible. For these shots you will often see the phrase level cue. On jump shots, masses and selected other shots, however, you must elevate your cue to the proper angle. This symbol gives the correct elevation without the need to read the text.

Speed of Stroke (B)

The correct speed of stroke is critical on many of the shots in the book. Speed of stroke is shown by the pool speedometer underneath the diagrams. The numbers on the poolometer (hey, there's another new word for pool players) correspond to the speeds given in the table below. The example B-1 shows a soft stroke on the 5 to 10 scale. Example B-2 shows a shot which could be played with a medium to medium hard stroke.

The Spectrum of Speed (Poolometer)

Speed	MPH	Speed	MPH
1 Extremely Soft	.5- 1.5	6 Medium Hard	6.0
2 Very Soft	2.0	7 Hard	7.0
3 Soft	3.0	8 Very Hard	8.0
4 Medium Soft	4.0	9 Extremely Hard	10.0 - 14.5
5 Medium	5.0	10 The Break	15.0-30.0+

Clock Cue Ball (C)

The clock above tells you exactly where you should strike the cue ball. Please remember that on some shots you may have to adjust your cueing slightly from that shown on the clock.

Essential Lessons on Pool

On the pages that follow I will discuss a number of items that are essential to your success on trick shots. As an added bonus, these lessons will also help you with your regular pool game. So before you rush into the chapters on trick shots, set up the situations in these diagrams and observe how the balls react. The more knowledge you have, the better you will be able to handle any situation that arises on a pool table.

Combination Throws

A majority of the multiple ball shots rely on an understanding of how the second ball in a combination can be thrown. When two object balls are frozen or very close you get what is called a throw effect when the first ball is struck at an angle. Normally balls can be thrown when they are up to an eighth of an inch apart. However, the throw effect can occur when the balls are up to a quarter inch apart when the balls are dirty. In Diagram #1, Part 1, the 1-ball and 2-ball are frozen together and are pointing at the center of the pocket. If the cue ball is aimed down Line A, the 2-ball will follow path A-1 into the pocket. Now, if the cue ball was shot down Path B and the 1-ball was contacted on the left side, the 2-ball would be thrown to the right down Path B-1.

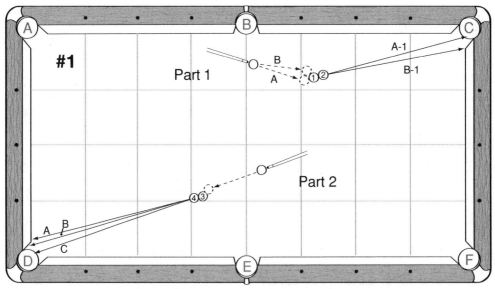

Speed is very important on throw shots. The balls will throw more when they are struck softly. In Part 2, the 3-ball and 4-ball are lined up along Line A. In the following three examples, the cue ball is aimed at the right side of the 3-ball as shown. If this combination was shot on the right side with a very hard stroke, the 4-ball would only be thrown slightly to the left of Line A. If the 3-ball was struck on the right side using a medium stroke, the 4-ball would likely follow Line B and hit the point of the pocket. Finally, if the 3-ball were cut on the right side with a soft stroke, the 4-ball would follow Line C towards the pocket. Again, the softer a throw shot is played, the more the object ball will veer off its original line.

When the balls are particularly clean or slick, less throw will result. If the balls have been cleaned with some cleaning agent or have been waxed, you will get very little throw until the balls have been used and handled for a while.

Throwing a Ball with English

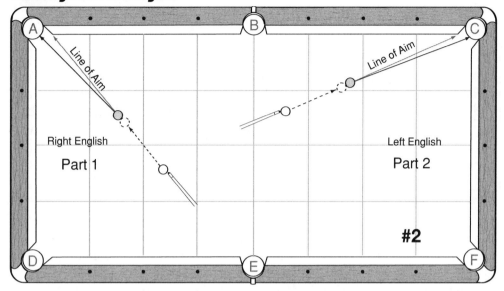

You can also get the balls to throw by applying english to the cue ball. Right english will throw the object ball to the left as shown on Part 1 of Diagram #2 Left english will throw the ball to the right as shown in Part 2. Speed and conditions also effect the amount of throw that results when using english. A soft hit results in more throw. The same hold true if the balls are dirty.

Transferring Spin to an Object Ball

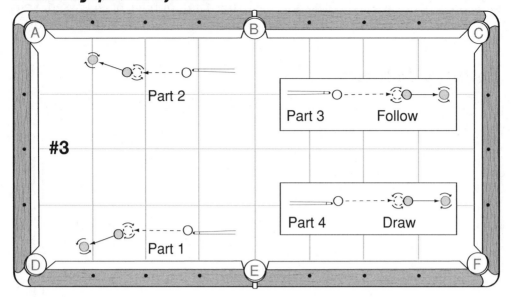

When the cue ball contacts the object ball, there is a very slight transfer of spin from the cue ball to the object ball. The transfer will cause a reverse effect on the object ball. Part 1 of Diagram #3 shows that left english on the cue ball imparts right english on the object ball. Part 2 demonstrates that right english on the cue ball leads to left english on the object ball.

Follow on the cue ball transfers stun (or even a very minute amount of draw) to the object ball, as shown by Part 3. Draw on the cue ball transfers follow to the object ball as demonstrated by Part 4. The effects of transfer are greatest when a soft stroke is used and/or the balls are dirty. The same applies to the speed and conditions of balls and cloth.

Anytime you play a cut shot it puts spin on the object ball. (Note: this effect, however, can be offset by using english.) When you cut a ball to the left, the object ball will pick up right english (or left spin because it's spinning to the left). And when you cut an object ball to the right, it will pick up right spin. I think that turn is a better word to use for the spin applied to an object ball. The amount of english transferred is very little, but it can be very effective when playing bank shots.

How Speed Effects Bank Shots

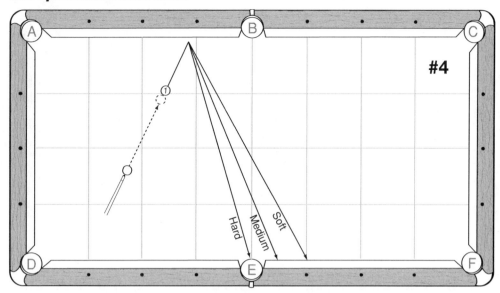

Speed is a very important factor on bank shots. For example, when you play a bank with a hard stroke, it will rebound at a narrower angle as shown in Diagram #4. The diagram shows how a bank shot aimed at the same spot will rebound at a different angle when played with a medium or soft stroke. When the cloth is worn or when the humidity is high, bank shots will rebound at a narrower angle.

It is always a good idea to test the cushions to determine if the table is banking average, long, or short. Bank shots such as the one in Diagram #4 are good for testing the cushions. Make sure you test all of the cushions.

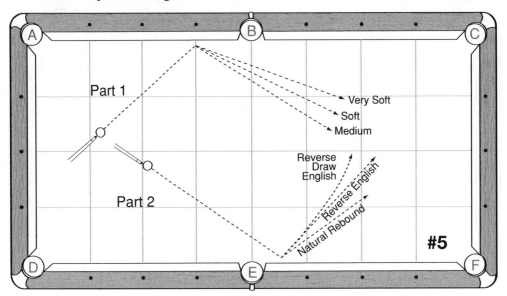

Speed and english exert a substantial influence on the cue ball's path on kick shots. The harder you shoot, the more sharply will be the rebound angle and vice versa. This is known as shortening up the angle. English on kick shots will also take more at slower speeds.

In Part 1 of Diagram #5 the cue ball has been shot with the same amount of right english on all three shots. Notice that a softer stroke results in a wider rebound angle. The harder you shoot, the shorter the rebound angle will be.

Part 2 of Diagram #5 shows that you can shorten up the rebound angle by using draw, reverse english, or a combination of these two. The natural rebound angle is shown. Notice how much more sharply the cue ball will rebound off the cushion when either draw or reverse english (in this case, right english) is used.

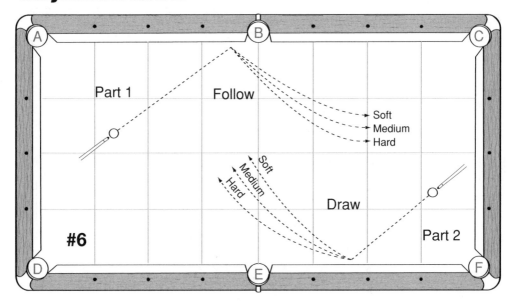

When you shoot into the cushion at an angle with topspin, the cue ball will arc forward, especially on new cloth. This is shown in Part 1 of Diagram #6. With draw you can make the cue ball bend back towards you as demonstrated in Part 2 of Diagram #6.

In both parts, notice the effect of speed on the rebound angle and the arc the cue ball traces out. The softer you shoot, the sooner the cue ball will arc. Conversely, the harder you shoot, the farther the cue ball will travel before it arcs. This holds true when either draw or follow is used.

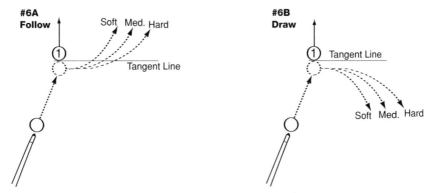

Diagram #6A gives you another look at how the cue ball curves after contact on a follow shot. Notice that the harder the shot is hit, the greater the distance the cue ball will travel down the tangent line before curving forward across it.

Diagram #6B illustrates how the cue ball curves away from the tangent line on draw shots. Once again, the harder the shot is hit, the longer the cue ball will travel along the tangent line before curving away from it.

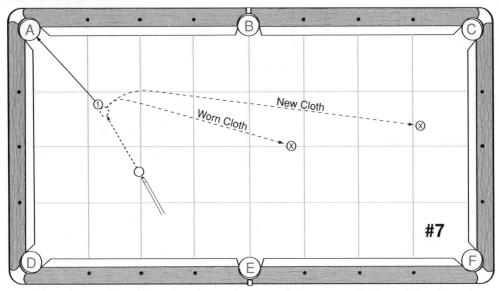

When playing on worn or dirty cloth, english will grab and take sooner than on new cloth. Although the english takes quicker, the spin doesn't last as long because of the additional friction. Diagram #7 shows an angled draw shot. The shot has been played with the exact same stroke in both cases. Notice how much quicker the cue ball reversed on worn cloth, and how much shorter it traveled. The shot on new cloth took longer to grab hold, but traveled much further.

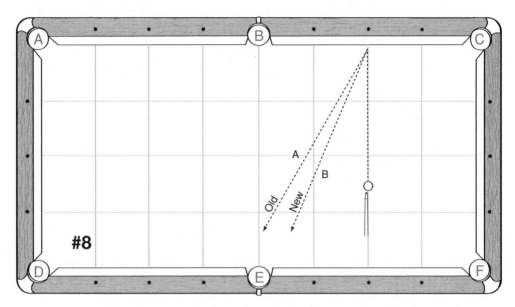

When the cloth is worn or dirty, english takes better off the cushions. In other words, you get more bite. In Diagram #8 the cue ball has been struck exactly the same on two shots. On a table with worn cloth, the cue ball would follow Path A.

When the cloth is brand new, english doesn't take as well. Instead, it spins off instead of biting. This results in a sliding effect as shown by Path B. And if the balls are clean, the cue ball will slide even more.

Tangent Lines

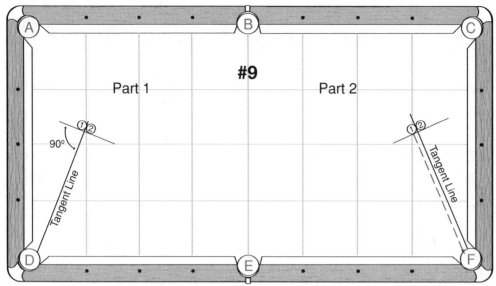

You will need an understanding of tangent lines to set up a lot of the shots in the book. Part 1 of Diagram #9 illustrates a line that runs at a 90-degree angle between the 1-ball and 2-ball. You can see that the so-called tangent line bisects the corner pocket.

In Part 2 the tangent line is pointing about an inch inside the edge of the corner pocket. The dashed line runs parallel to the tangent line and extends from the center of the 1-ball to the corner pocket.

When setting up most trick shots, you will need to position the balls so that the tangent line is pointing either to the center of the pocket (as in Part 1), or to the outside edge (as in Part 2).

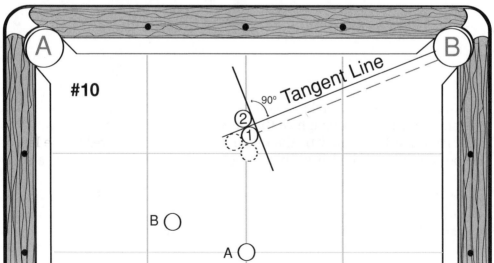

The tangent line in Diagram #10 is pointing just inside the corner pocket (as in Part 2 of Diagram #9). And the dashed line that runs parallel to the tangent line runs from the center of the 1-ball to the center of the pocket. When two object balls are frozen like those in the Diagram #10, you can make the ball (in this example, the 1-ball) by contacting it at the two points shown by the dashed cue ball, or anywhere in between the two dashed cue balls.

If you use a hard stroke and/or draw, the path of the object ball could be altered, enough to cause a miss. It depends largely on the location of the cue ball. If you aim for a full hit from Location A with a hard stroke and/or draw, you would miss the 1-ball to the left of the pocket. If the cue ball was in Location B, draw and/or a hard stroke would have less effect in throwing the 1-ball to the left of the dashed line.

Tangent Lines with Several Balls

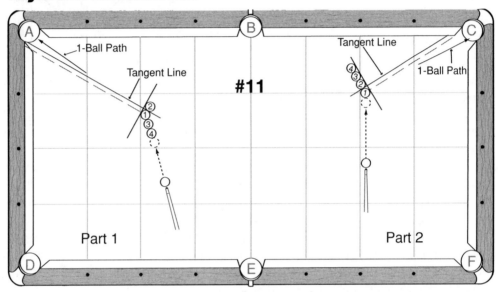

When there is more than one ball on either side of the object ball, the object ball's path will change. How much depends on speed, the contact point, and the number of balls. In Part 1 of Diagram #11 the tangent line is pointing to the left of the pocket. The 1-ball would ordinarily follow the path shown by the dashed line and miss to the left of the pocket. In this case, however, the extra weight provided by the 3-ball and 4-ball will help push the tangent line to the right at contact. As a result, the path of the 1-ball will shift to the right enough so that it will now go into the pocket.

In Part 2 of Diagram #11, the tangent line is pointing well to the left of the pocket. The dashed line that indicates the path of the 1-ball also is pointing far enough to the left that it looks like the 1-ball can't be made. However, this time the extra balls (the 3 and 4-balls) are on the opposite side of the cluster. Now when the 1-ball is contacted as shown, it will rebound slightly due to the weight of the 3-ball and 4-ball and travel to the right of the dashed line and into the pocket.

Now let's assume that the dashed line was pointing towards the pocket. This shot would likely be missed to the right because of the rebound effect caused by the extra balls on the opposite side. The shot can be made with draw, which counteracts the rebound effect caused by the 3-ball and 4-ball.

Using English - The Clock

When applying english to the cue ball it will help you to visualize the cue ball as a clock. Your tip should contact the cue ball within the circle in Part 1 as shown. Any contact outside the inner circle will result in a miscue. The shaded circle in Part 3 shows maximum english at 9:00.

#12
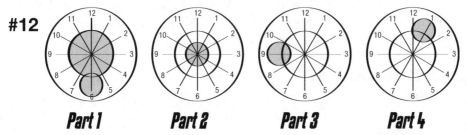

The line of the circle or clock is 9/16 of an inch from the edge of a 2.25 inch cue ball. This is shown by the shaded circle in Part 1.The distance of the clock line is always half from the center to the edge of the cue ball. Keep in mind that billiard balls, snooker balls, and Russian billiard balls would have a different distances since these balls are different in diameter from a cue ball.

Part 1 also shows tip placement when maximum draw is used. A miscue would likely result past this point. Part 2 shows a centerball hit. Part 3 demonstrates maximum left english while Part 4 shows top right english. These are but a few of the possible tip locations.

Although part of the tip will be past the clock line when using maximum english, the contact point will still be inside the clock since the cue ball is round. You will get good surface contact with the cue ball if you shape your tip to the radius of a dime.

The Clock and Elevation

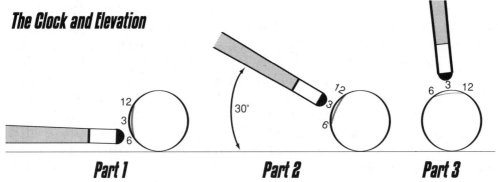

The contact points on the clock are all relative to the angle of elevation. When you are holding your cue in a level position, the clock face is facing you as shown in Part 1. On many shots in this book you will need to elevate your cue. Part 2 shows 30 degrees of elevation. Notice that the clock face has shifted to accommodate the cue's elevation. On extreme massé shots you will need to elevate anywhere from about 70-90 degrees. On these shots, the clock face will be pointing close to or even straight up. Part 3 shows the clock for a nearly vertical masse.

Stroke Shots

It is good to have a knowledge and understanding of the stroke shots, massé shots, banks, and kick shots. These shots are the product of experience and are played mostly by feel and instinct. To acquire a feel for these shots, you must put in hours of practice to gain any measure of consistency.

A number of the stroke, bank, kick and massé shots can be made with different hits on the cue ball. One example would be Mike's Power Draw Shot on page 142. To make this shot on new cloth you might use more draw and less spin as you will need to rely more on speed and bounce off the cushions. This shot also underscores the need to be able to adapt to the conditions: balls, cloth, cushions, and humidity.

On worn cloth more spin and less draw might be better. Maybe 5:30 maximum draw would be best on new cloth while draw at 4:30 would work best on worn cloth. On worn cloth since you get more bite, the cue ball doesn't lose as much speed when it contacts the cushion.

About Your Stroke Shots

This is not a book on basic fundamentals, but here are a couple of tips on the stroke. On most stroke shots the two most important factors are: complete your follow through and grip the butt end lightly. On power draw shots you must drop your elbow and follow through as far as possible. This will keep the tip from dipping too soon into the slate, which is what happens if you just use your forearm.

Some of the stroke shots in this book are very difficult even for most pros because they haven't practiced them. The reason they don't practice them is because the shots very seldom come up in a game. When some of these shots do appear in competition (other than Artistic Pool), there are usually other options such as a safety which are more reliable and more logical.

I believe almost anyone can make just about every shot in this book with enough practice, desire, and dedication. Of course, for some it will be much easier than for others. Some people have a natural stroke. There are those who are born to play pool, just like some people are gifted in art, music, etc. In those pursuits people with the knack find them to be much easier than for the person who isn't as gifted.

Knowing Your Cue

It is important to know how your cue plays. You must be able to allow for the squirt effect when using english. (Note: some people use the term deflection or pushes off instead of squirt.) When you use left english the cue ball will squirt to the right. And, of course, right english makes the cue ball deflect to the left. So you will have to make minor adjustments when using sidespin compared with what is diagrammed.

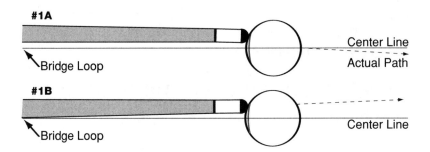

Example #1A shows the application of english. The person is aiming parallel and is not allowing for squirt. Notice that the cue ball is going to veer to the right away from the center line because of the left english.

In Diagram #1B shows the correct way to apply maximum english, which makes it much easier to compensate for squirt. The point at which your cue is in contact with your bridge hand is on the center line. Line up from the center out to the point of contact and then take your warm up strokes and final stroke along this line.

The best way to learn to allow for squirt is to practice shots using english. If you shoot the shots over and over eventually your instincts will tell you where to aim to compensate for the squirt. Experiment with one tip of english at 1:30, 3:00, 4:30, 7:30, 9:00, and 10:30. Also try using maximum english at the same clock readings.

On the shots that require english I will show you how I hit the shot with my cue and on cloth that is in very good condition, but that is not brand new. You probably will have to adjust, but if you're using cloth that is in good shape, are using good quality balls that are clean, you shouldn't have any trouble with sufficient practice.

Contents Overview

Chapters

Italicized bold type indicates a story.

18 *Trick Shot Listmania*

19 *Mike's Poolography*

Appendix

1 Hustler's Specials

If you have ever admired the talents of a carnival barker or if there is a con man or hustler side to you that you've been dying to turn loose, now's your big chance. The shots in this chapter will provide you with an outlet for what might otherwise be criminal activities. While learning these shots, you will have the opportunity to perfect your conversational skills. And, once they've been mastered, you may never have to buy a coke or your favorite beverage again.

Your audience will be led to believe that a number of these shots appear to be impossible. In fact, most are quite easy. On others, you will actually have to spend some time perfecting your skill with a cue in hand. Don't forget, however, that your main skill is in developing a line of chatter that will convince your "friends" to risk an appropriate wager.

The proper set up and a convincing line of patter are crucial to your success. However, if you insist on using these shots to hustle dough in less than reputable establishments, first try to strike up a friendship with the largest guy in the joint. A back up, a knowledge of the exits, a car with its motor running and a wheelman are also recommended. I'm kidding of course.

Jar the Table

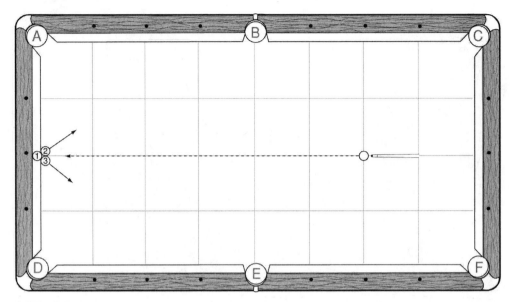

SUR: 1.0
EXR: 1.0
MSR: 99.9%

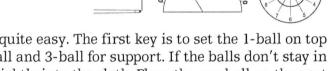

This proposition shot is quite easy. The first key is to set the 1-ball on top of the rail using the 2-ball and 3-ball for support. If the balls don't stay in place, try tapping them lightly into the cloth. Place the cue ball on the spot as shown or behind the head string.

The big key is to lay down a convincing line of patter. Tell your intended victim that you can do the impossible. You can hit the 1-ball first, even though the 2-ball and 3-ball are in front of it. Once you've made the wager, shoot the cue ball softly at the 1-ball. Then jar the table with your hip or fist. Make sure the table doesn't have any sharp edges or molding if you plan to bump it with your hip. The 2-ball and 3-ball will separate and the 1-ball will fall to the table in time to be struck by the slowly rolling cue ball. I recommend a one or two beverage limit. If you succumb to greed and bet more, be prepared to run fast after grabbing the cash.

This is a fairly easy shot on most home tables. You should, however, be aware of any roll off in the table since the cue ball will be traveling a long distance at a slow speed. On some commercial tables you may have to use more force. I once tried the shot on a Connelly table with two-inch thick slate. Even though I pounded my fist on the table, the balls refused to fall.

I was doing an exhibition at the Spirit Independent Movie Awards when James Woods came up to the table and said he wanted to show me a trick shot. This is the one he showed me. I didn't mention it was one I learned when I was only 13 years old.

The Intentional Miscue

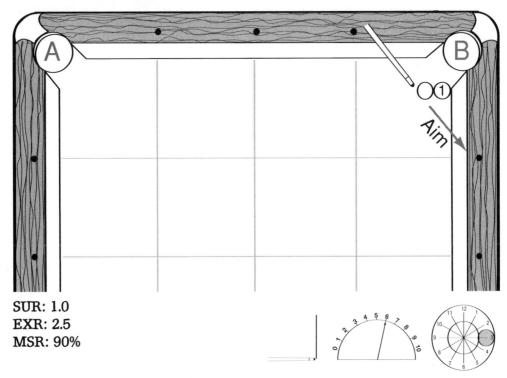

SUR: 1.0
EXR: 2.5
MSR: 90%

Place the cue ball and 1-ball as diagrammed. This is a difficult looking shot even if you were going to attempt to bank the 1-ball cross corner. Tell your opponent or audience you intend to shoot the 1-ball into Pocket B. This would appear to be all but impossible. Aim up the side rail as indicated. Use extreme right english. Strike the cue ball far enough towards the edge that a miscue is virtually assured. The cue ball will stay in place while the 1-ball kisses off it and goes into Pocket B.

Massey's Proposition Shot

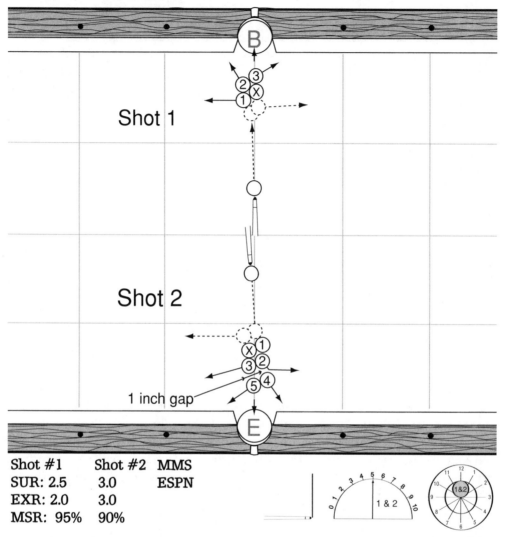

Shot #1	Shot #2	MMS
SUR: 2.5	3.0	ESPN
EXR: 2.0	3.0	
MSR: 95%	90%	

Shot #1 is one I learned when I first started playing pool. Set up the shot and then ask your "mark" if he can pocket Ball X in Pocket B. Unless he's seen the shot, he most likely won't be able to figure it out. Shoot into the 1-ball with a half-ball hit on the right side. Use a half tip of follow and a medium speed stroke. The 1, 2, and 3-balls will separate while the cue ball caroms into Ball X, making it in Pocket B.

Shot #2 features two more balls. I consider this creation of mine to be a proposition shot. There should be a one inch gap between the 2-ball and 4-ball and the 3-ball and 5-ball. In addition, the 4-ball should be about a half inch to the right of the 2-ball. Once again you will want to use a half tip of follow with a medium speed stroke. Aim for a half ball hit on the 1-ball. The 1-ball will start a chain reaction that will remove the 1-5 balls. The cue ball will billiard off the 1-ball into Ball X, cutting it into Pocket E.

Cue Is Quicker than the Eye

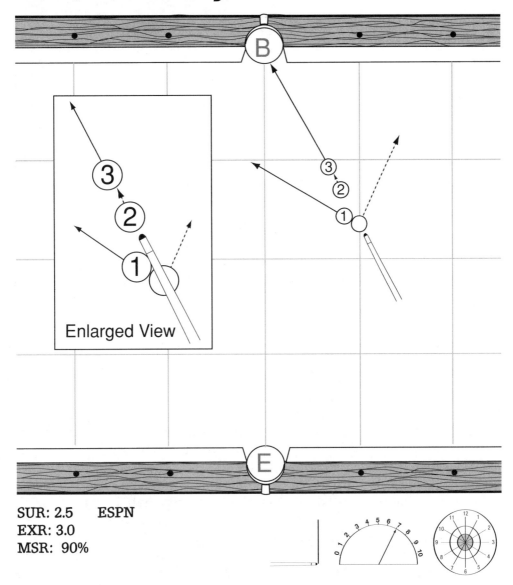

SUR: 2.5   ESPN
EXR: 3.0
MSR: 90%

Fast Eddie Felson made this shot while playing the notorious Minnesota Fats in the movie *The Hustler*. The Cue is Quicker than the Eye shot is illegal, but most people won't catch it, at least not at first.

Align the cue ball, 2-ball, and 3-ball in a straight line with Pocket B. Freeze the 1-ball to the cue ball so the tangent line is a little to the right of the 2-ball. Stroke the cue ball hard in the center and follow through far enough so that your cue tip hits the 2-ball. Grip the cue a little tighter than normal and use a firm closed bridge. The 3-ball will go straight into the side pocket.

It's Your Choice 8-Ball Shot

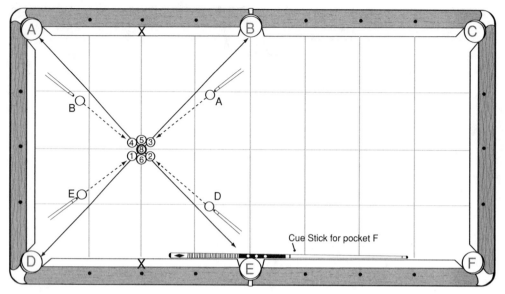

SUR: 3.5
EXR: 1.5
MSR: 95%

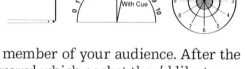

This rather ingenious shot involves a member of your audience. After the balls are set up, ask a member of the crowd which pocket they'd like to see the 8-ball shot into, A, B, D, or E. You can make the 8-ball in any of these four pockets. It all depends on where you place the cue ball.

The 8-ball is positioned on the spot. Make sure the 5, 8, and 6-balls are frozen and in a straight line with the diamonds marked X. The 3-ball and 4-ball are frozen to the 5-ball. They are both about a half-inch from the 8-ball. The exact same set up procedure applies to the 1, 6, and 2-balls. The table once again determines the exact set up for a successful shot. You may have to adjust the distance between the 8-ball and the four outside balls.

Now let's say the person who is going to call the shot wants you to pocket the 8-ball into Pocket A. Place the cue ball at Location A. Aim directly at the 3-ball. Strike the cue ball in the center with a medium speed stroke. The diagram shows the other three locations and their corresponding pockets.

The 8-ball can still be made even if the person calling the shot is a wise guy and chooses either Pocket C or F. Let them play the shot as if they were shooting for Pockets B or E. The speed must be increased to medium hard on this version, so be sure to tell the shooter to use a firm stroke. The second they shoot, lay a cue stick along the rail blocking the side pocket. When the 8-ball hits the cue it will roll into either Pocket C or F.

The Great Deceiver

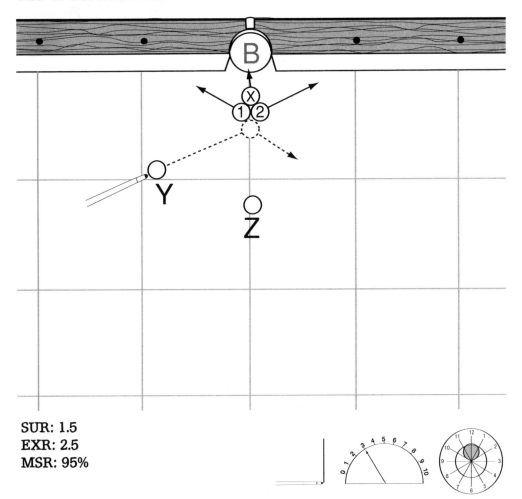

SUR: 1.5
EXR: 2.5
MSR: 95%

Here's a proposition shot that looks easy enough. But unless the shooter knows it, they will be surprised when they can't pocket Ball X into the side pocket.

When setting up this shot, make sure all three balls are frozen together. Next, hand your potential victim the cue ball and ask them to make Ball X in the side pocket. If they don't know the shot they will usually place the cue ball at Position Z. In fact, I have never seen anyone make the shot from this position. To make it from Position Z you would have to hit the 1-ball and 2-ball at the exact same instant, which is super difficult.

You can make this shot and display your knowledge of pool by placing the cue ball at Position Y to the left of the cluster. Hit the 1-ball very thinly with a soft stroke. This will move Ball X over slightly. When the cue ball caroms into the 2-ball, it will combo it into the side pocket.

Christopher Walken Take One

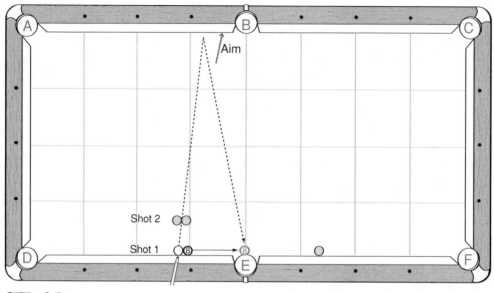

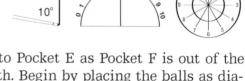

SUR: 2.5
EXR: 4.0
MSR: 50%

The object is to pocket the 8-ball into Pocket E as Pocket F is out of the question due to the blocker in its path. Begin by placing the balls as diagrammed. Aim at the point indicated by the arrow near the opposite side pocket. Elevate your cue about 10 degrees. Use a half tip of right english and cue a tip above center with a medium speed stroke. If the 8-ball crosses in front of the pocket too soon, move both balls a little to the right. Should the cue ball arrive before the 8-ball, move the balls a little to the left.

You will likely have to experiment with the shot for a while before you discover the ideal location for the cue ball and 8-ball.

I've seen Tom Rossman place the balls as shown in Shot #2 and jump them using a jump cue, pocketing the 8-ball as planned. Use a jump cue and elevate about 35 to 40 degrees. Aim the same way and yse a jump shot to clear the interfering balls.

Christopher Walken Take One

Even though this shot has been around for a long time, I decided to rename it the Christopher Walken Take One Shot because Walken made it on his first take while shooting *Pool Hall Junkies.* Walken was rehearsing when he told them to roll the cameras, saying they might get lucky. He made the shot and everyone else was in character so they used this take for the movie. He tried the shot a few times afterwards and missed it every time. Mars Callahan, who starred in the movie, made the shot one handed in the movie and it only took him about five takes, not bad for an actor. By the way, Mars happens to be a good pool player.

A Dab Will Do You

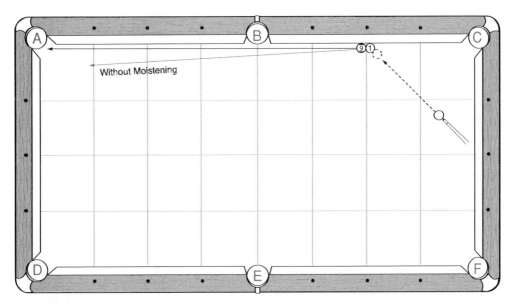

Without Moistening

SUR: 1.0
EXR: 1.0
MSR: 99.0%

This proposition shot has been around for ages. Set up a 1-9 combination with the two balls frozen to each other and to the cushion. Place the cue ball where indicated and ask your pigeon to shoot the combo. When they miss, boast that you can make the shot, no problem. When setting up the balls, secretly wet the contact point between the 1-ball and 9-ball with a little saliva. Aim straight at the 1-ball with a medium stroke.

You may be wise to test the table (in private, of course) as it could roll out or the point of the side pocket could get in the way. You should test the shot exactly the way you are going to play it.

Don't bet your house on this shot (unless you can set up the balls) as it is an oldie and they just might know it.

Michael Phelan's Challenge

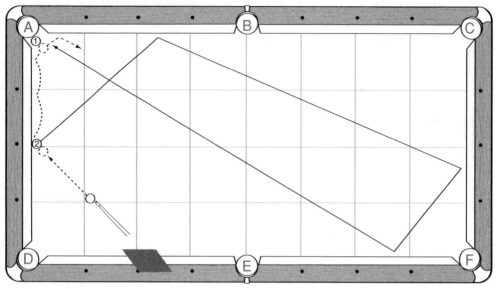

SUR: 2.0   **AP**
EXR: 4.0   **ESPN**
MSR: 50%
LMS

The object of this shot is to shoot into the 2-ball making the cue ball walk along the rail to pocket the 1-ball, meanwhile, the 2-ball goes four cushions into the same pocket.

I recommend placing the 1-ball a little to the left of the center of Pocket A. I feel this will give you a better chance for the cue ball to get out of the way. The shaded zone is my reference point for aiming this shot. The exact cue ball location depends on whether the table is playing long or short. Aim straight into the 2-ball and use a medium hard stroke.

If the 2-ball is hitting to the left of Pocket A, move the cue ball to the left a little. If the 2-ball is coming up short to the right of the Pocket A, move the cue ball a little to the right. A common mistake is to shoot too hard and lose control of the cue ball. Another error is to fail to allow for enough deflection, which results in hitting the 2-ball to the left.

Robert Byrne credits Michael Phelan with having created this shot in his book, *Byrne's Treasury of Trick Shots*.

1-2-3 Proposition Shot

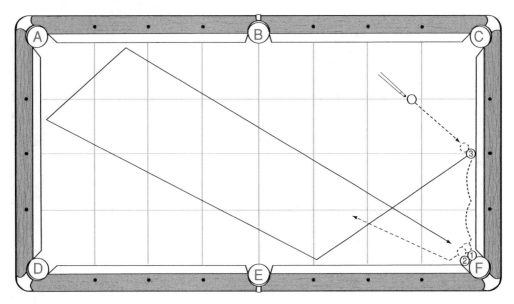

SUR: 2.5
EXR: 4.5
MSR: 40%
LMS

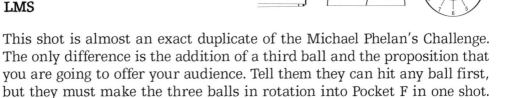

This shot is almost an exact duplicate of the Michael Phelan's Challenge. The only difference is the addition of a third ball and the proposition that you are going to offer your audience. Tell them they can hit any ball first, but they must make the three balls in rotation into Pocket F in one shot. Their natural inclination is to hit the 1-ball, then the 2-ball. That's easy enough. But making the 3-ball is another matter.

The correct way to play the shot is to aim for a full hit on the 3-ball with top right english. Use a medium hard stroke. The cue ball will hug the rail and pocket the 1-ball and 2-ball, then move out of the way. The 3-ball will travel four rails around the table and into the same pocket. I estimate that a decent player with a pretty good stroke should be able to make this shot once in every five or six tries.

Coin in the Glass Shot

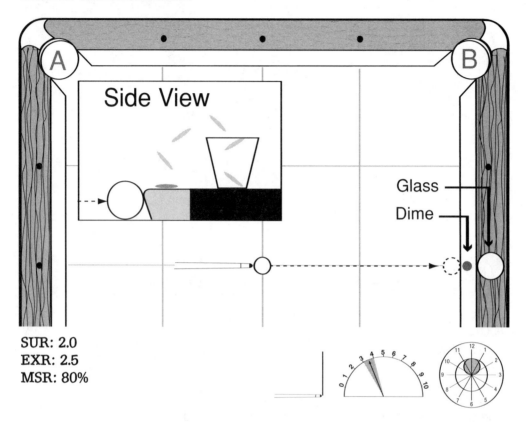

SUR: 2.0
EXR: 2.5
MSR: 80%

Place a dime a quarter to a half inch away from the edge of the rail. The distance depends on the liveliness of the cushions. Place a glass directly behind the dime on the rail. I recommend a double shot glass. A paper coffee cup would also work, but the sound of the coin settling in a glass sounds so much neater than a paper cup. The cue ball is placed on the head spot. Speed is everything on this shot. Shoot straight into the rail with a soft to medium soft stroke.

You can add another element of suspense to this shot by having an audience member call whether the coin will come up heads or tails in the glass.

Mr. Kimura's 57th Take

If you get real good at this shot you might try putting the glass on another table about 10 feet away. A quarter works best. Lest you think this version is easy, keep in mind that Mr. Yoshikazu Kimura, made this shot on his video *Mind-Boggling Trick Shots*. However, it required 57 takes! Considering it took him this long, it might take the average shooter 570 attempts. Don't say I didn't warn you.

Hit Your Hand on the Table Shot

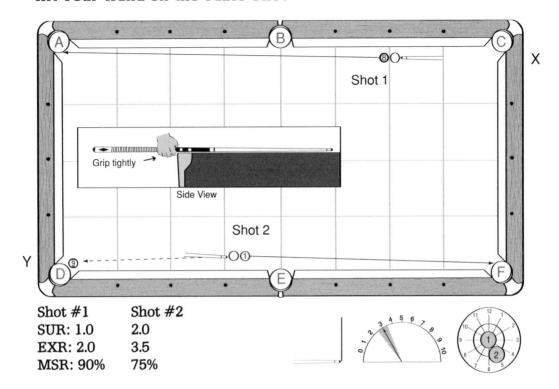

Shot #1	Shot #2
SUR: 1.0	2.0
EXR: 2.0	3.5
MSR: 90%	75%

Shot #1 is but another of the proposition shots I learned early in my career at Charlie and Henry's Poolroom in Loudon, Tennessee. I have won a lot of RC Colas and Moon Pies playing it.

The object of Shot #1 is to pocket the 8-ball while preventing the cue ball from rolling over the head string. Make sure you use a sturdy bridge and keep your cue level. Choke up on your cue as shown in the illustration. Keep advancing your tip until it is about a half inch from the center of the cue ball. Your grip hand should be touching the table at Location X. Grip the cue very tightly. Pull your hand back a few inches and then accelerate your hand into the table. This will prevent a double hit. Practice this shot by hitting the table softly at first. Then apply additional force in small increments. The goal is to use enough speed without hurting your hand.

After you master the stop shot in Shot #1, try Shot #2. In this version, you will make the 1-ball and draw back into the 9-ball. Use the same technique. Hit the cue ball at 5:00 as shown.

I want to emphasize again that you must use extreme care when learning these shots. It is possible you could hurt your hand if you hit the rail too hard. And make sure there are no sharp edges or anything else at the point where your hand will be striking the table that could cause damage to your hand.

Ball Out of the Rack (1)

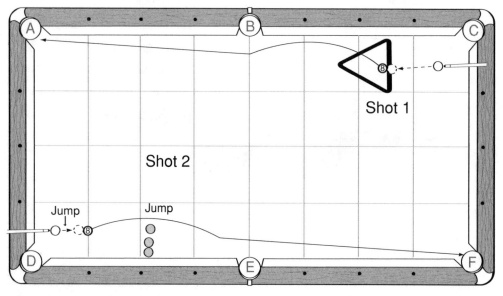

Shot #1	Shot #2		
SUR: 2.0	2.0	Video	
EXR: 3.5	3.5	ESPN	
MSR: 80%	80%		

The object in Shot #1 is to make the 8-ball in Pocket A. This is a fun shot that looks impossible to someone who hasn't seen it before. Place the balls as shown with the cue ball about 10 inches from the 8-ball. The shot works best if you position the balls so you have to cut the 8-ball slightly to the right. I recommend a 90% full hit on the 8-ball. This alignment will insure the balls don't hit each other when they come flying out of the rack.

Make sure the side of rack you select is not too wide. If the rack has rollers, lay the rack down so they are facing up. If you are using a plastic rack with a flanged edge, make sure the edge is on the bottom.

Even though this is a jump shot, your normal playing cue should work just fine. Elevate to about 30 degrees. Hit the cue ball in the dead center with a medium hard stroke. The cue ball will bounce over the edge of the rack, contact the 8-ball just above center and drive it into the slate. This will cause it to jump over the far edge of the rack and on towards Pocket A. If you are playing on Simonis 760, you may have to use a jump cue.

In Old Mexico

Sometimes when I do an exhibition I will set up this shot without the rack and tell a story about playing a Mexican in Old Mexico. I tell the audience as I'm getting ready to play the ball in the corner that my opponent placed a rack over the 8-ball and said, "No shooty." Then I made the ball out of the rack and said, "I shooty anyway."

Shot #2 is very similar to Shot #1. However, you may need to place the cue ball a little closer to the 8-ball. You might also need to use a slightly harder stroke. Sometimes the balls have been known to fly off the table on this shot. So as a precaution, be sure that no one is in front of you when you play this shot. And also make sure there are no mirrors, windows or any other breakable objects in the direction you are shooting.

I might add that this shot is one of the most practical trick shots as you could very easily be called upon to jump an object ball over an obstructer in an actual game, or at least over the edge of a ball.

A Miracle in Reno

I was giving an exhibition at the Sands in Reno during which I played Shot #2 on page 14. Something happened that I could not duplicate in a thousand years. I jumped the 8-ball over the obstructers, but I hit the shot so far off line that it missed the pocket by about four inches to the left. The 8-ball struck the short rail and flew way up into the air, bounced off the slate one time. and landed on the top of the rail right in front of me. It just froze there like a golf ball that has plugged in a sand trap or a wet fairway. I didn't miss a beat. I held out my arms and said, "Ta da!" Some people actually thought I was trying to have this happen!

Ball Out of the Rack (2)

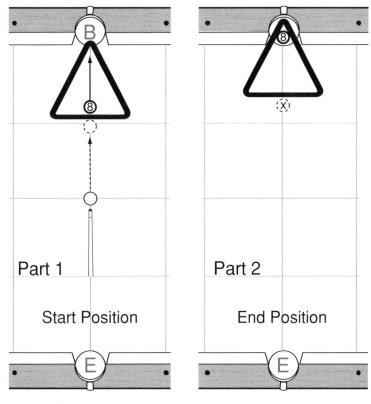

Part 1

Start Position

Part 2

End Position

SUR: 1.0   ESPN
EXR: 1.0
MSR: 100%

The fans love this shot, which is a cousin to the Ball Out of the Rack shot. This shot should earn you at least a few laughs.

Place the rack and 8-ball as shown in Part #1. Tell your audience you are going to once again perform a feat of magic by sinking the 8-ball in Pocket B. After viewing the previous shot, they will think you're going to jump the ball out of the rack. This time, however, all you have to do is force the ball into the pocket as demonstrated in Part #2. Strike the cue ball in the middle with a medium stroke. I suggest that you test the pocket beforehand to make sure the 8-ball will fall as shown in Part #2.

6 Balls in One Shot

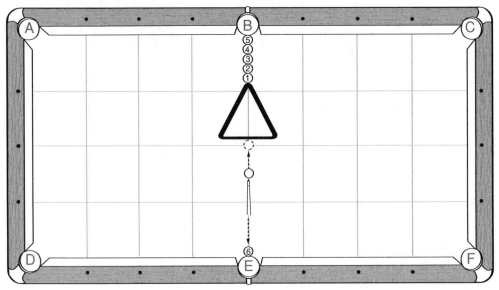

SUR: 1.5
EXR: 2.0
MSR: 99%

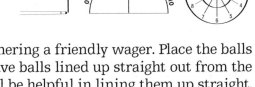

This simple shot can be used in garnering a friendly wager. Place the balls as diagrammed with the group of five balls lined up straight out from the side pocket. The side of the rack will be helpful in lining them up straight. Place the cue ball and six ball where shown. Now tell your friend to sink all six balls in one shot. They will no doubt fail. The next step is to tell them you can make the shot. Then secure a modest wager.

The set up for your attempt is exactly the same, with but one exception. You will be using the rack. Be sure the edge of the rack that the cue ball will be contacting is parallel with the long rail. Aim at the center of the rack, 1-ball, or pocket, whichever enables you to line up best for the shot. Hit the cue ball in the center using a medium stroke. The five balls will go into the side pocket and the cue ball will bounce back to pocket the 6-ball.

I recommend that you use a wooden rack or one made of sturdy fiberglass.

2 Three for the Price of One

I'll admit that the shots in this chapter are not as likely to bring down the house as some of the others in the book. And they are not as likely to win you a burger. They do, however, require the usual elements of correct set up and good technique if you wish to execute them successfully. And they are pleasing to novices who are easily impressed when even one, much less three balls find the pocket. On some of these shots, even the most knowledgeable of spectators will appreciate the modest amount of skill that is required to execute them, provided you play them perfectly.

Perhaps these shots might best be described as training wheels for the more difficult shots found elsewhere in the book. They are instructive in teaching you to line up tangent lines and combos correctly. And they will also demonstrate the importance of good shooting technique. Finally, on one of them, I even gained valuable ground on a competitor on my way to winning an important trick shot championship.

Three in One

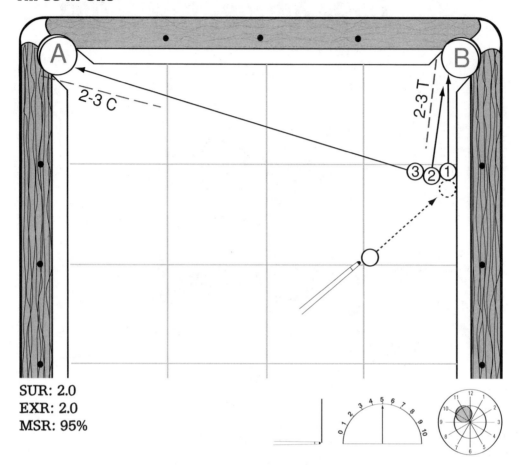

SUR: 2.0
EXR: 2.0
MSR: 95%

This shot has been around for a long time. It is fairly easy to set up and execute.

Be sure that all three balls are frozen. The 2-ball and 3-ball should be aligned with the left side of Pocket A to allow for throw. The tangent line between the 2-ball and 3-ball should point towards the left edge of Pocket B. Place the cue ball as diagrammed. Strike the cue ball with a half tip of high left english at 10:30. Keep your cue level and use a medium speed stroke.

One-Pocket Run Out

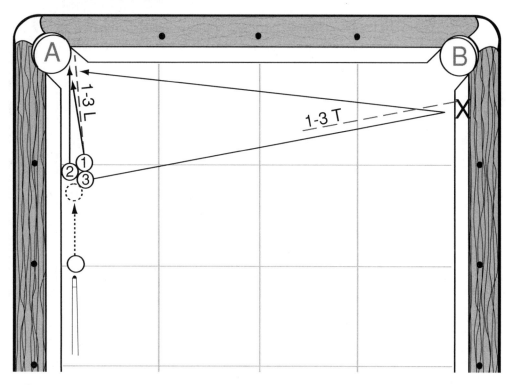

SUR: 3.5
EXR: 2.5
MSR: 75%
LMS

The idea is to pocket all three balls into Pocket A. This shot will come in handy should you ever encounter this layout in a game of One-Pocket (it might come up about as often as an eclipse of the moon). Position the balls as diagrammed. The tangent line between the 1-ball and 3-ball should be lined up at Position X, about a half diamond from Pocket B. Be sure all three balls are frozen together and that the 2-ball is frozen to the cushion.

Aim for a thin hit on the left side of the 3-ball. Use a half tip of left english and medium to medium hard stroke. The correct speed depends on the table.

PS: I'm still waiting for this shot to come up in a game.

Three for the Price of One

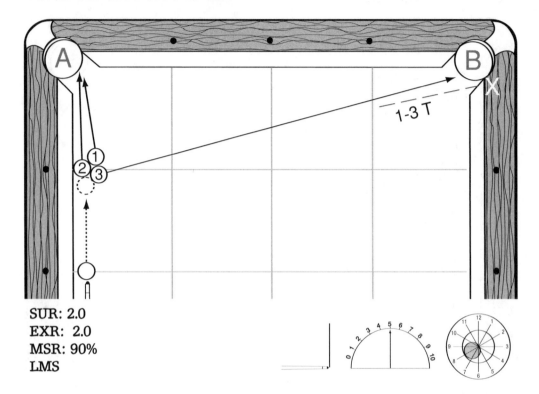

SUR: 2.0
EXR: 2.0
MSR: 90%
LMS

This shot is similar to the One-Pocket Run Out shot. The main difference is the set up. The 2-ball is directly centered on the first diamond instead of a half ball above the diamond. The tangent line between the 1-ball and 3-ball should point at Location X.

Aim for a thin hit on the 3-ball. Use a half tip of left english and a little less than a half tip of draw. Use a medium stroke. The 1-ball and 2-ball go into Pocket A. The 3-ball goes into Pocket B.

Three's Company

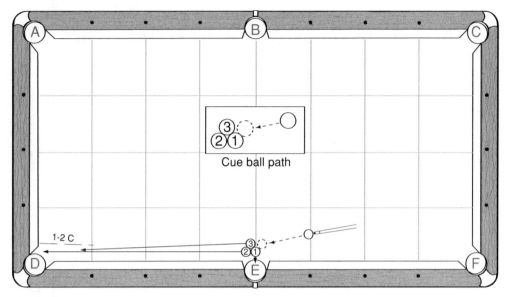

Cue ball path

SUR: 2.0
EXR: 2.5
MSR: 95%

It looks like there is no way to make the 3-ball unless it is pocketed on a slop shot. However, the 3-ball can go straight in thanks to a carom from the cue ball, which takes place after the 1-ball and 2-ball have departed. Place the balls as diagrammed with the 1-ball and 2-ball aimed to the right of the pocket. Make sure all three balls are frozen together. The cue ball is placed two ball widths from the rail opposite the first diamond to the right of Pocket E.

Aim for a half ball hit on the 1-ball. Use a half tip of right english and a medium stroke. The 1-ball will kiss off the 2-ball and into Pocket E. The 2-ball is comboed into Pocket D. The 3-ball is made in the same pocket.

Gerni's ESPN 3 Ball Shot

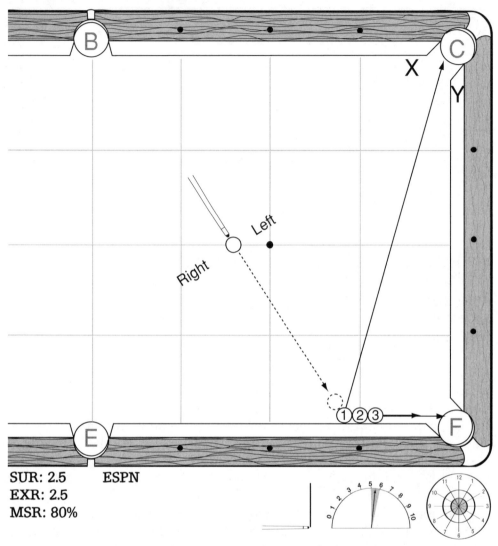

SUR: 2.5   ESPN
EXR: 2.5
MSR: 80%

Paul Gerni challenged me with this shot on ESPN. The challenger has to shoot first, which can sometimes work to his opponent's favor. I happened to notice Paul's mistake and was able to make the appropriate adjustment, gaining some ground in the competition.

On most tables this is not a very difficult shot. I have, however, tried it on tables where it was tough to make. It all depends on the cushions. The 1, 2, and 3-balls are frozen to each other and to the side rail as shown. Place the cue ball about five inches above the spot. Use center ball and aim for a full hit on the 1-ball. The 1-ball banks into Pocket C while the 2-ball and 3-ball go into Pocket F. Use a medium to medium hard stroke. From the shooter's perspective, if the 1-ball misses to the right (Y), move the cue ball to the left. And if the 1-ball misses to the left (X), move the cue ball to the right.

Straight and Narrow Three Ball Shot

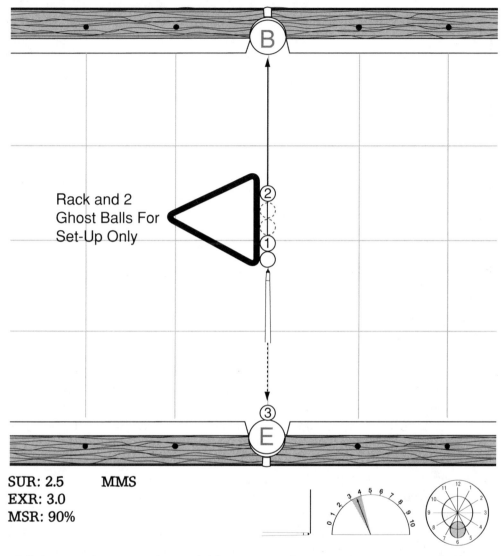

Rack and 2
Ghost Balls For
Set-Up Only

SUR: 2.5   MMS
EXR: 3.0
MSR: 90%

This is one of my creations which seems to impress even very good players.
The rack is used to line up the balls. Make sure the cue ball, 1-ball, and 2-
ball are lined up with the centers of the two side pockets. The cue ball
should be frozen to the 2-ball. When setting up the shot, place two balls
between the 1-ball and 2-ball to create the right gap. Then carefully
remove them.

Hit the cue ball a full tip below center with a soft to medium soft
stroke. The 1-ball will combo the 2-ball into the side pocket. Since the cue
ball is frozen to the 1-ball, it will stay extremely close to it. When the 1-ball
hits the 2-ball, the cue ball will collide with the 1-ball again. This will send
the 1-ball into the same pocket as the 2-ball. The backspin, which has been
retained by the cue ball, will cause it to draw back into the 3-ball.

Jerry Orbach's 3 Ball Shot

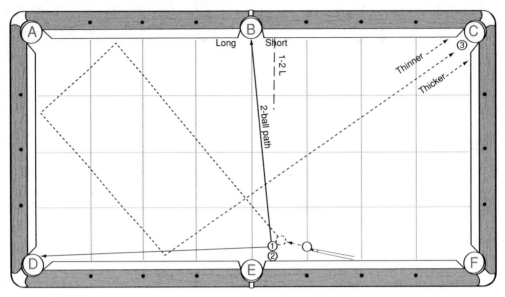

SUR: 2.0
EXR: 2.5
MSR: 95%

This neat three ball shot features a combination, a bank, a kiss shot, and a three-rail kick shot all in one. The set up is very simple. Just place the 1-ball and 2-ball near the side pocket. There should be a one-inch gap between the edge of the 2-ball and the point of the side pocket. Position the 3-ball in the jaws of Pocket C. The cue ball is even with the first diamond to the right of the side pocket and is a ball's width from the rail.

Hit the cue ball with a half tip of left english at 9:00. Use a medium speed stroke. You want the cue ball to contact the upper side rail about one to one and a half diamonds above Pocket A. The cue ball will travel three rails before sinking the 3-ball. If the cue ball misses to the left, hit the 1-ball a little thinner. And if the cue ball misses to the right, aim for a slightly fuller hit on the 1-ball.

If the 2-ball banks long (to the left of the side pocket) set up the 1-ball and 2-ball a little further from the edge of the side pocket. And if the 2-ball banks short (to the right of the side pocket) place the 1-ball and 2-ball a bit closer to the side.

Jerry's Friend the Con Man

Jerry Orbach of *Law and Order* was taping a popular TV show 25-30 years ago. Minnesota Fats was a guest on the program. Jerry beat Fats in a game of 8-Ball. Then he made this trick shot. Jerry told a friend about these successes. Later that same night when the show came on his friend was in a bar having a drink. Everyone in the bar thought they were watching the show live. Jerry's friend bet some sucker five or six hundred dollars that Jerry would beat Fats and make the shot on his first attempt. This would certainly have appeared to be a bad bet for Jerry's friend, but that was obviously not the case.

The National Geographic TV Program we did together is one of my fondest memories. I've also done a few charity events with Jerry, who is one of the best pool players among the actors who play the game. He's also one of the nicest people I've ever met.

Three Off the Spot

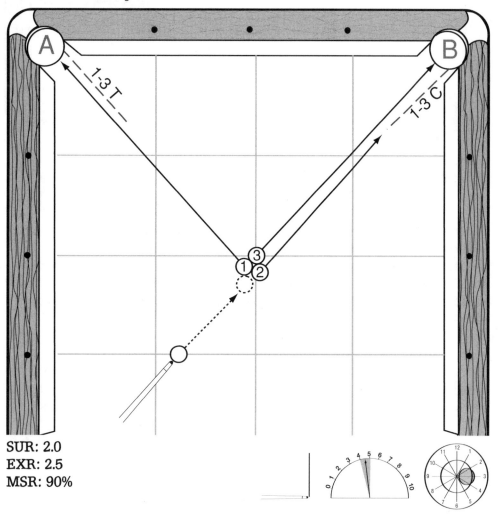

SUR: 2.0
EXR: 2.5
MSR: 90%

This shot is very closely related to Three's Company and to one of the shots in the Artistic Pool program, only it doesn't have a fourth object ball. Place the 3-ball on the spot. The tangent line between the 1-ball and 3-ball should point at the right edge of Pocket A. Aim for a half ball hit on the 1-ball. Use a half tip of right english and a medium soft to medium stroke.

The Disappearing Shot

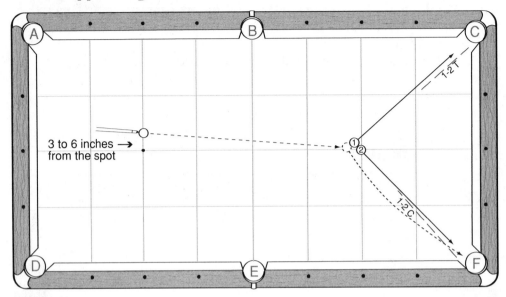

3 to 6 inches → from the spot

SUR: 1.5
EXR: 2.5
MSR: 90%

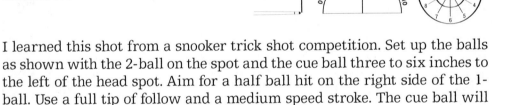

I learned this shot from a snooker trick shot competition. Set up the balls as shown with the 2-ball on the spot and the cue ball three to six inches to the left of the head spot. Aim for a half ball hit on the right side of the 1-ball. Use a full tip of follow and a medium speed stroke. The cue ball will arc forward after contacting the 1-ball and scratch (on purpose, of course) in Pocket F.

3 *Prop Shots*

You could call these shots the Hollywood Shots of pool, for they require special effects. Balls will drop on the table, only to be pocketed shortly thereafter. Balls will collide in midair before scurrying to their destinations. And on several shots the cue ball will take a ride on the Pool Railroad.

You will need to assemble a bag of tricks to play the shots in this chapter. Coin wrappers, doctored object balls, bottles, and extra cues will be needed. The reward for acquiring these items will be the ability to dazzle your friends with a series of offbeat and highly entertaining feats of wizardry.

All of the items you will need are readily available. Nickel coin wrappers can be secured at your bank. The hand tools in your workroom will help you apply surgery to extra object balls. A top quality wooden rack is also vital to your operation. On one shot in this chapter you will need four of them. Extra balls and racks can be purchased at almost any billiards supply store.

Connected Balls

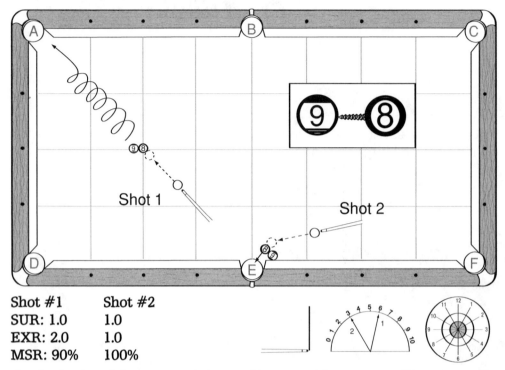

Shot #1	Shot #2
SUR: 1.0	1.0
EXR: 2.0	1.0
MSR: 90%	100%

I've had a lot of fun entertaining audiences with the two offbeat shots in the diagram above.

Take an 8-ball and a 9-ball and drill a small hole about an inch deep into both balls (you can purchase individual balls from a billiards supply store). Make sure the holes are aligned with the center of the balls. Take a screw that's two inches long and screw it into one of the balls. Cut the head off and screw the other ball into the part of the screw that is sticking out.

When you set up these shots you have to be a little sneaky. You don't want your fans to recognize that you are using a set of connected balls. In Shot #1, place the 8-ball on the spot with the 9-ball directly behind it. Place the cue ball 8-10 inches from the 8-ball aligned straight into Pocket A.

Aim as though you are trying to shoot the 8-ball straight into the pocket. Use centerball and a medium hard stroke. Both balls will spin like a top before scurrying into the pocket as long as the pockets aren't too small.

Shot #2 also makes superb use of your new set of gaffed balls. Position the 8-ball and 9-ball as shown. Now cut the 8-ball into the side pocket. As the 8-ball is entering Pocket E, the 9-ball will swing out from the rail and then follow the 8-ball into the pocket. For maximum effect I suggest that you shoot this with a soft stroke. I've even had some excellent players act very confused while trying to figure out what happened. (Of course, you must once again not let your audience see that you are using a doctored set of balls prior to playing the shot.) I also suggest that shooting Shot #2 first may result in a better effect.

The Perplexed Teenager

When I'm done with these shots I normally show the audience that the balls are connected. About ten years ago I gave an exhibition in Switzerland. Everyone was in shock when I made these shots. This time I unfortunately had to rush off. I forgot to show the crowd that I was only able to make these shots because the balls were connected.

The next year I gave a show in the same location. A young teenager came up to me before the show and asked how it was possible for me to make one of these shots. He said he had been practicing it with no success ever since he saw my exhibition. You should have seen the look on his face when I showed him the connected balls. I gave him the balls and now he's an expert at using connected balls.

The Flying Three Ball Shot

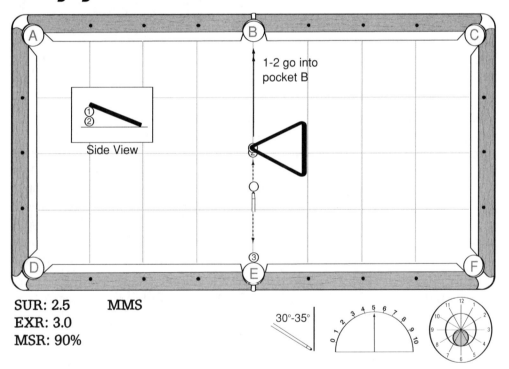

SUR: 2.5   MMS
EXR: 3.0
MSR: 90%

The object of this shot is to sink the 1-ball and 2-ball into Pocket B and draw back to make the 3-ball in Pocket E.

Place the four balls as shown. The 1-ball is placed on top of the 2-ball and is held in place by the rack (see side view). A wooden rack is recommended. Elevate your cue to 30-35 degrees. Strike the cue ball about a half tip below center with a medium speed stroke. The cue ball will jump and make contact with both the 1-ball and 2-ball before drawing back to pocket the 3-ball.

Edgar Nichol's Bottle Shot

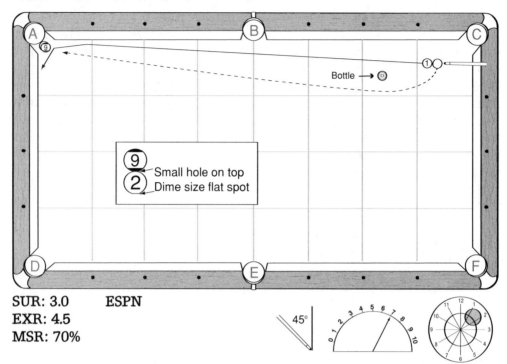

Bottle → ⊙

9 — Small hole on top
2 — Dime size flat spot

SUR: 3.0   ESPN
EXR: 4.5
MSR: 70%

45°

I fell in love with this shot the first time I saw it played by Edgar Nichol, who was giving an exhibition in Germany. Edgar and I wound up doing many shows together, and he has always been one of my favorite people to perform with. Edgar has an excellent stroke and he's great at massés. But mostly he's a nice guy and an excellent entertainer. Edgar's Bottle Shot is one of the shots that helped me win the 2000 Trick Shot Magic competition.

The object is to shoot the 1-ball into the 2-ball, knocking it out from underneath the 9-ball. The 2-ball goes into Pocket A. The 9-ball falls in front of Pocket A and stays in place. The cue ball curves around the bottle (or an object ball) before traveling down table to pocket the 9-ball.

Set up the shot as shown. The 2-ball must be gaffed (doctored with a small flat spot and indentation). You could also use two reinforcements for notebook paper. Make sure there is an eighth of an inch gap between the cue ball and the 1-ball. Aim the cue ball and 1-ball so the 1-ball will hit the long rail just ahead of the 2-ball. First try using 45 degrees of elevation. If the cue ball curves too much, reduce the angle down to 35-40 degrees. Aim almost straight at the 1-ball or for about 90% of the left side. Use an open bridge and stroke through the cue ball with a hard stroke. The right english should make the cue ball deflect to the left. When stroked properly, the cue ball will massé around the bottle and go up table to pocket the 9-ball.

This shot will probably take quite a bit of practice before you can make it consistently. In addition, the shot plays much differently on worn cloth or new cloth.

Bottle Shot

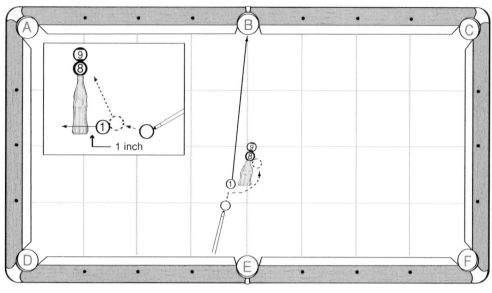

SUR: 3.0   ESPN
EXR: 4.0
MSR: 75%

You will need a gaffed 8-ball for this shot. The indentation on the 8-ball enables the 9-ball to be balanced on top of it. The shot is much easier with a Snapple bottle. If you use a pop bottle, you will also need to make an indentation on the cap as well.

Place the cue ball about five inches from the 1-ball. Elevate your cue about 30 degrees. Strike the cue ball a little less than a half tip above center with a medium hard stroke. The cue ball will pocket the 1-ball in Pocket B and jump up and knock the 8-ball from underneath the 9-ball when executed properly. The 9-ball will fall onto the Coke bottle and stay put.

Coin Wrapper Shot

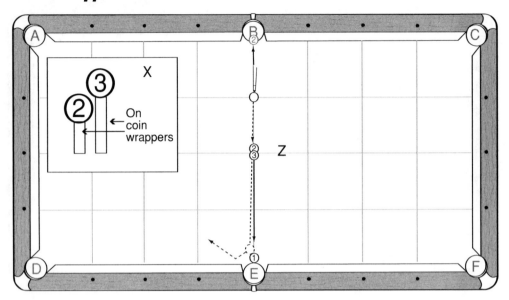

SUR: 2.0
EXR: 1.5
MSR: 95%

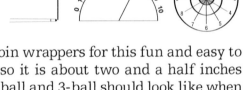

You will need to acquire a couple of coin wrappers for this fun and easy to make shot. Cut one of the wrappers so it is about two and a half inches long. Illustration X shows what the 2-ball and 3-ball should look like when set up side-by-side. The 2-ball is on top of the short wrapper and is very close to the 3-ball, which is on the taller wrapper. Make sure the balls on the wrappers are in a straight line that runs between the centers of the side pockets. Place the cue ball and 1-ball as diagrammed in Illustration Z.

Aim to hit the 1-ball three quarters full on either side. Cue just above center and use a hard stroke. The cue ball will travel underneath the 2-ball and 3-ball, knocking the wrappers out from beneath them. The two balls will collide upon landing and roll into the opposing side pockets.

Mid Air Collision Special

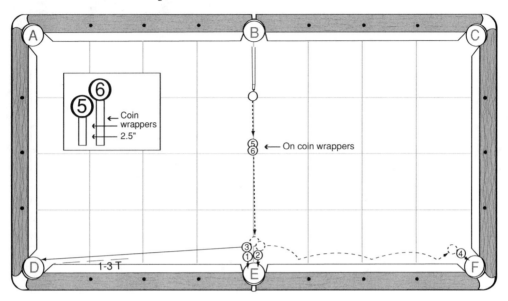

SUR: 3.0
EXR: 3.5
MSR: 85%

The 5-ball and 6-ball are placed in the middle of the table as shown on top of two coin wrappers. The coin wrapper the 5-ball sits on should be cut so it is two and a half inches long. You will be shooting the cue ball underneath these balls and into a thin hit on the left side of the 3-ball. Apply a half tip of maximum top left english. Hold your cue as level as possible and use a medium hard stroke. The cue ball will carom into the 2-ball and then hug the rail on its way to pocketing the 4-ball. The 5-ball and 6-ball will collide upon falling to the table and proceed into Pockets B and E.

The Skyscraper Stop Shot

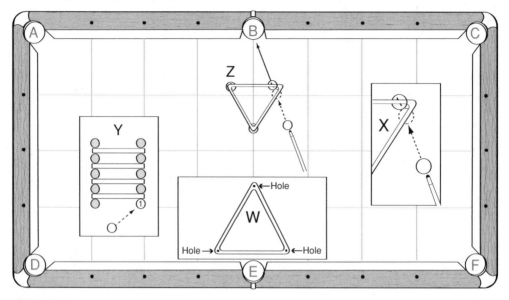

SUR: 2.5
EXR: 2.0
MSR: 98%

Four wooden racks are required for this shot plus all 15 balls and the cue ball. You will need to make a small indentation on all three corners (See Inset W) and on both sides of all four racks. Use a one eighth inch drill bit. All you want is an indentation that is deep enough so that the balls will stay in place.

Tap the bottom three balls into the cloth just a little. Place the 1-ball as shown in Inset X. Carefully stack the rest of the balls and racks as shown in Inset Y. The location for the shot is Position Z. Now place the cue ball where shown and shoot the 1-ball straight into the side pocket. Use a medium stroke and hit the cue ball in the dead center. The balls and racks will barely move, if at all, when the shot is executed properly.

A Slight Miscalculation

My good friend, great trick shot artist and entertainer Bogdan Wolkowski and I gave an exhibition in Poland. Bogdan decided to do the Skyscraper Shot with 30 racks and 93 balls! Now that's about a 14-foot tall structure, not counting the table. While he was setting up the shot I gave a 30-minute interview. He had to be very careful as you might have imagined or the whole thing could have easily collapsed during construction.

When Bogdan got ready to shoot, he didn't want me to feel left out of the glorious finale to our show, so he decided we would both shoot at the same time and dislodge and replace two balls simultaneously. To do this the balls under the rack have to be positioned just right. While we were trying to move the 2-ball into position our building collapsed and we barely escaped without being pummeled by falling pool balls and racks. The place was packed with spectators and I believe our blooper earned us a bigger ovation than any of our previous shots!

About 30 minutes later after Bogdan set up the shot again he made it alone and we all celebrated.

Time Will Tell 9-Ball Shot

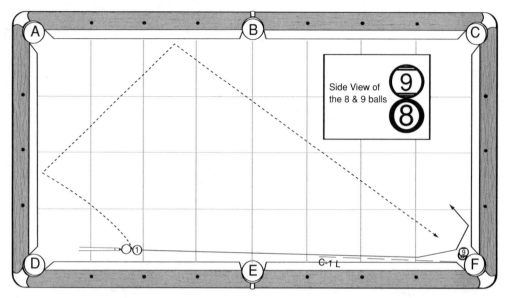

SUR: 2.0   MMS
EXR: 5.0   Video
MSR: 80%

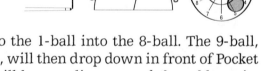

The object of this shot is to combo the 1-ball into the 8-ball. The 9-ball, which is sitting on top of the 8-ball, will then drop down in front of Pocket F. In the meantime the cue ball will be traveling around the table on its way towards the newly positioned 9-ball.

You will need a gaffed 8-ball (one with a small flat surface on one side and an indentation on the other). The 9-ball is balanced on top of the 8-ball. Place the cue ball and 1-ball in line with the right side of Pocket F. The cue ball should be about two inches from the cushion. Apply lots of low right english at 4:30. Use a closed bridge and a medium hard stroke. Aim straight at the 1-ball. Make sure you stroke through the cue ball like when you are playing a normal draw shot. Don't hold back on your follow through.

When the shot is properly stroked, the cue ball will squirt to the left and then draw back to the end rail before continuing around and down the table towards the 9-ball.

The Mysterious Flying 8-Ball Shot

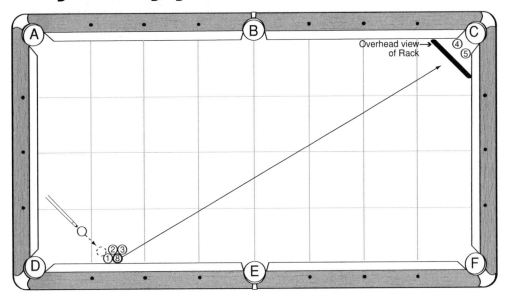

SUR: 3.5
EXR: 2.5
MSR: 85%

Set up the 1, 2, 3, and 8-balls as shown. Make sure all four balls are frozen with the 1-ball and 8-ball frozen to the cushion. Start with the 8-ball about a diamond and a half from Pocket D. Play the shot first without using the rack and the two balls in front of Pocket C. Use a medium hard stroke about a half tip of draw. Aim for a full hit on the 1-ball. The 8-ball should travel into the center of the pocket. If it doesn't, adjust the position of the four balls.

If the 8-ball goes to the right of Pocket C, move the four balls a little closer to Pocket D. If the 8-ball hits to the left of Pocket C, move the balls a little further from Pocket D.

Once you've located the correct spot for the four balls, place two balls in front of Pocket C. Position a wooden rack on its side in front of the two blockers. The 8-ball will jump over the balls and into Pocket C.

The Ball Tray Shot

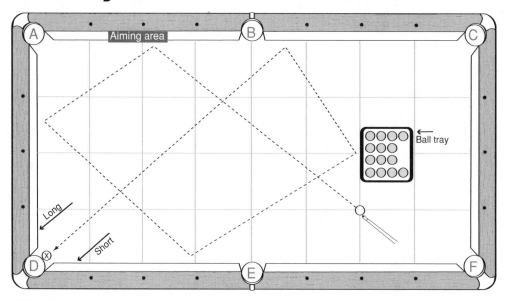

SUR: 2.5
EXR: 3.5
MSR: 80%

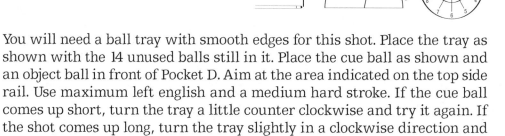

You will need a ball tray with smooth edges for this shot. Place the tray as shown with the 14 unused balls still in it. Place the cue ball as shown and an object ball in front of Pocket D. Aim at the area indicated on the top side rail. Use maximum left english and a medium hard stroke. If the cue ball comes up short, turn the tray a little counter clockwise and try it again. If the shot comes up long, turn the tray slightly in a clockwise direction and try it again.

The Moving Cue Shot

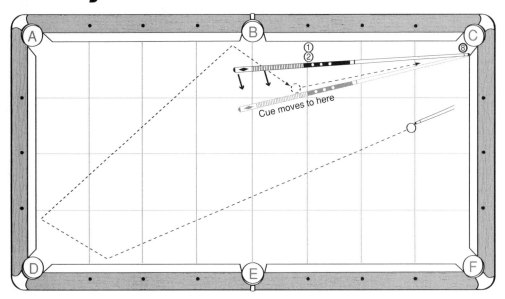

Cue moves to here

SUR: 2.0
EXR: 2.5
MSR: 90%

The proposition you are going to offer is to make the 8-ball without touching either of the two object balls and without jumping over the cue. Use a full tip of right english. Shoot with a medium hard stroke. The cue ball will travel three rails before rebounding into the cue. The cue will slide over enough so that the cue ball will clear the object balls on its way to the 8-ball.

I set up this shot for Alex Corretja, a top tennis player from Spain. He made it when he was a guest of the Carom Christmas show in Barcelona.

The Chattanooga Choo Choo Shot

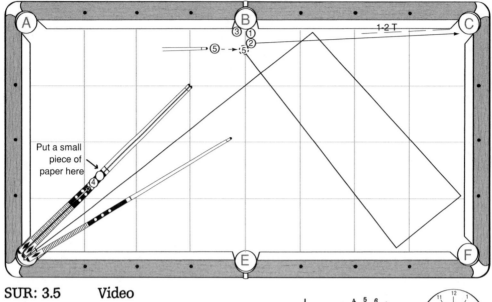

SUR: 3.5   Video
EXR: 3.0
MSR: 95%

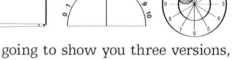

Everyone loves the railroad shots. I'm going to show you three versions, two of which are my creations. However my favorite, The Chattanooga Choo Choo Shot, is one I learned from Norm Webber.

You will need three extra cues, two of which must be straight and the same length. The third cue doesn't have to be so straight. Place the two straight cues into the corner as shown. Take the third cue and place the butt into the corner pocket. It also must be opened up as diagrammed. Now roll the cue ball up into the open part and see if it will turn the corner and roll down between the two closely spaced cues. If the cue ball doesn't make the turn, keep adjusting the cue until you get it right.

Place the 3-ball up against the left side of Pocket B. Now adjust the cues so when the cue ball rolls down them, it will make the 3-ball and then carom to the right and out of the way. After you've completed this test, place the cue ball and 4-ball on top of the cues as diagrammed. Fold up a small piece of paper and use it to keep the cue ball and 4-ball in place.

Place the 1-ball and 2-ball as shown. The 5-ball acts as the cue ball. Aim for a half ball hit on the right side of the 2-ball. Use top left english and a medium speed stroke. This works best on most tables. The 1-ball goes into Pocket B, the 2-ball goes into Pocket C. The 5-ball will travel three rails and up onto the cues before turning the corner and rolling down into the 4-ball and cue ball. The cue ball then rolls down the cues and pockets the 3-ball, moving out of the way for the 4-ball and 5-ball, which will both go into Pocket B.

Mike's Three Ball Railroad Shot

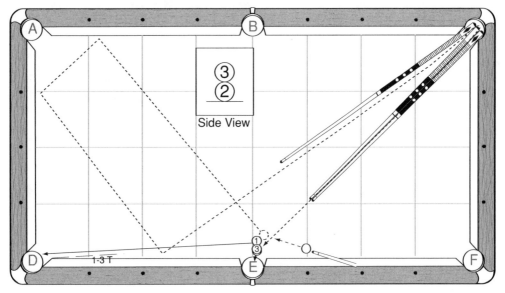

SUR: 2.5   MMS
EXR: 2.5   Video
MSR: 95%

This is one of my creations. Place the gaffed 2-ball as diagrammed with the 3-ball on top. The 1-ball is frozen to the gaffed ball with the tangent line aligned to the left edge of Pocket D. The cues should be set up the same way as in the Chattanooga Choo Choo Shot.

Place the cue ball a little closer to the cushion for this shot. Aim for a half ball hit on the 1-ball. Use top left english and a medium to medium hard stroke.

The 1-ball will go into the corner and the gaffed ball into Pocket E. The 3-ball, which was positioned on top of the 2-ball, will fall straight down and stay in place. The cue ball will circle the table, climb up the cues, turn the corner, and end its journey by pocketing the 3-ball.

Bar Table Railroad Shot

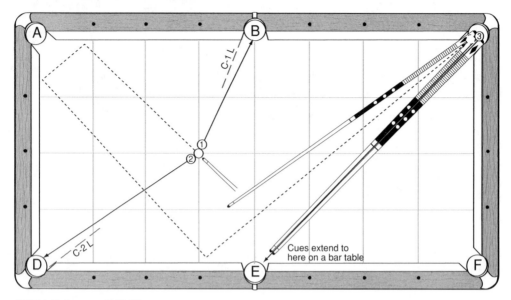

Cues extend to here on a bar table

SUR: 3.0   MMS
EXR: 2.5   Video
MSR: 95%

I use this shot when I'm giving an exhibition on a bar table and I get a request for a railroad shot. I specially created this shot for the 3.5' x 7' tables because standard length cues are too long for the previous versions. You can, of course, also play this shot on a regulation table.

Place the cues as diagrammed. Balance the 3-ball between the open cue and the one next to it. Make sure the cue ball, 1-ball, and 2-ball are frozen. You will have to allow for a lot of throw when lining up both object balls because of the left english. You'll also need to shoot a little harder so the cue ball will dislodge the 3-ball and knock it onto the right set of tracks.

Four Balls in Rotation with a Bank & Kick

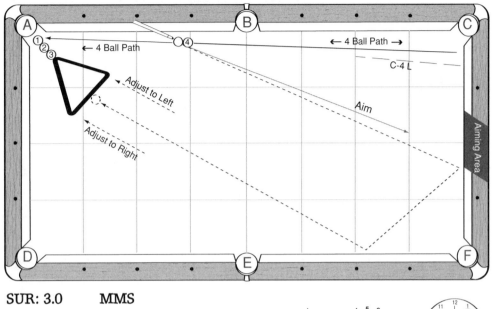

SUR: 3.0   MMS
EXR: 4.0
MSR: 85%

45°-55°

You're given the opportunity to make four balls in rotation with this shot. Be sure to elevate your cue to 45-55 degrees. Start by aiming at the center of the aiming area. If that works, you've found the correct target. If not, start adjusting in small increments to either side of the aiming area. Hit the cue ball at 1:30. Use a medium to medium hard stroke. When executed properly the cue ball will go two cushions, hit the rack and pocket the 1, 2, and 3-balls before the 4-ball arrives at Pocket A,

This shot is much easier when you only use two balls next to the rack instead of three. The 4-ball now has a better chance of going. It may hit the rack and still find the pocket.

Luke's 8-Ball Shot

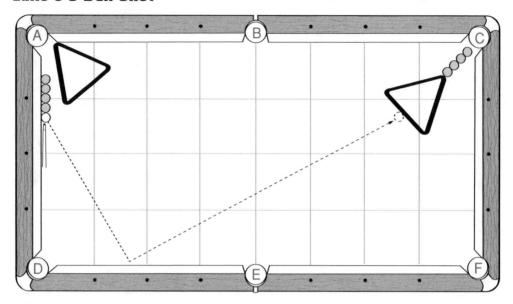

SUR: 2.0
EXR: 3.5
MSR: 85%

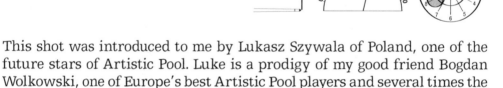

This shot was introduced to me by Lukasz Szywala of Poland, one of the future stars of Artistic Pool. Luke is a prodigy of my good friend Bogdan Wolkowski, one of Europe's best Artistic Pool players and several times the world trick shot champion in snooker.

Set up the balls and racks as shown. Aim straight into the line of four balls in front of the cue ball. Use maximum english at 8:00 and a medium hard stroke. The cue ball should deflect to the right, draw back into the side rail with good speed, and travel down the table and before striking the rack, pocketing the remaining four balls into Pocket C.

Roy's Psychic Energy Shot

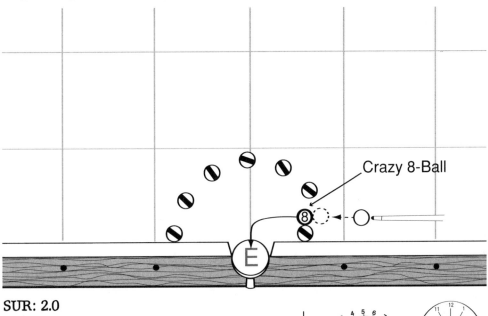

Crazy 8-Ball

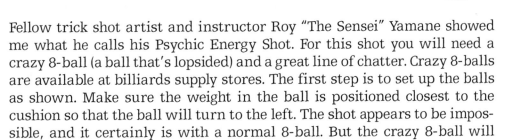

SUR: 2.0
EXR: 1.0
MSR: 100%

Fellow trick shot artist and instructor Roy "The Sensei" Yamane showed me what he calls his Psychic Energy Shot. For this shot you will need a crazy 8-ball (a ball that's lopsided) and a great line of chatter. Crazy 8-balls are available at billiards supply stores. The first step is to set up the balls as shown. Make sure the weight in the ball is positioned closest to the cushion so that the ball will turn to the left. The shot appears to be impossible, and it certainly is with a normal 8-ball. But the crazy 8-ball will turn at a right angle to the left and disappear into the side pocket.

Once you've got the balls set up, ask the crowd if they have seen or heard about how psychic energy has been used to bend forks and such. Most will know about it. Now tell them that you will need their help to make the 8-ball. They must put their energy to work so that when you shoot the 8-ball it will bend to the left and into the pocket. A very soft stroke and excellent conversation are the keys.

The Silver Dollar Proposition Shot

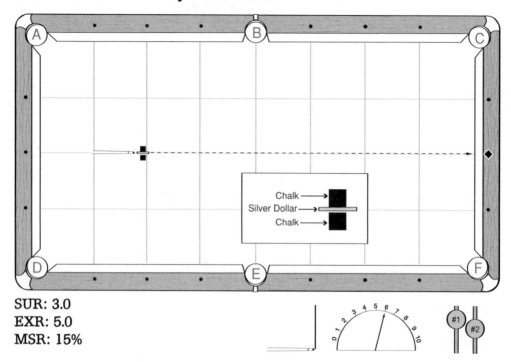

SUR: 3.0
EXR: 5.0
MSR: 15%

You will need a silver dollar for this shot. The object is to have the dollar hit the far end rail and rebound back between two closely spaced pieces of chalk. Place the chalk at the foot spot. The gap between them should be about twice the width of the dollar. The dollar is placed against one of the pieces of chalk in a nearly perfectly upright position. Aim at the middle diamond on the far end rail. You may wish to put a piece of chalk on the rail as shown as this will make aiming a little easier. Cue above the chalk on the top half of the dollar. Use a medium hard stroke. This is a very difficult shot. So if you are having trouble making it, try moving the chalk and dollar a diamond closer to the end rail.

I was fortunate enough once to have the dollar split the pieces of chalk, bounce off the left end rail, and then rebound between the pieces of chalk a second time.

You can turn this shot into a proposition shot. Here's how. In the likely event that you miss it a couple of times, offer a wager on the next attempt. Once the bet has been made, make a slight adjustment in setting up the shot. This time strike the dollar in the middle. The two pieces of chalk will go flying in opposite directions, leaving a huge gap for the dollar to negotiate.

If you have trouble locating a silver dollar, you might try shooting the shot with a quarter as shown in Chef Anton's *The Pool Hustler's Handbook*. He advises that you set it up and aim for the side rail (two diamonds away) instead of the distant end rail.

The Curving Silver Dollar Shot

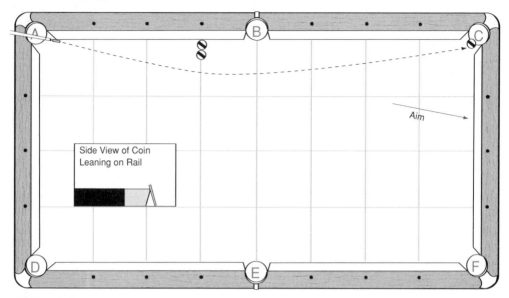

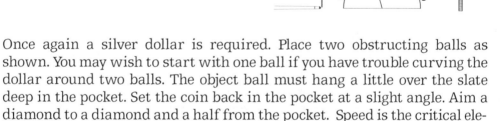

SUR: 2.5
EXR: 2.5
MSR: 90%

Once again a silver dollar is required. Place two obstructing balls as shown. You may wish to start with one ball if you have trouble curving the dollar around two balls. The object ball must hang a little over the slate deep in the pocket. Set the coin back in the pocket at a slight angle. Aim a diamond to a diamond and a half from the pocket. Speed is the critical element to this shot. Use a medium soft stroke. If the dollar dies short of the pocket, add a little more speed. Use a softer stroke if the dollar strikes the far end rail.

Capelle's Rocket Launcher Shot

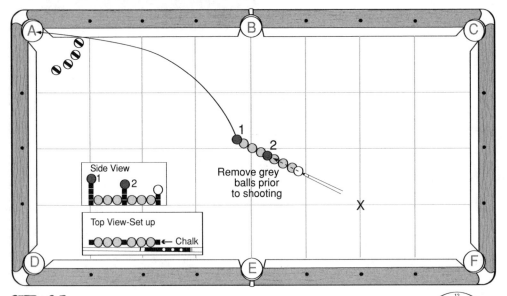

SUR: 3.5
EXR: 4.0
MSR: 70%

Phil Capelle dreamed up this fast moving shot. The sight of balls mounted on the three towers will pique your fans interest and then they be amazed at how quickly the shot unfolds. The object is to make the 1-ball on the highest stand fly over the obstructers and land in Pocket A on the fly. The shot is actually a flying straight in combination on chalk.

You will need nine pieces of new chalk. Lay your cue on the table with the tip a half-inch to the left of the center of Pocket A. The butt should be over the middle of the table. Place three balls along side the end of the cue. Build a tower with four pieces of chalk on the side closest to Pocket A. Place the 1-ball on top. Construct another tower for the 2-ball with three pieces on the other side of the three balls. Remove the balls next to the cue.

Extend your cue towards Pocket F so it will act as a guide for building the third tower. Put the three set up balls along side the cue. Place two pieces of chalk next to the cue and place the cue ball on top. Remove the set up balls. Get down near table level at Position X and check to make sure the shot is lined up straight. Place the blockers in front of Pocket A.

Use an elevated open bridge. Raise your hand up enough so you can hit the cue ball in the dead center with a level stroke. Aim to hit the 2-ball fully. Use a hard stroke. Both speed and accuracy are required. An accurate hit ensures the 1-ball will fly directly towards the pocket. The correct speed enables the 1-ball to fly the correct distance into Pocket A.

As a word of warning, be sure no spectators or breakable objects are near the opposite side of Pocket A.

4 *Crowd Pleasers*

After traveling for nearly 30 years entertaining audiences worldwide I have discovered the select group of trick shots that seem to especially delight spectators. I call them crowd pleasers. There is just something about the movement of the balls that makes these shots especially delightful. They are to pool what the slam-dunk is to basketball, the tape measure home run to baseball, and the long bomb to football.

Crowds love action, and these shots provide it in spades as a goodly number of them feature several balls in motion at once. On one version of the Just Showing Off Shot, eight balls will find the pocket. On Earl's and my Beijing 14-Ball Shot, 14 balls will be pocketed in less than three seconds. And on another shot, a dime will fly off the cushion and into a glass.

Many of these shots take some time and effort to set up. And on several of them you will have to spend some time perfecting the execution of the shot. The big keys are in the set up and in making the necessary adjustment(s) should you miss your first attempt. As always, it will improve your act if you have an escape line ready should the shot fail on your first or subsequent attempts.

If you take the time to learn these shots, your loyal fans will shower you with applause well out of proportion to the difficulty of the shots.

Rempe's Eight in One

Version With 8 Balls
SUR: 3.0 for 8 ball version.
EXR: 2.5 for 8 ball version
MSR: 90%

The first time I saw this shot was at a billiard trade show in Germany. I immediately liked the shot as played by Jim Rempe, so I just happened to take a few notes. What makes this such a neat shot is that the balls disappear so quickly.

The cue ball is placed on the spot and is frozen to the 1-ball and 2-ball. When the conditions are good try aligning the right edges of the cue ball and 2-ball with the left edge of the 5-ball. Similarly, align the left edges of the cue ball and 1-ball with the right edge of the 3-ball. The edge of the 6-ball is hanging over the slate and is frozen to the 5-ball. The 6-ball and 5-ball are aligned straight across the table at a 90-degree angle to the long rail. Place the 3-ball and 4-ball the same way on the opposite side of the table. Tap all of the balls lightly so you can easily repeat the shot should you somehow fail to pocket all eight balls on your first attempt. The 7-ball is a ball's width from the center of the spot. It is frozen to the 8-ball as shown.

The main challenge is in the set up, but you must also be very precise with your speed of stroke. Hit the cue ball a little less than a half tip above center with a medium hard stroke. The 5-ball and 7-ball should reach Pocket F at almost exactly the same moment. The same goes with the 3-ball and 8-ball as they race for Pocket E. The precise timing of these two sets of balls is just one more reason why this is a difficult shot. If one of the balls happens to jar the pocket it will usually keep the other ball from falling.

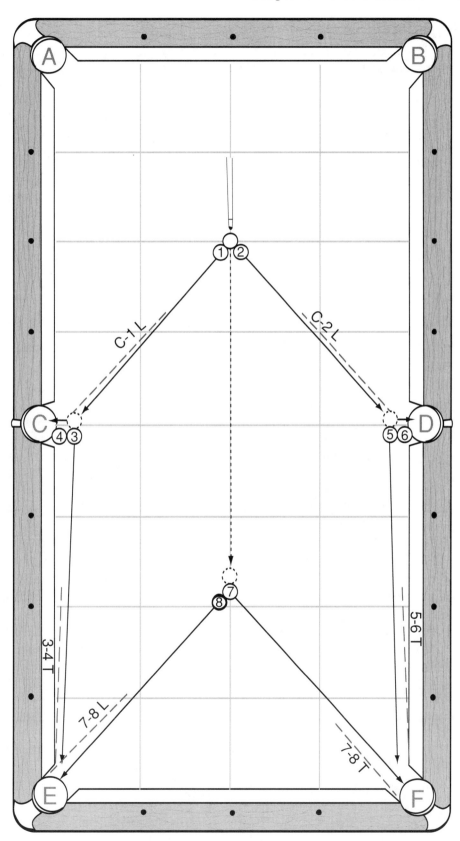

The Butterfly

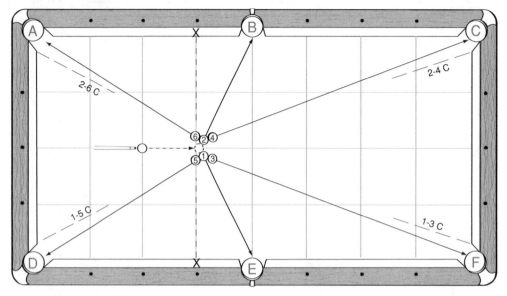

SUR: 3.5   Video
EXR: 2.0   ESPN
MSR: 95%

The Butterfly has been around forever and is one of the most requested and well known trick shots. People are always interested in learning how to set it up, which happens to be the big key to the shot. Start the set up procedure with the 1-ball and 2-ball. Place them about an inch and a half apart and one inch to the right of Line X, which connects the two diamonds adjacent to the side pockets.

Carefully place the remaining four balls. Be sure to allow for throw as indicated on the diagram. I recommend that you use the numbering sequence shown in the diagram. Just in case a ball or two fails to drop, you will know which ball(s) was not set up properly. Then adjust accordingly for your next attempt.

Strike the cue ball a little more than a half tip below center. I recommend using a medium hard stroke because then you won't have to allow for as much throw on the four outside balls.

The Half Butterfly

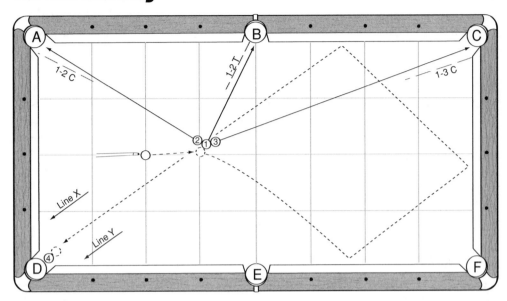

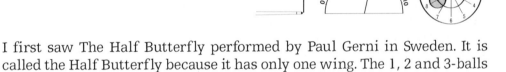

SUR: 2.5
EXR: 3.0
MSR: 90%

I first saw The Half Butterfly performed by Paul Gerni in Sweden. It is called the Half Butterfly because it has only one wing. The 1, 2 and 3-balls are set up exactly as in the Butterfly shot.

The 4-ball is placed in front of Pocket D. Aim for about a half ball hit on the 1-ball. Use nearly a full tip of low left english at 8:00 and a medium hard stroke. The big challenge is in pocketing the 4-ball. If the cue ball follows Line X aim for a fuller hit on the 1-ball. And if the cue ball is following Line Y, hit the 1-ball a little thinner.

Titanic Shot (aka The Dream Shot)

SUR: 5.0   Video
EXR: 4.0
MSR: 75%

The Titanic is a combination of the Rempe Eight in One and The Butterfly shots. However, it also features two additional balls in front of each side pocket. The set up is the biggest challenge to the Titanic Shot because so many things can go wrong. But the shot is worth the effort as you'll treat your fans to the sight of 14 balls going in on one shot!

Place two balls so that they are hanging over the edge of Pockets A and B. Aim down the exact the center of the table. Strike the cue ball just a little above center with a medium hard to hard stroke (it depends on the table). Then get set to watch balls start flying into all six pockets.

An Iceberg in Barcelona

I used to call this shot the Dream Shot, but while preparing for a TV special called Carom Christmas in Barcelona the name was changed to the Titanic. The show was an hour of entertainment that featured trick shots on a pool table and a billiard (carom) table. I performed the pool shots and Danny Sanchez and Mr. Perea executed the billiard shots. They also had a number of celebrities on the show.

The show had a live audience of about 100 people and 11 cameras. It took about 10-12 hours to be taped. The show appeared on TV3, which is one of their top government channels. For the month of December Carom Christmas got better ratings than any other program.

I sent diagrams of the shots I was going to use to the producer and writer about a month before the show so they could write the script. Jose Farras, the creator and writer of the show, changed the name to the Titanic. For the program, I was scripted to say that, "I call this shot the Titanic Shot and I'm going to sink every ball in one shot." I was successful in making all of the balls on my first attempt as planned. Now Farras, who was also the MC, picked up the cue ball and says, "Mike, you didn't sink all of the balls. What about this one?" I replied, "Farras, that's the iceberg." The crowd loved it.

I now like to call this shot the Titanic because I have an out in case all of the balls fail to drop. Should one or more remain on the table, I call them the survivors.

Bill "Weenie Beanie" Staton made the shot on the TV show *I've Got a Secret*, pocketing 16 balls. He placed two extra balls in the far corners.

I've set the Titanic Shot for other celebrities. Mars Callahan made it when we were in Las Vegas promoting the movie *Pool Hall Junkies*. Scott "Chachi" Baio from the *Happy Days* TV series, and my good friends Rick Rodgers and James Tolkan (*Top Gun*) have also performed it successfully.

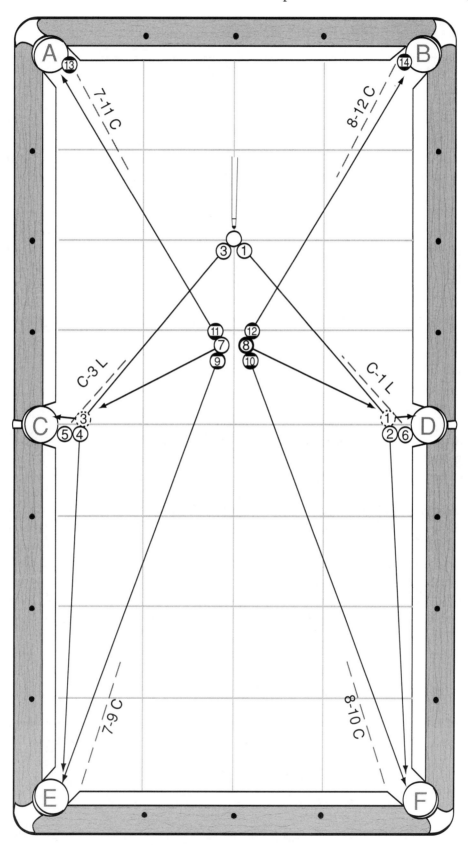

The Football Shot

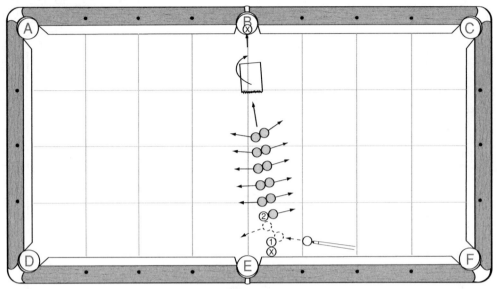

SUR: 4.0   Video
EXR: 3.0   ESPN
MSR: 90%

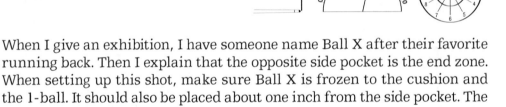

When I give an exhibition, I have someone name Ball X after their favorite running back. Then I explain that the opposite side pocket is the end zone. When setting up this shot, make sure Ball X is frozen to the cushion and the 1-ball. It should also be placed about one inch from the side pocket. The 2-ball should be about two ball widths from the 1-ball. Angle the six pairs of balls as diagrammed. There should be an inch of separation between each pair.

Place a small paper bag where indicated. The bag should be 5-6 inches long and the opening should be just big enough for a ball to roll into easily. Aim for a half ball hit on the right side of the 1-ball. Use a tip of follow and a medium hard stroke. The cue ball will carom into the 2-ball, clearing the six pairs of balls. Ball X will bank across the open field into the paper bag. The bag will flip over and the running back (Ball X) will emerge in the end zone.

Parting of the Red Sea

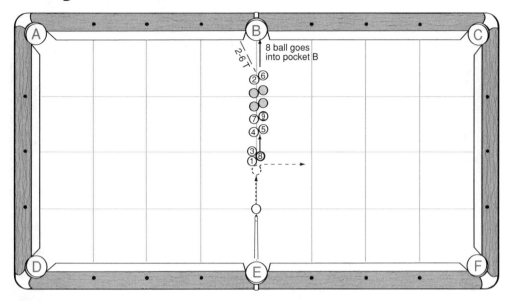

8 ball goes into pocket B

2-6 T

SUR: 3.5
EXR: 3.5
MSR: 90%

Align the 1, 3, and 8-balls as diagrammed. The 1-ball and 3-ball should line up straight for the left side of the Pocket B. Freeze the 8-ball with the 1-ball and 3-ball. Angle the 4-ball and 5-ball as shown. The 4-ball and 3-ball should be about a ball's width apart. The 4-ball should be positioned so the 3-ball will hit it about three quarters full on the left side. Make sure the tangent line between the 2-ball and 6-ball points slightly to the left of the point of the side pocket. Place the cue ball half the distance between Pocket E and the 8-ball. Aim for a half ball hit on the right side of the 1-ball. Strike the cue ball in the center with a medium stroke.

Speed Demon

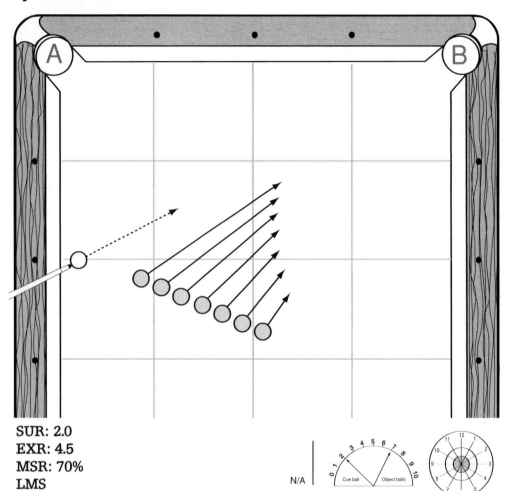

SUR: 2.0
EXR: 4.5
MSR: 70%
LMS

N/A

I learned this shot in England while in a snooker trick shot competition. You must shoot the cue ball very slowly into Pocket B. Use a very soft stroke. Before it arrives you must shoot the other seven balls into the same pocket. These are played with a hard stroke. The shot takes lots of practice. I suggest that you start with four balls until you get the feel of it.

This shot is easier on a snooker table because you have more room to work with. I've seen Dennis Taylor, a former world snooker champion, sink twelve balls before the cue ball arrived. Talk about a machine gun shooter!

Air Raid

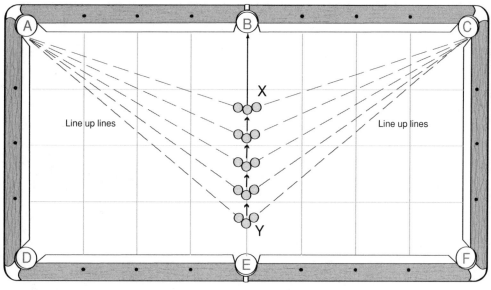

SUR: 4.5
EXR: 3.0
MSR: 90%

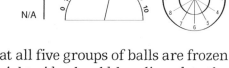

N/A

Make sure when setting up this shot that all five groups of balls are frozen as diagrammed. The five balls on the right side should be aligned to the right edge of Pocket C to allow for throw. Similarly, the five balls on the left side should be pointing towards the left edge of Pocket A.

Aim the center balls at the center of Pocket B. Now for the hard part. You must shoot while your bridge is held in the air above each cluster. Start with Group X and work your way back towards Group Y. Use a medium hard stroke. Try to shoot each group within one-second intervals.

Just Showing Off Shot

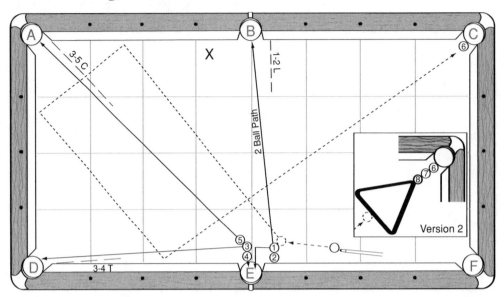

Version With 6 Balls
SUR: 3.5   Video
EXR: 3.5
MSR: 90%

The set up is not too difficult. Place the 1, 2, and 6-balls the same as you would for the Jerry Orbach 3-Ball Shot on page 26. The 1-ball and 2-ball go near the side pocket. There should be a one-inch gap between the edge of the 2-ball and the point of the side pocket. Position the 6-ball in the jaws of Pocket C. The cue ball is a diamond and a half to the right of the side pocket and is about a ball's width from the rail.

When setting up the 3-ball and 4-ball, be sure that the 3-ball is an eighth of an inch further out towards the center of the table than the 1-ball. This placement enables the 1-ball to carom into Pocket E. The 3-ball goes in Pocket D while the 4-ball goes in Pocket E. Freeze the 5-ball to the 3-ball so they are aligned with the right side of Pocket A. Use a half tip of left english and a medium to medium hard stroke.

You can spice up this shot by placing the 7-ball and 8-ball in a straight line with the 6-ball. Make sure they are frozen. Then place a wooden rack as shown in the diagram. When the cue ball hits the rack, the three balls near Pocket C will all disappear.

This is the shot from the Miller Lite commercial that Steve Mizerak made famous, and that made him a well-known figure in mainstream America.

No Time for Kissing

In my one of my videos I set up this shot on both sides of the table. Then my wife Francine and I shot simultaneously and pocketed all 12 balls. Francine and I also shoot this shot together at a lot of my exhibitions. After we make it, we meet in the middle for a quick kiss. We were busy doing a lot of exhibitions one time and of course we would always do this shot. During this busy period I was doing a show at a tournament while she had gone shopping. I got a good friend of mine named David Howard, a great player and former U.S. Open champion, to play the shot with me. We nailed it, even making the cue balls go three cushions into the corners at the same time. David met me in the middle to shake hands and I almost kissed him.

When I made the shot in the movie *The Night the Lights Went Out in Georgia*, a stunt man laid across the table instead of a beer like in Steve's commercial. I was going to grab his collar and lift him off the table so the cue ball would make the ball in the corner. Instead he told me to lift him up by the hair of his head. I did as I was told. I then dropped his head down into the slate after the shot had been made. Man, those stunt men sure are tough.

Half Beijing

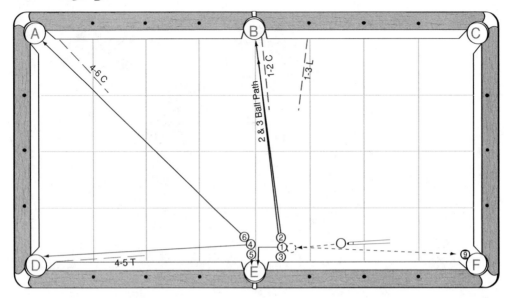

SUR: 3.5   Video
EXR: 3.5
MSR: 85%

To set up this shot you will need to place the 4, 5, and 6-balls exactly as in the Just Showing Off Shot on page 62. The 3-ball should be half the distance from the middle of the side pocket and the first diamond. You may have to adjust the 1, 2, and 3-ball cluster a little.

Place the cue ball about one and a half ball widths from the rail. Aim to hit 90% of the 1-ball. Favor the left side. Hit the cue ball a full tip from center at 7:00. Use a medium hard stroke. If the 3-ball strikes the rail to the right of Pocket B, move the 1-ball very slightly to the right. Should the 3-ball miss to the left of Pocket B, move the 1-ball a little to the left.

I usually tell the crowd to focus hard on the balls at the other end of the table. This enables me to tip the 9-ball into the pocket just in case the cue ball veers away from the rail.

Bachnine 10-Cent Special

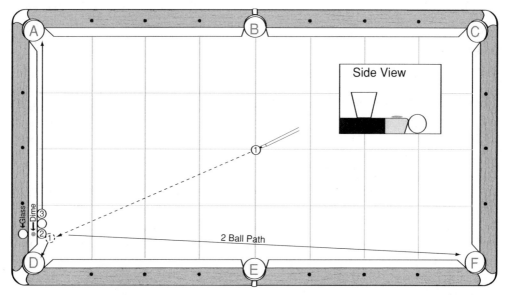

SUR: 3.5   MMS
EXR: 3.5   ESPN
MSR: 80%

The 2-ball, cue ball, and 3-ball are frozen together and to the end rail. The 1-ball is placed in the center of the table. The 1-ball is shot into the 2-ball with a medium hard to hard stroke. Use a half tip of follow and english at 10:30. Aim for between a quarter and a half ball hit on the 2-ball. The correct speed depends on the table.

The 1-ball will carom off the 2-ball and into Pocket D. The 2-ball is banked into Pocket F. And the 3-ball goes into Pocket A. The cue ball stays put. Perhaps because of this, Steve Lillis calls this the *Be Still Shot* when doing his Trick Shot Ministry.

When I was in Bachnine, Germany in 1993 I came up with a different version which I call the Bachnine 10-Cent Special. Set the balls up exactly as before. Now place a dime on the rail opposite the center of the 2-ball. There should be a half-inch gap between the edge of the rail and the coin. Next place a four inch tall glass or coffee cup on the rail where shown. When hit correctly, the dime will jump up into the glass. Normally you have to shoot hard for this to work.

I made this shot against Paul Gerni on ESPN during the Trick Shot Magic 2001 competition. It turned out to be a tremendous crowd pleaser. Even the cameraman loved it.

Mike and Earl's Beijing 14 Ball Shot

SUR: 4.0   MMS
EXR: 4.5
MSR: 60%

I devised this shot in Beijing, China and was lucky enough to have five times U.S. Open winner Earl Strickland as my partner. This shot is particularly impressive when two people shoot it at the same time from opposite sides of the table.

The 1-ball is frozen with the 2-ball and 3-ball. The 3-ball is frozen to the cushion centered on the first diamond from the side pocket. Make sure the 4-ball is a little left of center near Pocket C and about a quarter inch out from a line that connects the points of the side pocket (see Inset X). Align the balls as indicated in Inset X. Place the cue ball in position for a straight in shot on the 1-ball into Pocket A. Use a lot of draw and a little less than a half tip of left english. Use a medium hard stroke. Now you know the first half to the shot.

Now for Mike and Earl's Beijing 14 Ball Shot, which results in 14 balls being pocketed! The shot requires two shooters. The set up is a mirror image of the shot using the 8-14 balls. Place the 7-ball on top of a 2.5 inch tall coin wrapper in front of Pocket E. Repeat the process with the 14-ball in front of Pocket B.

Make sure you and your partner shoot at the same time. Try counting down out loud: 3 – 2 – 1 – shoot. If the shot is executed properly, the balls on top of the coin wrappers will fall down in front of the opposite corner pockets after a ball has rolled under each ball. This will happen just in time for the two cue balls to draw back and pocket them.

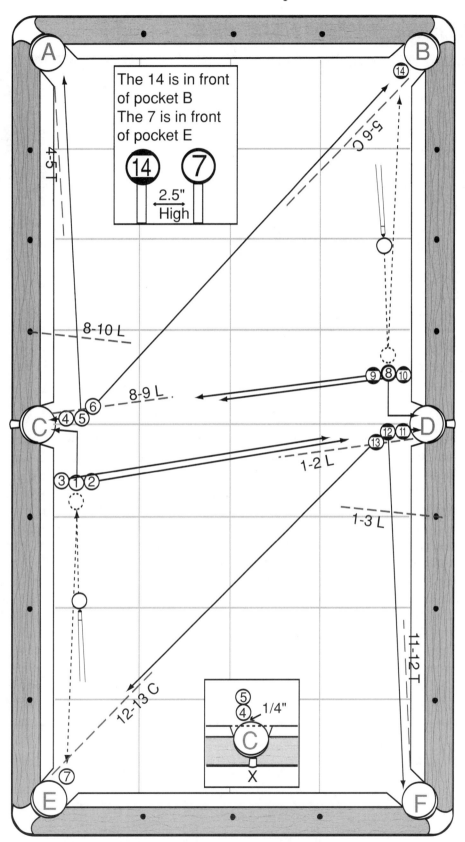

The 14 is in front
of pocket B
The 7 is in front
of pocket E

14   7

2.5"
High

4-5 T

8-10 L

8-9 L

5-6 C

9 8 10

6
4 5
C

8-9 L

3 1 2

12 11
13
D

1-2 L

1-3 L

11-12 T

12-13 C

7

5
4   1/4"
C

X

Windshield Wiper and Broken Wiper

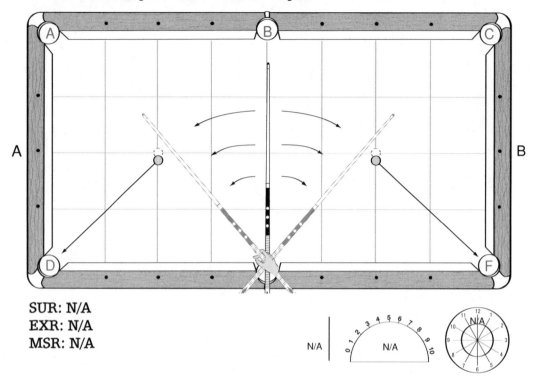

SUR: N/A
EXR: N/A
MSR: N/A

N/A

N/A

N/A

Here is a fun "shot" that I learned in Manila from a Filipino player named Snooky when my wife Francine and I were there. Place an object ball about 1.5 inches from the foot spot and another the same distance from the head spot. Take a house cue and hold it as shown with the cue aligned across the center of the pocket. Now keep your forearm still. Just by hinging your wrist you can make the cue swish to the left and right. The object is to make the balls into Pocket D and then Pocket F over and over again. Have a couple of friends stand at locations A and B. Their job is to replace the balls after they've been pocketed. I usually do ten balls, five on each side.

If you are only able to recruit one volunteer, you could call the shot the Broken Wiper and only shoot to one side over and over. However, your volunteer had better have fast hands for this version of the shot.

The Sideswipe Special

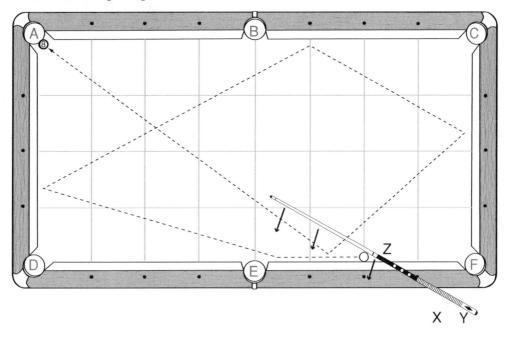

SUR: N/A
EXR: N/A
MSR: N/A
LMS

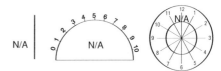

You don't even have to chalk up for this neat little shot. Place the 8-ball in the jaws of Pocket A. Freeze the cue ball adjacent to the first diamond. Stand at Location X. Hold your cue with your left hand at Location Z and your right hand at Location Y. Now pull with your left hand sharply forcing the cue ball up the rail. It should take the path in the diagram to pocket the 8-ball. Note: This shot will sometimes not work on new cloth.

A Friendly Shot

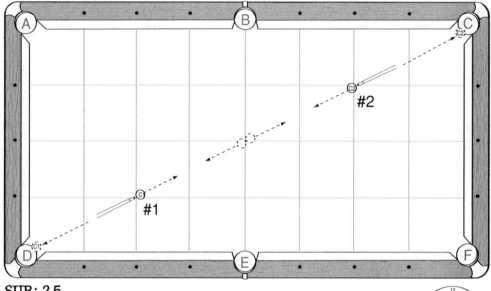

SUR: 2.5
EXR: 4.0
MSR: 50% (with a good partner)

Place two cue balls in the positions shown, which are along a diagonal line between Pocket D and Pocket C. The cue balls are shot directly at each other by two players at opposite ends of the table. The object is to make Cue Ball #1 in Pocket D and Cue Ball #2 in Pocket C.

Aim as though you are trying to make the other cue ball straight into the middle of the opposite corner pocket. Use a dead center hit on the cue ball with a medium speed stroke. Timing is crucial on this shot. I like to say one, two, shoot and anticipate shooting. Try this or look for another sequence that works best for you and your partner. The main thing is to shoot at the same time.

The Big Miscommunication

I saw a video in which two people played a similar shot. In their version, however, one person was supposed to jump over the other's ball. They must have forgot who was supposed to jump and who was going to simply roll the ball across the table because they both played jump shots. The balls met in the middle of the table about six inches above the slate. However, one cue ball was a little higher than the other, and it ricocheted into the florescent lights over the table. The other ball bounced hard into the slate before soaring up into the lights as well. The lights burst into a million pieces and covered the table with glass.

I think it was in Atlanta, Georgia with Larry Grindinger and Rick Wright. They could have named the shot *The Night the Lights Went Out in Georgia*.

The Machine Gun Shot

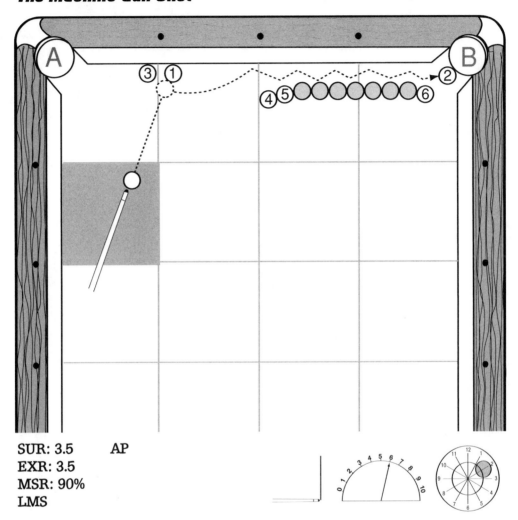

SUR: 3.5   AP
EXR: 3.5
MSR: 90%
LMS

Both Willie Mosconi and Robert Byrne called this the Machine Gun Shot in their books on trick shots. Make sure to keep your cue level. The first couple of balls in the line should be a little more than a ball's width from the rail. The rest should be a ball's width from the cushion. Strike the 1-ball about 80-90% full on the left side. Use a medium hard stroke with top right english. The cue ball should carom off the 3-ball and follow the path in the diagram, making contact with most of the balls on its way to pocketing the 2-ball.

Typical mistakes include shooting too hard, not hitting the cue ball high enough, or not putting enough spin on the cue ball.

In Artistic Pool, the cue ball must make contact with at least four balls in the row. The 5-ball and 6-ball should be about an eighth inch further from the cushion than the others in the row.

Flying 8-Ball Shot

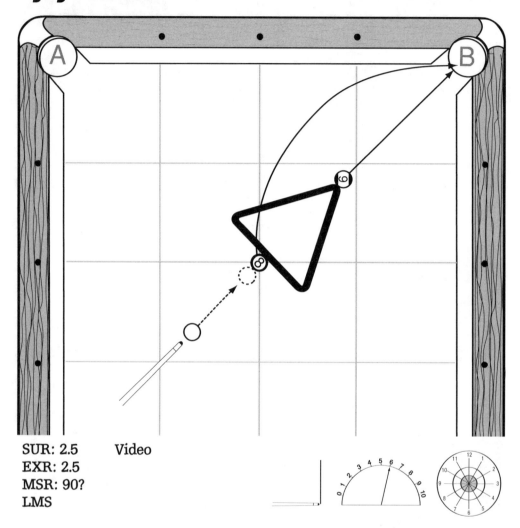

SUR: 2.5   Video
EXR: 2.5
MSR: 90?
LMS

Rick Wright, an excellent trick shot artist from Georgia, taught me The Flying 8-Ball Shot. This crowd pleaser is not very difficult and it will earn you a warm applause. Place a piece of chalk on the spot and place the 8-ball on top of it. Then place a wooden triangle as diagrammed up against the 8-ball. Make sure they are touching. Place the 9-ball so that it touches the point of the wooden triangle. Now take your cue ball and place it in a straight line about eight inches from the 8-ball. Make sure all three balls are in a straight line with the pocket.

Shoot straight into the 8-ball with a medium hard stroke. When stroked properly, the 8-ball will pop up in the air and go into the corner on the fly. The 9-ball will follow in behind it. Speed is the crucial element to the shot, particularly when there is something on the other side of the table that could easily be shattered should the 8-ball fly over the table.

5   *Great Escapes & Gamewinners*

Every shot except one in this chapter is perfectly legal. So should lightening strike and you are confronted with any of these hellish positions in actual play, you need not hesitate to play them. Master these shots and you'll have one of the most complete arsenals in pool. Remember, even if you only need one of them in your entire career, which is a distinct possibility, but the shot helps you win an important championship, your efforts at learning these shots will be worth it. Besides, while you are waiting for one or more of them to appear in competition, you can use them to entertain your friends, relatives and admirers during your shows.

After you set up these shots, challenge your onlookers to find the solution to these seemingly impossible situations. Ask them what they would do. Let them try shooting them if they've got the nerve. After they've given up, it's your turn to show them how to accomplish the impossible. Obstacles that looked to be insurmountable will be overcome. Cushions will give way, balls will be hurdled, and corner hooks will be no problem. All in a days work.

Knowledge and skill are the keys to these shots. And, as always, your mental dexterity at setting up the crowd for your grand solution will only add luster to your accomplishments.

Corner Hooked (Escaping a)

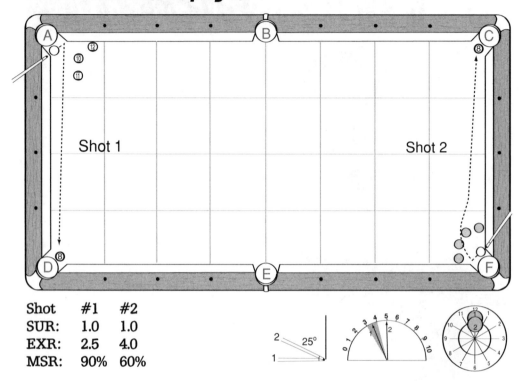

Shot	#1	#2
SUR:	1.0	1.0
EXR:	2.5	4.0
MSR:	90%	60%

In Shot #1 you are in a jam. It's your shot on the 8-ball and you're corner hooked. Furthermore, the three striped balls prevent you from kicking for the 8-ball. However, lucky for you there is a way out of this trap. Hold your cue level with the tip positioned for maximum follow at 12:00. Aim at the point of the corner pocket and use a soft to medium soft stroke. If the cue ball comes back into the cushion, aim a little further to the right.

Shot #2 is similar to Shot #1, only this time the cue ball is completely surrounded. Once again, however, there's hope. Aim at the point the same as before. This time, elevate your cue to 25 degrees. Hit the cue ball one tip above center (not as high as in Shot #1). Stroke down on the cue ball with medium speed. Use a quick jab so you won't double hit the cue ball.

The cue ball will jump over the object balls and go straight across the table to pocket the 8-ball.

Snake Shot

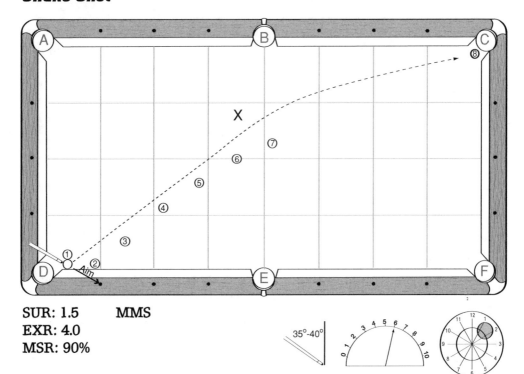

SUR: 1.5   MMS
EXR: 4.0
MSR: 90%

35°-40°

I call this the Snake Shot because the path of the cue ball gives spectators the illusion the cue ball curves twice on its way down table.

With the cue ball pinned to the rail by the 1-ball and several blockers stationed across the table, it appears as if making the 8-ball is out of the question. Not so. Aim at the first diamond as shown. Elevate your cue to 35-40 degrees. Apply maximum english at 1:30 and use a medium hard stroke. You've got to stroke over the top of the cue ball. This is what makes the cue ball massé. If you play the shot only with topspin, the cue ball won't curve nearly as much.

The cue ball will cross the table and trace out a very eye-pleasing arc with a big curve at Position X on its journey to the 8-ball. If the cue ball curves too soon and it hits the blockers, try aiming a little further to the right of the diamond. If the cue ball strikes the rail to the left of Pocket C, adjust your aim a little to the left of the diamond.

The Possible Dream 8-Ball Shot

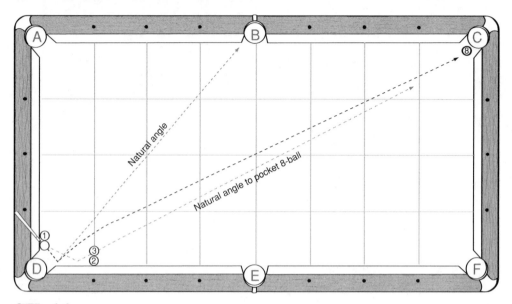

SUR: 1.0
EXR: 3.5
MSR: 85%

Imagine you're in a game of Eight Ball and your opponent has the cue ball locked up tight. If you don't make the 8-ball now, you'll certainly lose the game. The diagram shows the natural angle if you could bank the cue ball off the side rail and down towards the 8-ball. This route is unfortunately blocked by the two solids. If you bank the cue ball to avoid the obstructers, it will travel towards Pocket B. The solution? Set up with your cue as level as possible. Use a soft to medium soft speed. The cue ball will arc around the obstructers as shown in the diagram. Note: You might not be able to make this shot if the cloth is very worn.

The Corner Hooked 3-Railer

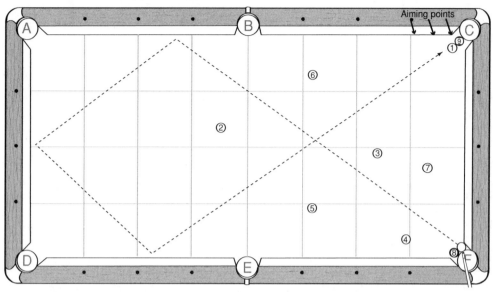

SUR: 2.0   MMS (with 8-ball)
EXR: 3.0
MSR: 90%

The game is Nine Ball and the cue ball is corner hooked and pinned against the 8-ball in Pocket F. In this position you can't push the cue ball out without moving the 8-ball. If you did strike the 8-ball first, your opponent would have ball in hand on the 1-9 combo.

Most people think this shot is impossible, and with good reason. However, there is a way for you to escape this trap and win the game. Here's how: aim into the cushion with a center ball hit on the cue ball. Use a hard stroke. The cue ball will compress the cushion enough to clear the 8-ball before traveling three rails on its way to the game winning 1-9 combo.

Magical Four Rail Kick

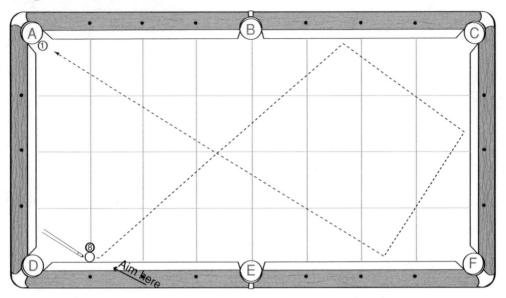

SUR: 1.5   AP
EXR: 3.0
MSR: 90%

I recommend that you use a very firm closed (looped) bridge. The bridge length is only five to six inches. Keep your cue level and use lots of english. You may have to adjust your aiming point slightly depending on the table.

The most difficult part of this shot is avoiding contact with the 8-ball (it does not move when the shot is executed correctly). Use a medium hard stroke and shoot directly into the cushion.

Off the Point Three Railer

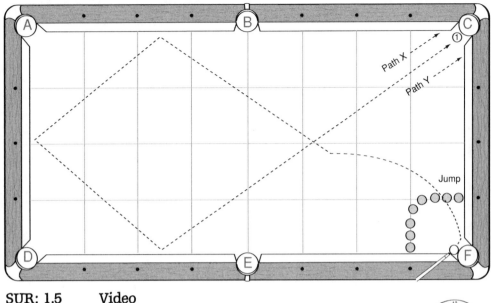

SUR: 1.5   Video
EXR: 3.5   ESPN
MSR: 85%   AP

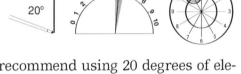

This shot is not as hard as it looks. I recommend using 20 degrees of elevation. Be sure to avoid elevating too much, which is a common mistake on this shot. Aim a little left of the center of the point of the corner pocket. Use a medium to medium hard stroke. You will need to use a punch stroke because your follow through is restricted, unlike a normal shot. A punch stroke will avoid a double hit.

If the cue ball comes up short (Path X), aim a little more to the right. And if the cue ball comes up long (Path Y) aim a little more to the left.

Mr. 60/60

The first time I saw this shot was when Norm "Farmer" Webber gave an exhibition while passing through Chattanooga, Tennessee. Norm's show was extremely fast paced and entertaining as he was able to shoot 60 shots in 60 minutes! I was just getting into exhibitions at the time, so he turned out to be a big influence on my life. Norm is a great showman with a wonderful and always cheerful personality, which is exactly what it takes to do a good exhibition. In fact, showmanship is just as important as having the skill to make the shots.

Pocket Ball X Three Ways

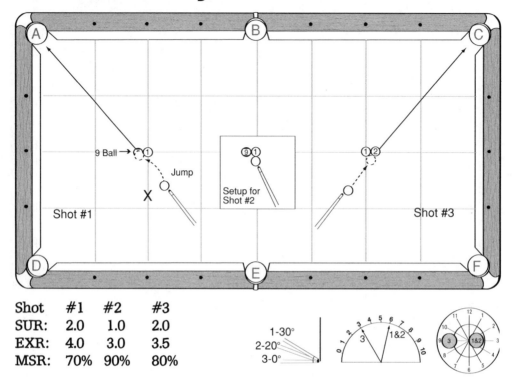

Shot	#1	#2	#3
SUR:	2.0	1.0	2.0
EXR:	4.0	3.0	3.5
MSR:	70%	90%	80%

1-30°
2-20°
3-0°

At first glance it looks like the 9-ball in Shot #1 won't go into Pocket A. After we're through, you'll know three ways you can make it. On two of the three shots, the 1-ball does not even move. The first way is to place the cue ball at Location X. Now play a jump shot over the edge of the 1-ball, hitting the 9-ball on top. The big trick is to keep the cue ball from jumping the table. Elevate your cue to about 30 degrees and apply a half tip of right english. Use a medium hard stroke. If you own a jump cue, you might get better results by using it and only elevating your cue to about 20 degrees.

Shot #2 is the easiest. The 1-ball and 9-ball are set up near the spot as in Shot #1. Freeze the cue ball up against the 1-ball in the position shown in the inset. Aim at the point where the 1-ball and the 9-ball touch. Elevate your cue about 20 degrees and apply a half tip of right english. Use a medium hard stroke.

The third way (Shot #3) is to apply chalk to the side of the 2-ball that is facing you (the area that the cue ball will be contacting). The blue 2-ball obscures the chalk. Use extreme left english. Hit as much of the 2-ball as possible without contacting the 1-ball first. Use a soft stroke. The chalk on the 2-ball will create extra friction, which increases the amount it can be thrown to the right.

The Johnny Cash Special

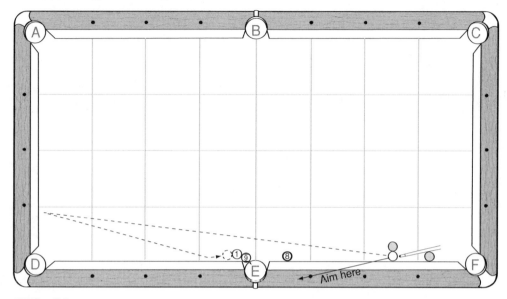

SUR: 2.0
EXR: 2.5
MSR: 95%

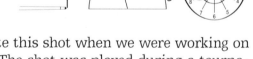

I taught Johnny Cash how to execute this shot when we were working on the movie *The Baron and the Kid.* The shot was played during a tournament scene. As I recall, he made it on the first take.

Place the balls as diagrammed. Aim into the cushion while applying lots of left english. Use a medium soft stroke. If you hit the 8-ball, adjust your aim a little to the left until the cue ball clears it.

The Jerry Briesath Karate Chop Draw Back

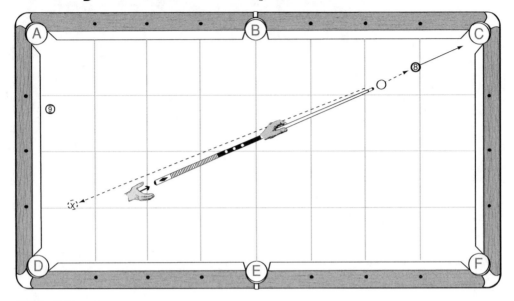

SUR: 2.5
EXR: 3.0
MSR: 90%

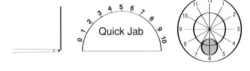

Quick Jab

I learned this shot from Jerry Briesath who has long been considered one of pool's top instructors. This neat little shot is one you could use in a game if no mechanical bridge is available.

The object is to pocket the 8-ball and draw back to Position X for shape on the 9-ball without using the mechanical bridge. This might seem like a difficult task unless you are a great one-handed player or happen to be eight feet tall. However, once you learn this shot, you'll discover it is not too difficult.

Place your cue on the table straight in line with the cue ball and 8-ball. Lean over and reach out as far as you can with your bridge hand. Now use your thumb and pointing finger to raise the shaft so the tip is aimed to hit the cue ball as shown. You should have the tip about one inch from the cue ball. Place the heel of your right hand on the cloth behind the butt of your cue. Now pull your right hand back slowly about eight inches leaving the heel on the cloth. Strike the butt of your cue with a quick jab of the heel of your hand.

It takes some practice to get the feel of the shot. But once you do, you'll have a lot of fun showing it off to your friends. Note: this shot works better on a 4 1/2' x 9' table, because on a smaller table you don't have much room to work with.

The Boomerang Shot

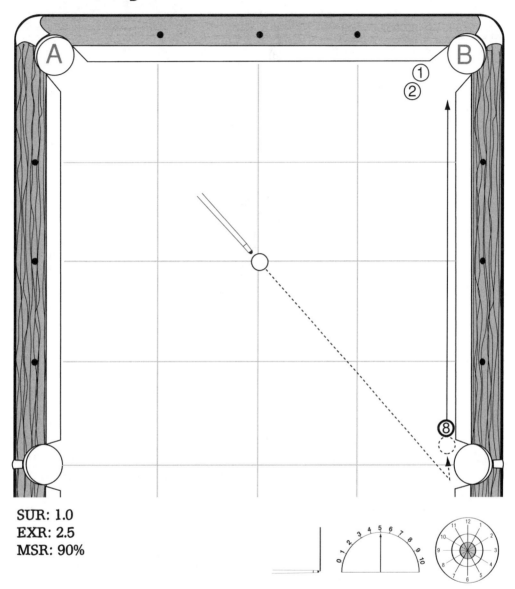

SUR: 1.0
EXR: 2.5
MSR: 90%

The big key to this shot is to find the correct spot for contacting the point of the side pocket. The right spot will vary since the pockets are cut differently on some tables.

Once you find the correct aiming point, the shot is not very difficult. Hit the cue ball in the dead center with a medium speed stroke. This shot could actually come up some day while you are in competition, so learning it is a bonus for your regular game.

The Double Kiss 8-Ball Shot

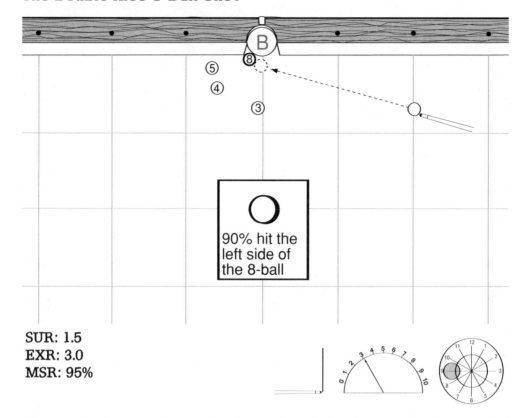

SUR: 1.5
EXR: 3.0
MSR: 95%

Once again it looks like you're doomed to defeat in a game of Eight Ball unless you know the secret to this tricky little shot. Since a kick shot is out of the question, you're going to have to shoot straight at the 8-ball and make it into the side pocket. No problem. Hit the cue ball with maximum left english. Hold your cue as level as possible. Aim to hit the 8-ball 90% full on the left side. Use a soft stroke. Once you find the exact speed, the 8-ball will double kiss the cue ball and the left spin will throw the 8-ball into the side pocket. The keys are speed and lots of spin.

After you've made the shot from the location on the diagram, try to make it with the cue ball closer and closer to the rail.

John DiToro's Lament

I was playing in a Nine Ball tournament in Florida in the early 1990s'. My match with John DiToro reached double hill and I was faced with the shot on the 8-ball we've just discussed above. The 9-ball was close by, so if I made the 8-ball, I would essentially win the match. I played the Double Kiss 8-Ball Shot, made it and won the match. He was, shall we say, a bit surprised at the outcome.

Kiss Back to Win

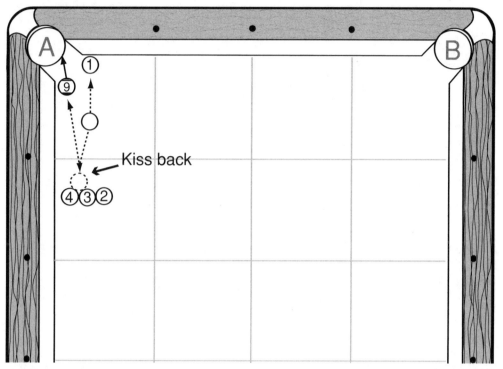

Kiss back

SUR: 3.0
EXR: 4.0
MSR: 75%
LMS

You'll get some second looks when you make this shot. Make sure to place the 2, 3, and 4-balls as diagrammed. To get the necessary action on the cue ball, you must use a half tip of right english and maximum follow with a medium speed stroke. Aim directly at the 1-ball. The cue ball will bounce back, strike the 3-ball and then rebound back into the 9-ball! Make sure to avoid elevating your cue any more than is necessary.

The 9-ball can be made by kissing any of the three balls (the 2, 3, or 4-balls). Nevertheless, you'll typically get the best results by hitting the 3-ball solidly.

On the Rebound

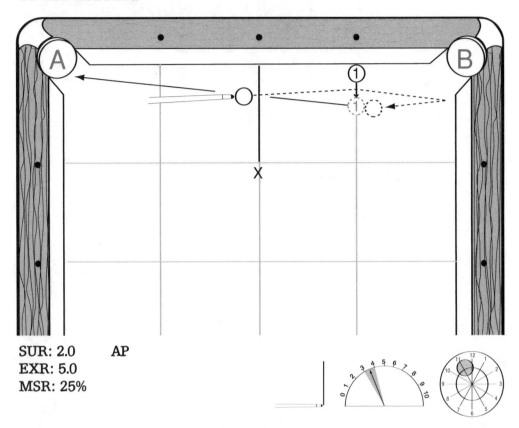

SUR: 2.0   AP
EXR: 5.0
MSR: 25%

The rather simple looking setup to this shot should not deceive you into thinking this in an easy shot. It takes equal doses of skill and luck to make this rascal. Bank the 1-ball softly away from the rail. The cue ball is then supposed to knock the 1-ball into Pocket A after it has rebounded off the side rail.

Place the cue ball about a ball and a half from the cushion. In Artistic Pool the cue ball must be to the left of Line X. Aim for a very thin hit on the 1-ball. Keep your cue nice and level. Speed is critical. Use a soft to medium soft speed stroke. Typical mistakes include hitting the 1-ball too thick and shooting too hard.

6 *Mystery Shots*

There is an aura of mystery about these shots that's similar to those in the previous chapter. One of the main differences, however, is that most of these shots are either illegal or so outrageous that they will virtually never appear in a game should you live to be a thousand years old.

Once again, try to draw your audience into the act. Which ball is going to go? Where? And how? Make them venture a guess as to the solution, or better yet, have them try the shots themselves. After they've failed to guess the solution or make the shot, it's your turn to be the hero by making the impossible possible. Perhaps the most enjoyable shot of the lot is The 8-Ball Riddle Shot, which requires that you spew out a line of chatter at lightening speed prior to executing the shot.

Ultimate Trap Shot

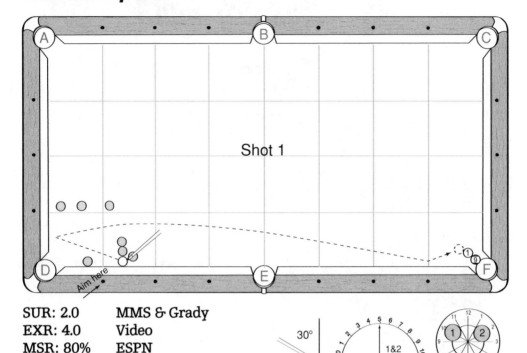

Shot 1

SUR: 2.0   MMS & Grady
EXR: 4.0   Video
MSR: 80%   ESPN
LMS

Grady Mathews came up with shot #2 below. I then improvised on his creation to come up with shot #1.

To make shot #1 you must lean out across the table to get in position for this shot. Elevate your cue to about 30 degrees. Aim at the first diamond, hit the cue ball a full tip off center at 10:00, and use a medium stroke.

Speed is very important on this shot. If you shoot too hard, the cue ball will not curve enough to make the shot. And if you shoot too easy, the cue ball will run into the blockers. Shot #2 is made by using top right english and a medium stroke. Be sure to elevate your cue to 30 degrees.

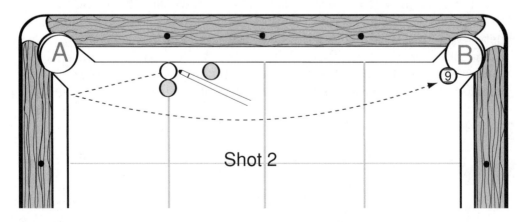

Shot 2

The Mysterious 9-Ball Shot

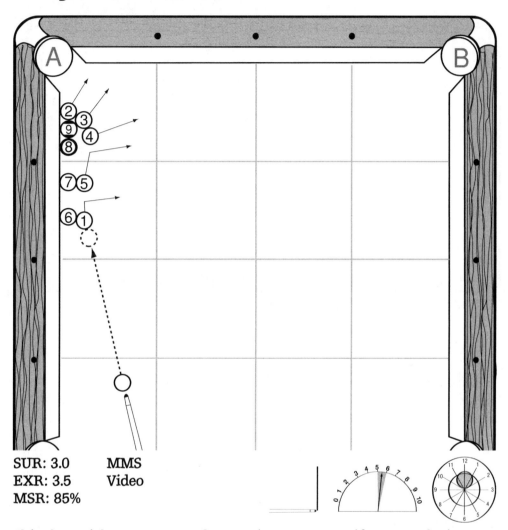

SUR: 3.0   MMS
EXR: 3.5   Video
MSR: 85%

This shot might come up maybe once in your career if you are playing on a table that is lopsided. Shoot straight into the 1-ball. The 9-ball will go into Pocket A without pocketing the 2-ball. Place the balls as diagrammed. The 8-ball is about a ball's width from the 7-ball. And the 7-ball is also a ball's width from the 6-ball. Make sure the five ball cluster is set up properly. The 3-ball, 2-ball, and 9-ball are frozen to each other.

Be sure to angle the 1-ball and 6-ball slightly. Do the same with the 5-ball and 7-ball. You want the 5-ball to kiss into the 4-ball, hitting it full. Line the cue ball up straight with the 1-ball and 8-ball.

Use follow with a medium to medium hard stroke. The 1-ball, 6-ball, 7-ball, and 5-ball will vacate the area so the cue ball can continue into the 8-ball, making the 9-ball on a combination. Before the cue ball hits the 8-ball, the 5-ball will strike the 4-ball, causing the 4-ball, 3-ball, and 2-ball to clear a path for the 9-ball.

The 8-Ball Riddle Shot

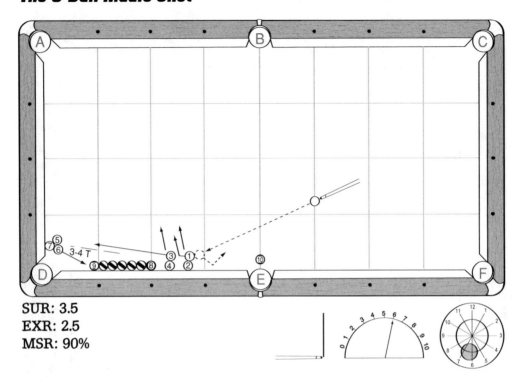

SUR: 3.5
EXR: 2.5
MSR: 90%

The main ingredient to this crowd pleaser is the set up. Freeze the 8-ball on the cushion straight out from the middle diamond. Freeze six striped balls in a line along the cushion between the 9-ball and 8-ball. (Note: on a 4'x 8' or 3 1/2' x 7' table, line up five striped balls instead of six.) The 5, 6, and 7-balls are frozen so that the 6-ball and 7-ball are in line for a full hit on the 9-ball. The 10-ball needs to be close to the side pocket so the 8-ball will kiss off it and go into Pocket E.

You want a ball's width between the 8-ball and 4-ball, and also between the 4-ball and 2-ball. Freeze the 3-ball to the 4-ball so the tangent line is pointing at the left edge of the 5-ball. Freeze the 1-ball with the 2-ball with a slight angle to the right. Place the cue ball as shown. Aim to hit the 1-ball as though you are shooting it straight into the 8-ball. Use a medium hard stroke with 6:30 english on the cue ball. When hit properly, the cue ball should hit the cushion and bounce out of the way.

Tell your friends that you are going to make the 8-ball in Pocket E. See if they can then figure it out before you wow them. In most cases they'll fail to solve the mystery, so you may wish to give them a clue. Tell them you're going to hit the 1-ball first. Unless they are pretty good players, they may still have trouble solving the riddle.

Now explain it real fast like this: the 2-ball moves out of the way. The 1-ball hits the 3-ball, moving the 4-ball out of the way. The 3-ball hits the 5-ball, sending the 7-6 combo into the 9-ball, which makes the 8-ball go straight up the rail into a kiss off the 10-ball and into the side pocket.

The Magical Helper Shot

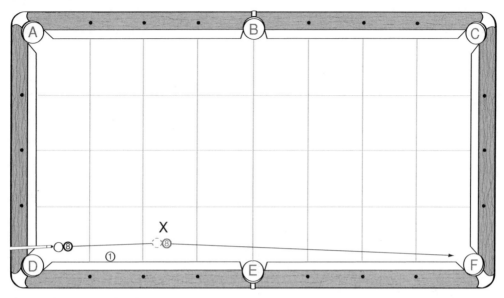

SUR: 2.0   MMS
EXR: 3.5
MSR: 80%

The cue ball is exactly a ball's width from the cushion. The 8-ball is about a sixteenth of an inch more than a ball's width from the side rail. The 1-ball is frozen to the rail about one and a half diamonds from the Pocket D. The cue ball and 8-ball are frozen.

Aim straight into the 8-ball with a level cue. Use a lot of follow with a touch of left english. Use a medium speed stroke. When properly stroked, the cue ball and 8-ball will separate for a short distance. The cue ball will then catch up with the 8-ball because of the topspin. The cue ball will nudge the 8-ball to the right of the original line of aim just enough to make it in the corner. You can hear a click when the balls are at about Position X. Sometimes the balls will make contact two or three times. It actually appears as if the 8-ball is curving around the 1-ball.

This shot is sort of like fooling someone with a magic trick. After the shot is setup, have someone check to see if the 8-ball will go straight in. It won't as the 1-ball is slightly blocking its path. When you make it, they will of course want to see it again and again.

The Jimmy Reid Sneaky 8-Ball Shot

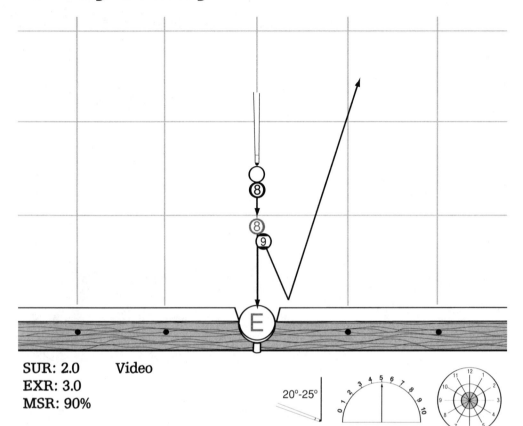

SUR: 2.0   Video
EXR: 3.0
MSR: 90%   20°-25°

Jimmy Reid showed me this sneaky little 8-ball shot quite a few years ago. The 9-ball is placed about eight inches from the side pocket and about a quarter ball to the side of a line running between the centers of the side pockets. The cue ball and 8-ball are frozen together with the 8-ball about six to eight inches from the 9-ball. They should be lined up for the side pocket.

Elevate your cue about 20-25 degrees. Grip your cue a little tighter than normal. Hit the cue ball in the center with a medium stroke. Make sure to aim straight down the line between the center of the 8-ball and cue ball. The key is to have the feeling that your tip is staying on the cue ball for as long as possible without double hitting the cue ball. You and your friends will be pleasantly surprised to see the 8-ball split the pocket.

This shot is another example of the collision effect. The cue ball stays extremely close to the 8-ball. A 100th of a second after the 8-ball contacts the 9-ball, the cue ball will contact the 8-ball again, driving it into the side pocket before it has the chance to be caromed off line.

When good players witness this shot, they invariably request that I play it again, wanting to know the secret.

It Almost Looks Legal

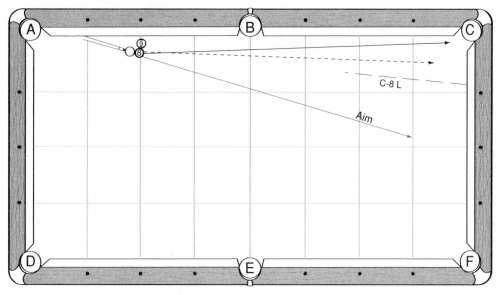

SUR: 2.0   MMS
EXR: 3.5   ESPN
MSR: 70%

Hard Shove

This is a very unusual looking shot. At first glance it appears to be impossible to make the 8-ball in Pocket C because it is frozen to the 9-ball and is aligned well to the right of the pocket as shown. It would be impossible to shoot the 8-ball directly into the corner without moving the 9-ball if you tried to play it directly without using the cue ball, unless you made it curve.

However, if you aim where indicated and play this push shot properly, you can pocket the 8-ball without even moving the 9-ball! The cue ball will stay with the 8-ball and the two balls will realign themselves once they pass by the 9-ball. Place your tip right next to the cue ball and give it a shove with a touch of right english. You will need to apply a bit of force when you shove the cue ball into the 8-ball. When the shot is executed properly, it looks perfectly legal!

Which Goes First

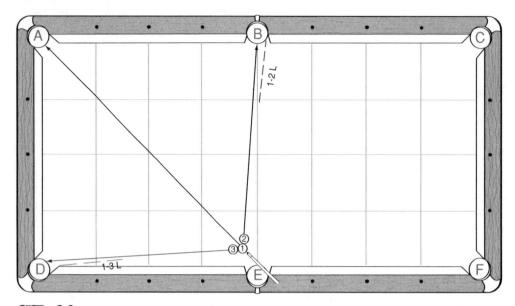

SUR: 2.0
EXR: 2.0
MSR: 95%

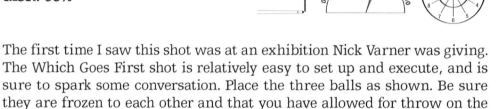

The first time I saw this shot was at an exhibition Nick Varner was giving. The Which Goes First shot is relatively easy to set up and execute, and is sure to spark some conversation. Place the three balls as shown. Be sure they are frozen to each other and that you have allowed for throw on the 2-ball and 3-ball. Hold your cue as level as possible and hit the 1-ball a half tip above center. Use a medium hard to hard stroke.

Before shooting, ask your fans if they can tell you which ball will go in first. The 1-ball, amazingly enough, will reach the pocket first even though it has to travel the furthest.

Air Bridge Position Shot

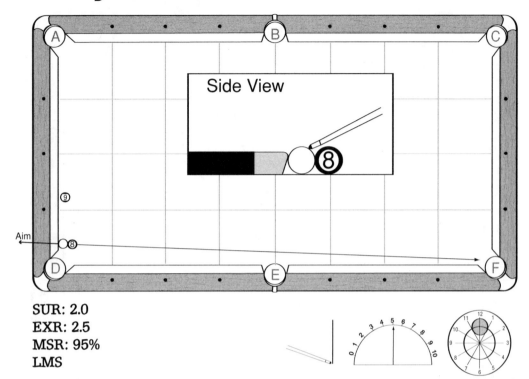

SUR: 2.0
EXR: 2.5
MSR: 95%
LMS

The object of this shot is to make the 8-ball in Pocket F and play position on the 9-ball. You will need to assume your stance along the side rail. Use an air bridge and shoot over the top of the 8-ball. You will be aiming away from the table as shown. Hit the cue ball well above center with a medium stroke.

Paul Newman made this shot in *The Color of Money*.

Sarge's Astounding 8-Ball Shot

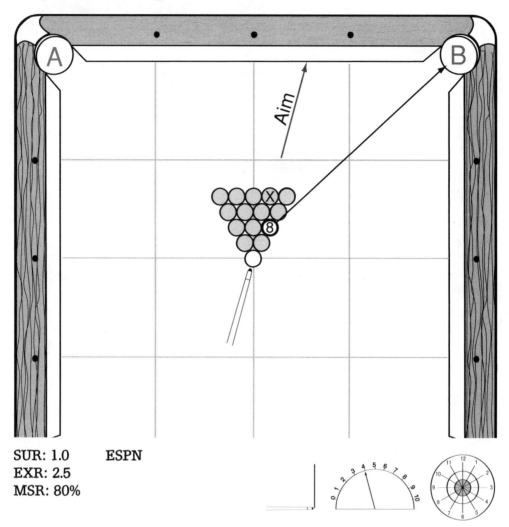

SUR: 1.0   ESPN
EXR: 2.5
MSR: 80%

Ken "Sarge" Aylesworth, a good friend and fellow trick shot artist, showed me this shot at Harvey's Billiards prior to the finals of the 2001 Trick Shot Magic competition. It helped me win a valuable point against Paul Gerni.

The object is to make the 8-ball in Pocket B. Rack up fourteen object balls and the cue ball as shown. The cue ball goes at the top of the rack, and the 8-ball in the middle of the outside row. Aim at the X-ball with your tip about an eighth of an inch away from the cue ball. Use a fluid forward stroke with a medium soft speed. If you are missing to the left, aim a little more to the right, and vice versa.

1 Curve Balls

If you are close to as old as I am, you no doubt marveled at Sandy Koufax's sweeping curve ball. And the younger set has probably witnessed Tiger Woods play a 50-yard intentional hook or slice up on to the green. This chapter offers but a few of pool's answers to these wonders of nature.

When you play pool, your goal of trying to win the game puts severe limitations on your decision-making and shot selection. As a result, you usually get to witness only a small part of the cue balls potential magic. On most shots in real pool, the cue ball curves very little. Any curve usually takes place a split second after contact and is over in a flash. A couple of exceptions are power draw cut shots and power follow shots. These shots often trace out a very wide arc that is quite pleasing to the eye.

In this chapter we're going to make up for the deficiencies inherent in pool games by offering you a series of shots in which the cue ball veers widely off its initial path on its way to making a ball near a pocket. The cue ball will curve its way around numerous assortments of object balls.

These shots are not hard to set up correctly. The real secret lies in your technique. You've got to give these shots your best stroke. After you've successfully executed the shots, should the audience doubt your skill, have them give the shots a try. They will quickly gain a greater appreciation for your wizardry with a cue.

Long Distance Curve Ball

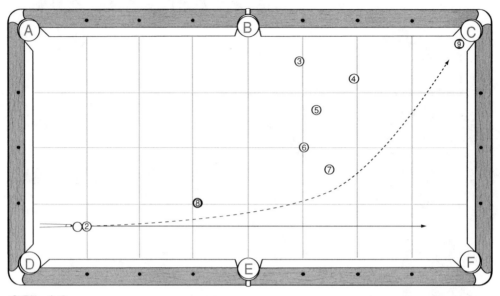

SUR: 1.5
EXR: 3.5
MSR: 80%

45°-50°

Your friends will really be impressed with the huge arc the cue ball makes in route to pocketing the 9-ball. Set the shot up as shown. Elevate your cue to about 45-50 degrees. Apply maximum english at 8:00. Aim straight down the table as shown by the path of the 2-ball. Use a medium speed stroke.

The Sweeper Draw Shot

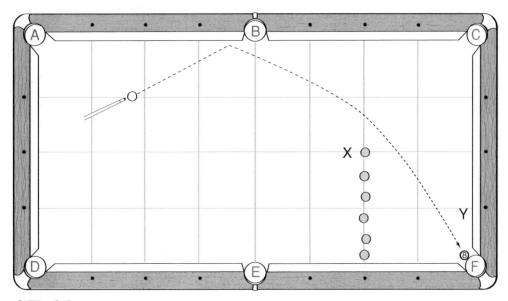

SUR: 1.5
EXR: 4.0
MSR: 70%

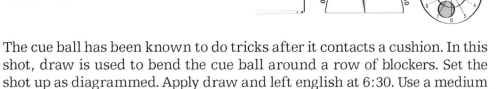

The cue ball has been known to do tricks after it contacts a cushion. In this shot, draw is used to bend the cue ball around a row of blockers. Set the shot up as diagrammed. Apply draw and left english at 6:30. Use a medium soft to medium speed stroke. Notice the widely sweeping curve the cue ball makes as it nears the obstructer on the spot.

If the cue ball hits at Side Y, shoot softer and lower. If you hit Ball X, shoot a little harder and closer to the side pocket.

Topspin Curveball

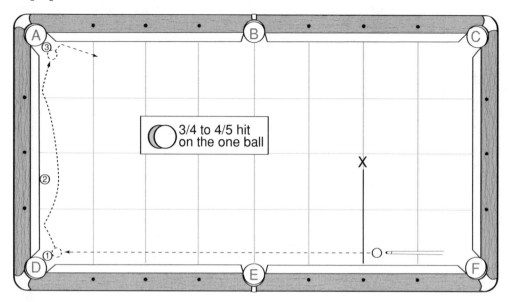

3/4 to 4/5 hit
on the one ball

SUR: 1.0   AP
EXR: 3.0
MSR: 75%

You can place the cue ball anywhere behind Line X in Artistic Pool. However, I recommend that you position the cue ball near the cushion as shown. Aim for about an 80% hit on the right side of the 1-ball. Use a level stroke with medium hard speed. Strike the cue ball well above center with a half tip of right english.

If the english takes too quickly the cue ball will strike the 2-ball. In this case, aim for less of a hit on the 1-ball. If the cue ball fails to arc around the 2-ball, aim to hit the 1-ball a little fuller or hit the cue ball a little higher. Common errors include hitting the 1-ball too thin or stroking too hard.

Walking the Dog

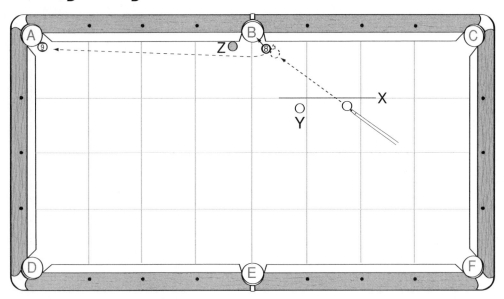

SUR: 2.0   ESPN
EXR: 2.5(A) 3.5(B)   AP
MSR: 80%

Aim to hit the 8-ball about 80-90% full. Cue at 10:30. Use a medium to medium hard stroke. Avoid the tendency to use excessive speed on this shot. Make sure your cue is level. In Artistic Pool you are allowed to position the cue ball anywhere behind Line X. I feel the cue ball location I recommend is much easier than Position Y, which is shown in the Artistic Pool book.

You can place a ball at Point Z and make the cue ball go around it on its way to the 9-ball. Hit less of the 8-ball and use a slightly harder stroke. This variation is much more difficult but is also more impressive.

Through the Great Wall

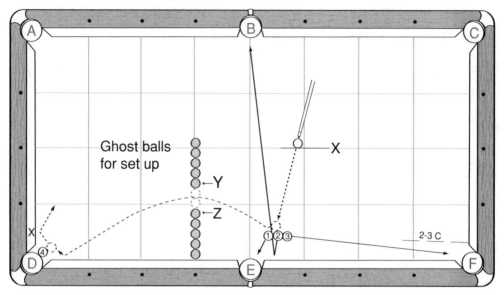

SUR: 3.5   ESPN
EXR: 3.5   AP
MSR: 80%

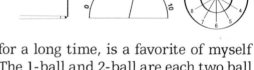

This shot, which has been around for a long time, is a favorite of myself and of audiences around the world. The 1-ball and 2-ball are each two ball widths from the cushion. The left edge of the 1-ball is in line with the point of Pocket E. The 3-ball is aligned as diagrammed to allow for the throw.

In Artistic Pool the cue ball must be placed behind Line X. It is important to hit half of the 2-ball, so aim with care. Use a medium hard stroke. If the cue ball hits Ball Y, you are shooting too hard. If the cue ball runs into Ball Z, you are shooting too easy. If the cue ball strikes the rail at Point X, you're not hitting the cue ball high enough or you're shooting too hard.

The Follow Bender

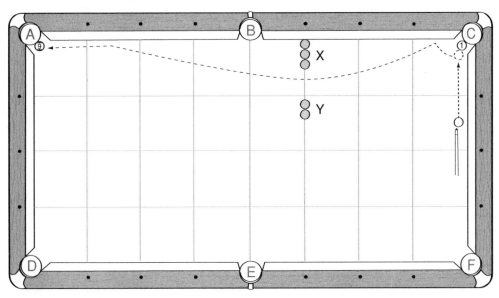

SUR: 1.5   Video
EXR: 4.0
MSR: 70%

This shot is a cousin of the shots on pages 100-102. It takes a good stroke. After pocketing the 1-ball, the cue ball will hit the cushion and bounce out before curving around the interfering balls on its way to making the 9-ball.

Aim for a three quarters hit on the left side of the 1-ball. Use a medium hard to hard stroke. The correct speed depends on the table. Hold your cue as level as possible. This will help keep the cue ball from flying off the table. If the cue ball curves too quickly and hits Row X, try hitting a little less of the 1-ball or use a harder stroke. Should the cue ball run into Row Y, hit the 1-ball a little fuller or use less speed.

The Koufax Curve Ball

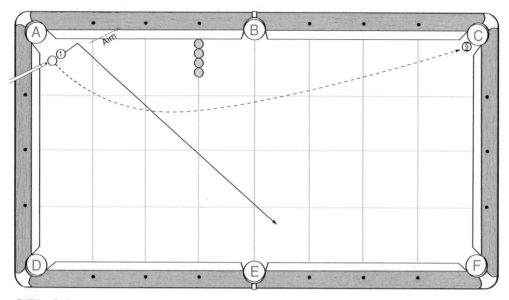

SUR: 2.5
EXR: 4.0
MSR: 75%

This is a new shot I came up with recently that will test your skills. The 1-ball is a ball's width from the cushion. There is an eighth of an inch gap between the cue ball and 1-ball. The object is to pocket the 9-ball in front of Pocket C.

Aim down the line shown in the illustration. Elevate your cue to about 25-30 degrees. Use maximum english at 10:00 and an open bridge. Use a medium hard stroke. Stroke through the ball like you would when playing Scratching With Style (see page 177). When struck properly, the cue ball will bend like a Sandy Koufax curve ball.

8   Lots of Balls In Action

In good old boring normal pool you will be doing well to make a single ball on most shots unless, of course, you have the unfortunate tendency to scratch on a regular basis. Spectators, on the other hand, have always enjoyed seeing numerous balls scurry across the table on their way to any and all pockets as we discussed in Chapter 4 on Crowd Pleasers. That's why we offer you these shots in which numerous balls get into the act.

Any trick shot that requires you to make several balls should be your warning that the set up procedure is going to be a big key to your success. You've got to make sure the tangent lines point where they are supposed to. And you must line up most combos with great care.

Multi-ball shots will often fail on the first attempt. So you must become adept at noticing the misses and making the necessary adjustments. Should you miss, you must also have your escape lines ready so you can quickly quiet any hostilities in the crowd should they have the nerve to give you a hard time.

Again, patience and care in the set up process are big keys to these shots. The reward is an explosion of balls racing for the pockets, to the delight of your fans.

What Happened Shot

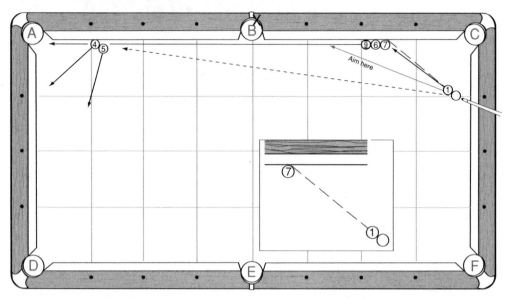

SUR: 2.0   MMS
EXR: 2.5
MSR: 95%

The object is to make the 9-ball on a legal shot into Pocket A. Set up the shot as shown with the cue ball about a ball's width from the end rail. The 1-ball is frozen to the cue ball. A line through the center of both balls should point at the right side of the 7-ball.

Aim at Location X. Strike the cue ball about one tip above center. Keep your cue level and use a medium hard stroke. The cue ball will race ahead and clear a path for the 9-ball by knocking the 4-ball and 5-ball out of the way.

The Scatter Gun

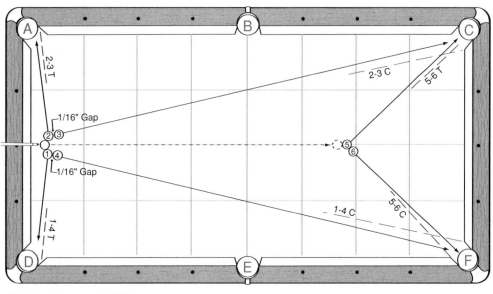

SUR: 4.0   ESPN
EXR: 3.5
MSR: 70%

The cue ball should be about a ball's width from the cushion. You want a sixteenth inch gap between the 2-ball and 3-ball, and also between the 1-ball and 4-ball. The 5-ball is a ball's width above the spot. Aim straight at the 5-ball. Use a half tip of follow and a medium hard to hard stroke. The big challenge is to keep the cue ball from running into either the 3-ball or 4-ball after it contacts the 5-ball.

The Jeff Carter Showed Me Shot

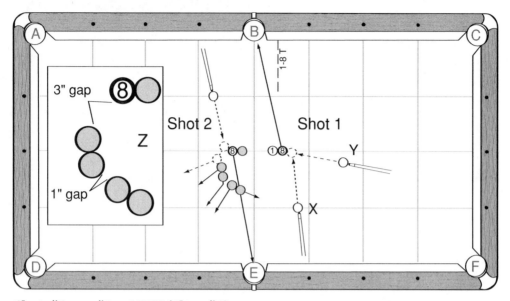

Shot #1   #2   MMS (Shot #2)
SUR: 1.5   2.5   ESPN (Shot #2)
EXR: 3.0   3.5
MSR: 90%   85%

The first person I saw make Shot #1 was Jeff Carter at the Sands 9-Ball Tournament in Reno. For 25 years I did not realize that it was possible to make the 8-ball straight into Pocket B (Shot #1) with the cue ball in Position X. I showed the shot to a lot of top players that also didn't know it.

Notice the tangent line between the 1-ball and 8-ball is pointing about two and a half to three inches to the right of the point. The cue ball in Position X is a little less than a diamond from the side pocket and about a diamond from the side rail. You can make the 8-ball in the side by hitting it very thinly on the right side with follow and a hard stroke. This is a practical shot for your regular game

Shot #1 on the 8-ball is much easier with the cue ball in Position Y. Shoot directly into the 8-ball. Strike the cue ball a tip below center with medium speed. You can also make the 8-ball by shooting hard with a center ball hit from this position.

After you learn Shot #1 from Position X, you are ready to play the trick shot (Shot #2). Add the four balls as shown. Aim for a thin hit on the 8-ball using a hard stroke the same as with Shot #1. The cue ball will eliminate the blockers and the 8-ball will proceed into Pocket E.

The Four in Three Shot

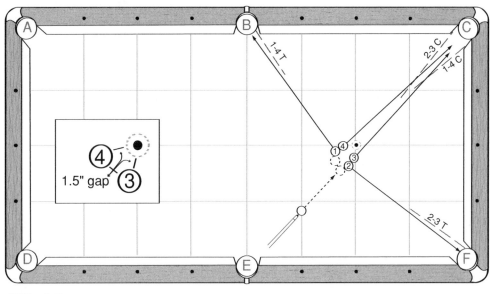

SUR: 3.5
EXR: 2.0
MSR: 90%

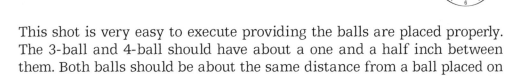

This shot is very easy to execute providing the balls are placed properly. The 3-ball and 4-ball should have about a one and a half inch between them. Both balls should be about the same distance from a ball placed on the spot.

After you've used a ball to measure the correct ball placement, be sure to remove it. Now align the 1-ball and 4-ball to the right of Pocket C to allow for throw. Align the 2-ball and 3-ball to the left of Pocket C to allow for throw. Strike the cue ball a full tip above center. Shoot into the 2-ball with a little more than a half ball hit with medium speed.

Jesse Cue Shot

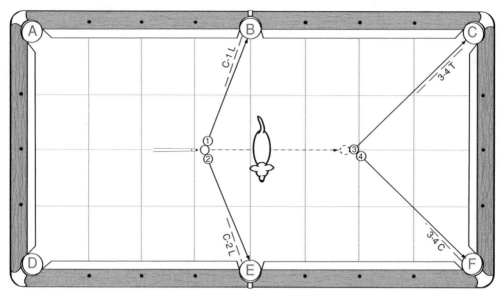

SUR: 1.5   Mike's Shot (with dog)
EXR: 1.5   Video
MSR: 100%

This shot is an oldie but goodie. To liven it up, I decided to add a unique feature by placing one of my dogs as shown. Thus, the shot was renamed the Jesse Cue Shot in honor of our dog. I've even taught Jesse to bow after the shot's been played. If you have a well-behaved dog, perhaps you can use him as I have. You might even wish to rename the shot after your pet.

Position the balls as shown. Be sure to allow for throw on the 1, 2, and 4-balls. Hit the cue ball a half tip above center with a level cue. Use a medium hard stroke, A firm hit makes the shot much more impressive than when its played with a softer stroke.

The Celebrities Love It Shot

There seem to be a lot of colorful stories that go along with this shot. Although this is a very easy trick shot, I have had a lot of fun by having members of the audience shoot it. One day while working on the movie *The Baron and the Kid* starring Johnny Cash, I was giving him some pointers when June Carter came up to watch. I set up the shot and she made it on her first attempt. She was so excited she almost jumped over the table. She sure was a wonderful lady. The time I got to spend with them is one of my most treasured memories.

I was in Moscow, Russia giving an exhibition for some people connected with the Olympic Committee when I had former Olympic President Juan Antonio Samaranch shoot the Jesse Cue Shot for Russian TV. The way his eyes lit up when he made the shot you'd have thought he'd just won the world championships!

I set up the shot for Jennifer Tilly, who is even more beautiful in person than in the movies. She got down low and aimed like she was shooting a rifle with one eye closed. Her technique caused her no problem as she also was successful on her first attempt.

While I was a guest on *The Best Damn Sports Show*, our dog moved just before Tom Arnold played the shot. You can just imagine the result.

The Double Double

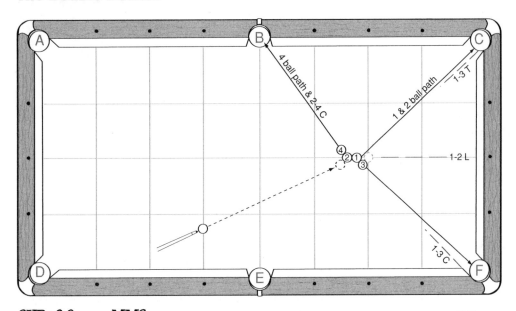

SUR: 3.0   MMS
EXR: 2.0
MSR: 95%

I devised this neat little shot, which features two kisses and two combos. Set it up in order of the ball's numbers. You will need to wet the contact point between the 2-ball and 4-ball. Hit the cue ball a full tip below center with a medium hard stroke. Aim straight into the 2-ball. The 1-ball and 2-ball go into Pocket C, the 4-ball goes into Pocket B, and the 3-ball goes into Pocket F.

Make sure the 1-ball is one ball's width up from the spot. The 1-ball and 2-ball must be in a straight line. For the 2-4 tangent line to point in the right direction you can't allow for throw on the 4-ball so they need to be aligned straight into the Pocket B.

4 Balls in 4 Pockets

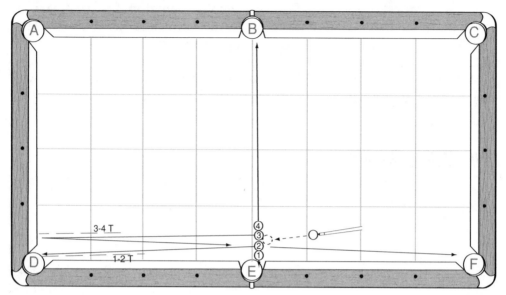

3-4 T

1-2 T

SUR: 2.5   Video
EXR: 2.5
MSR: 90%+

This old timer is one of the first shots I learned as a teenager. Over forty years later, when people want me to show them how to execute a trick shot, this one invariably comes up. I suspect this shot is one of the first that an average player learns who is into trick shots.

Place the four object balls in a line straight out from the right side of the side pocket. There should be a very small gap between the 2-ball and 3-ball. The cue ball goes about a diamond from the 3-ball and about the same distance from the rail as the 3-ball. Aim to hit the 3-ball slightly first. Hit the cue ball a full tip below center with a medium hard to hard stroke.

The 3-ball is the toughest to make since it has to be banked the length of the table. If it hits the long rail try using a little left english. You could also increase the gap between the 2-ball and 3-ball just a little bit. If the 3-ball hits the end rail first, try using a little right english or angle the 3-4 combo to the center of Side Pocket B.

Carom Christmas Revisited

Earlier in the book I talked about my appearance on Carom Christmas, a TV show in Barcelona, Spain. Jose Farras, the producer, added a twist to this shot. He convinced a hostess to lie on the table long ways with the small of her back in the middle of the table. When I played the shot, she arched her back so the 4-ball would go under the small of her back and into the side pocket.

4 Plus 4 (or 5) with Rack

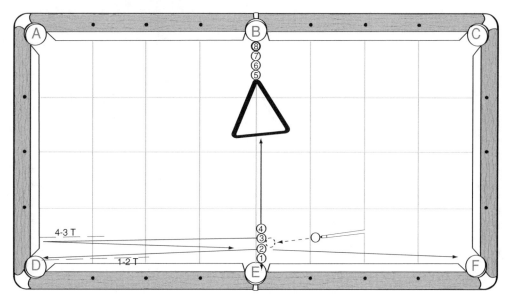

SUR: 3.0   MMS
EXR: 4.0
MSR: 70%

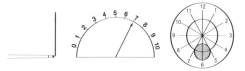

Once you've mastered the previous shot, it's time to tackle this advanced version. Once again, set up the 1, 2, 3, and 4-balls as before. Now line up the 5, 6, 7, and 8-balls with the opposite side pocket. If you want to be even more adventuresome, you could add the 9-ball next to the 8-ball. Place a wooden triangle as shown. It is best to use a rack that is not too bulky. The rack should be angled slightly to the right.

Cue a full tip below center. Use an even harder stroke in this version. The 4-ball will hit the rack, driving the 5, 6, 7, and 8-balls into the side pocket. The 4-ball is then supposed to rebound back and into the Pocket E. This shot seems to work best on a 4' x 8' table, because the 4-ball doesn't have to travel as far.

3-4-5 Shot

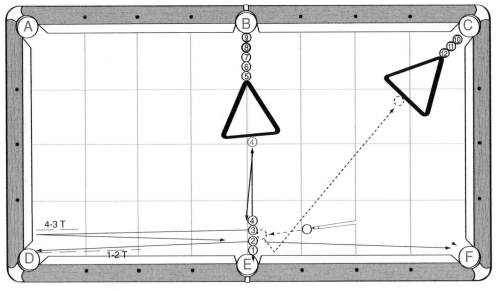

SUR: 3.5   MMS
EXR: 4.0
MSR: 65%

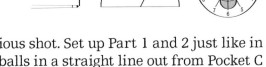

Here's another version of the previous shot. Set up Part 1 and 2 just like in the previous shot. Then add three balls in a straight line out from Pocket C with a rack placed as shown. Shoot hard like before and keep your fingers crossed.

The Big X Shot

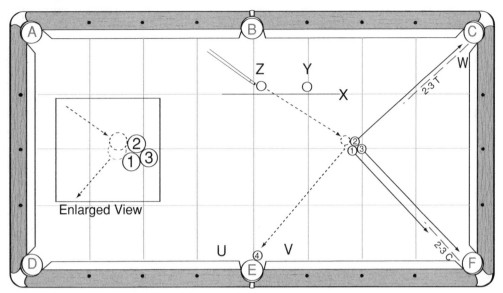

SUR: 2.5   ESPN
EXR: 3.0   AP
MSR: 85%

The cue ball must be placed above Line X. In the Artistic Pool book they have the cue ball at Position Y but I recommend that you place it at Position Z. Aim for a half ball hit on the right side of the 2-ball.

Use right english with a medium stroke. If the 2-ball hits at Position W, you may be hitting it too full. You could also be hitting the cue ball below center. If you miss the 4-ball at Position U, you are hitting too low. And if the cue ball strikes the rail at Position V, you are hitting the cue ball too high. If you think you are aiming properly and are hitting the 2-ball too full, you are probably not allowing for the squirt caused by the use of a full tip of right english.

Slam Dunk (aka Smiley Face or Half Moon)

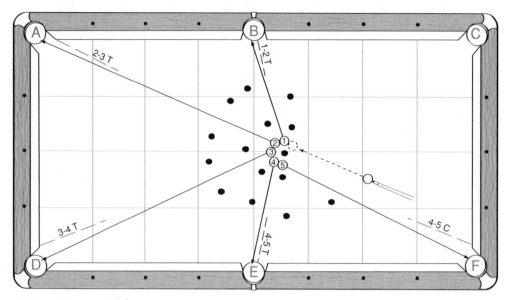

SUR: 3.5   Video
EXR: 2.5   ESPN
MSR: 95%

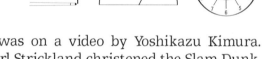

The first time I saw this shoot was on a video by Yoshikazu Kimura. Everyone loves this shot, which Earl Strickland christened the Slam Dunk. Others call it the Smiley Face or Half Moon Shot.

The set up is the big key to this shot because three of the balls must travel long distances to the corner pockets. So take care in lining up the combos and tangent lines as shown on the diagram. Hit the cue ball in the center and aim for a full hit on the 1-ball. Use a hard stroke. When practicing this shot, it helps to have a friend watch closely so they can tell you where each ball that misses hits the rail. This will help you to make the necessary adjustments. For instance, if the 2-ball hits to the left of Pocket A, you will need to move it clockwise just a little so that the tangent line points a little farther up the long rail.

You can place a series of object balls where the dots are located. This makes the shot even more impressive because the balls in the cluster appear to explode out of the center of the table. Once you've mastered this shot, you might try placing glasses of water where the dots are located. But be aware that an error could possibly damage the cloth.

Getting Waxed in Japan

I was in Japan for a TV show when disaster struck on the Slam Dunk. Before an exhibition I always go over the table and check out my shots, especially the set-up shots. After evaluating the table I decided to go to dinner before the show. While I was gone the organizers waxed the balls to a bright shine. The producers wanted them to look their best for the show.

Before I left for dinner the balls looked immaculate. So when I went back to the table I didn't think the waxing would affect my shots. I was wrong. I set up the Slam Dunk with 13 shot glasses full of water spaced so that the balls would go between them.

When I shot hard into the 1-ball, it forced through a little more than I had planned for and hit the point of the side pocket. It then bounced out across the table, breaking four of the glasses. I was reminded of why 13 is the unluckiest of numbers.

It was so quiet you could have heard a pin drop. Now when I do an exhibition and use glasses of water, I always leave this shot for last just in case. In all of the times I've played this shot, this is the only time I've spilled a drop. Whew!

9 *Multi-Rail Masterpieces*

The shots in this chapter can be likened to a 50-foot putt that's bearing down on the cup. As the ball gets closer, the gallery gets set to groan for a near miss or to cheer wildly for a holed putt. The same is true on these multi-rail masterpieces. The good news is that your odds of success should be much higher than those of the golfers. All eyes will be glued to whitey as it circles the table while the suspense rises steadily. Will the cue ball obtain its long distance objective, or will you be wiping egg off your face?

A couple of shots will require you to hit the cue ball several times while it is rolling around the table. On the Dollar Bill 9-Railer the cue ball will strike nine rails and cover an estimated 33 feet before hopefully coming to rest on a dollar bill. Highrollers who like to impress people with their big bankrolls are certainly welcome to substitute a C-Note for the dollar providing there are no fleet footed scoundrels in the crowd. On the grand finale to this chapter, a shot I've named the Traveling Music Shot, three cue balls will be propelled three, four, and five rails into three balls set in the jaws of the pockets. The total distance covered by the three cue balls is nearly 70 feet!

Once you have mastered these shots, the big key is to learn how the table plays should you take your show on the road. So pay special attention to your initial points of aim. That will help you to make the necessary adjustments.

Nine-Rail Kick Shot

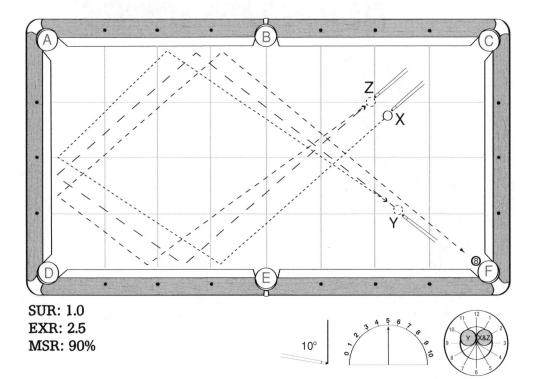

SUR: 1.0
EXR: 2.5
MSR: 90%

10°

This neat little nine-rail kick is not all that difficult. Place the 8-ball near Pocket F. Shoot the cue ball as though you are playing a three-rail kick from Position X. Immediately after shooting, step over behind Pocket F and prepare to shoot from Position Y. When the cue ball arrives, shoot it three rails in the other direction. Immediately move over behind Pocket C to Position Z and get ready to strike the cue ball again when it arrives at approximately Position Z.

If you are successful, the cue ball will travel the remaining three rails before pocketing the 8-ball in Pocket F. Use a medium speed stroke each time. Try to apply a little natural english on each shot. (Right, left, then right.)

12-Rail Kick Shot

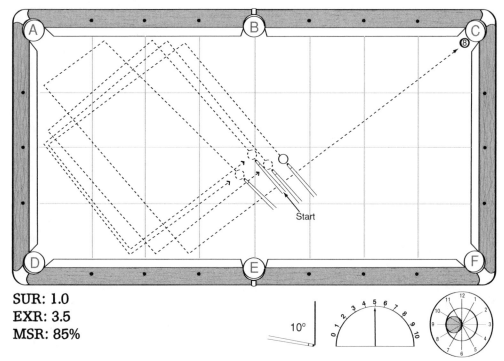

SUR: 1.0
EXR: 3.5
MSR: 85%

10°

This is a more difficult cousin of the previous shot. This time you must strike the cue ball while it is passing across in front of you. As you'll recall you had to strike the cue ball while it was coming straight at you in the previous shot. On this shot you do not need to run around the table.

Use a closed bridge with your arm in the air. Don't play this shot with your bridge on the table. You will be striking the cue ball at an angle of about 10 degrees. Shoot the cue ball three rails with a medium speed stroke. When the cue ball returns to the original location, shoot again. When you shoot, count out loud: 1, 2, 3, shoot again, 4, 5, 6, shoot again, 7, 8, 9, shoot again, 10, 11, 12 and make the ball. Your eventual goal is to make the 8-ball in Pocket C. The diagram shows an approximation of the cue ball's path for the second, third, and forth times it is struck. Be sure to make clean contact with the cue ball, and be sure the fourth stroke is in a direction that will enable it to go three rails and into the 8-ball.

Counting helps establish your rhythm. Don't try to aim too carefully. Let your instincts take control. You'll be amazed at what you can do without trying so hard.

The most difficult part of the shot is applying running english on the cue ball while it is moving. But after enough practice you will get a feel for it. Soon you'll discover the shot is not as difficult as it looks.

Before you shoot, tell everyone you are going to kick 12 rails to the 8-ball. Get down and act like you are going to hit the cue ball really hard. It's fun to watch people clear out of the area in which you are aiming.

Going for the Cheese

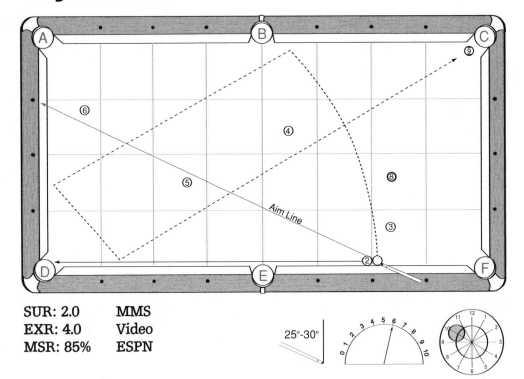

SUR: 2.0   MMS
EXR: 4.0   Video
MSR: 85%   ESPN

25°-30°

With blockers everywhere it looks like you have no chance to make the 9-ball. There is a shot on the cheese, however, hidden in this mess.

The 2-ball and cue ball are frozen to the cushion and are about an eighth of an inch apart. Start your search for the ideal point of aim by aiming at the first diamond below Pocket A. Elevate your cue to 25-30 degrees. Use maximum english at 10:00 and a medium hard stroke. You want the cue ball to still be spinning when it strikes the third rail.

When you stroke the shot correctly and it fails to go, it's time to adjust your aim. If the cue ball hits to the left of the 9-ball (indicating that the table is playing short) adjust your aim to the left. If the cue ball misses to the right of the 9-ball (goes long) adjust your aim to the right.

The Lose Your Opponent Shot

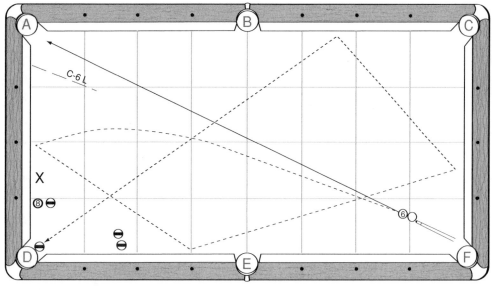

SUR: 2.5   MMS
EXR: 4.0
MSR: 75%

The goal on this shot is to pocket the 6-ball and play position on the 8-ball for Pocket A. If you ever get this shot and make it, however, your opponent will probably quit playing you!

Align the cue ball and 6-ball about a half diamond to the left of Pocket A as shown. Aim straight into the 6-ball with english at 7:30. Elevate 30 degrees and use a medium hard stroke. The cue ball should curve to the left and strike the middle of the end rail. It will continue three more rails around the table and into the striped ball in front of Pocket D or this vicinity for perfect position for the 8-ball!

A word of warning: this is a very difficult shot. In fact, it may not even work if you are trying it on new cloth. The tendency on new cloth is for the cue ball to go too long on the last cushion, resulting in a miss to the right of the 8-ball at Location X.

Position Wizard Shot

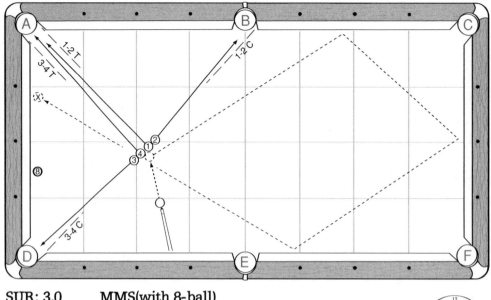

SUR: 3.0   MMS(with 8-ball)
EXR: 3.0   Video
MSR: 95%

I've been playing this crowd favorite for ages. The objective is to pocket the four solids (the 1, 2, 3, and 4-balls) while playing position for the 8-ball.

Begin the set up procedure by placing a ball on the spot. This ball helps ensure proper placement of the 1-ball and 4-ball. Both balls should be a half a ball's width distance from the set up ball, and there should be an eighth of an inch gap between them. Imagine a line going between the 1-ball and 4-ball that extends from Pocket A to the center of the Pocket E.

The next step is to line up the 2-ball and 1-ball with the right side of Pocket B. Line up the 3-ball and 4-ball with the edge of Pocket D as diagrammed. Make sure the 3-ball and 4-ball are frozen, and that the 1-ball and 2-ball are frozen as well.

Place the cue ball as diagrammed. Aim to hit about a fifth of the 4-ball on the right side. Use high right english and a medium stroke. When executed successfully, all four balls will go and the cue ball will travel three cushions for perfect position on the 8-ball at Position X.

George Middleditch's Relay Shot

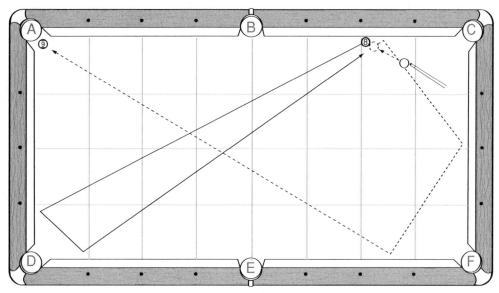

SUR: 2.5
EXR: 5.0
MSR: 5%

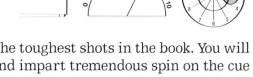

I must warn you that this is one of the toughest shots in the book. You will need to shoot hard into the 8-ball and impart tremendous spin on the cue ball. The cue ball must stop dead in its tracks near the cushion and spin like a top. The 8-ball goes three rails and comes back to hit the cue ball. The cue ball then travels three cushions to pocket the 9-ball.

You must hit the 8-ball 100% full. Use lots of right english and cue a little below center. Hold your cue as level as possible and use a hard stroke. Be sure to allow for deflection (since you are shooting so hard) by aiming a little to the right of a full ball hit. Note: this shot is even more difficult on a slow table or on one with new cloth.

George and Mike's Lucky Days

The first time I saw this shot was in Lansing, Michigan. Jimmy Mataya was giving George Middleditch 50 tries for $100. As I recall, George made it on his 46th attempt. I decided to call it George Middleditch's Relay Shot because the 8-ball runs the first leg of the race and the cue ball runs the second leg.

I actually made this on my first attempt on TV once. I'm just glad the cameraman didn't make a mistake. We might have been there for quite awhile if I had had to shoot it again.

Three and Three Shot

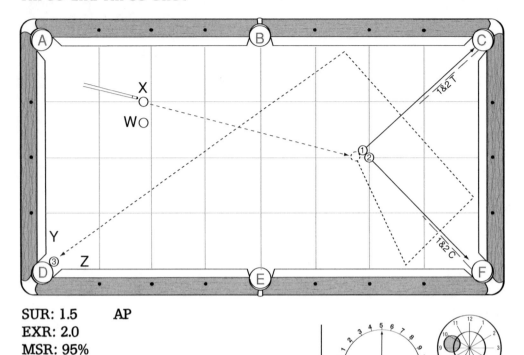

SUR: 1.5   AP
EXR: 2.0
MSR: 95%

This is probably the easiest shot in Artistic Pool. The 2-ball is on the spot with the 1-ball aligned as shown. In the Artistic Pool book the cue ball is placed in Location W. With the cue ball in this position, it is difficult to avoid double kissing the 2-ball. In addition, the cue ball will also travel long on new cloth. I prefer to place the cue ball at Location X.

Play this shot with medium speed, left english, and a touch of follow. A thin hit on the 1-ball will allow the cue ball to cross safely in front of the 2-ball, avoiding a kiss. If the cue ball strikes the rail at Position Y, then adjust by moving the cue ball a little above Location X. You might also try hitting the 1-ball a little thicker. If the cue ball hits the side rail at Position Z, move the cue ball a little below Location X.

1, 2 and a 3-Ball

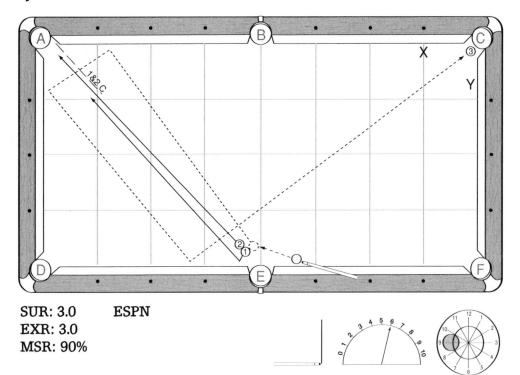

SUR: 3.0   ESPN
EXR: 3.0
MSR: 90%

The 1-ball is a ball's width from the cushion. The right edge is in line with the left edge of Pocket E. Make sure the 1-ball and 2-ball are frozen and aligned as diagrammed. Place the cue ball about one inch from the cushion and hit the shot medium hard with a thin hit on the 1-ball. A typical mistake is to hit the 1-ball too thick.

The 2-ball should be rolling slowly when it goes into Pocket A. If the 1-ball hits to the left of Pocket A, try aligning the 2-ball a little to the left. And if that doesn't work, move the 1-ball and 2-ball to the right a little.

If the cue ball hits on Side X of the 3-ball, move the cue ball a little farther from the cushion or hit the 1-ball a little thinner. And if the cue ball hits on Side Y of the 3-ball, move the cue ball a little closer or try hitting the 1-ball a little thicker.

This shot can be quite a challenge on some tables. I've played the shot on brand new cloth, which made it difficult to get the 1-ball to bank short enough. This meant that it kept hitting the left side of Pocket A.

Dollar Bill 9-Railer

SUR: 2.0   AP
EXR: 3.5
MSR: 70%

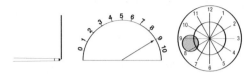

The best way to make this shot is to find a dollar bill that is 1' x 3' in size! I'm joking, of course. Aim one and a half diamonds to the right of Pocket E as shown. The cue ball will actually strike the rail two and a half diamonds to the above Pocket E as shown.

You need to hit this shot with an extremely hard stroke. The force required may in fact be nearly equal to your break speed. An exception would occur if you break like Francisco Bustamante, whose break exceeds 30MPH.

When hit properly, the cue ball will travel nine rails and die on the dollar bill! Make sure to keep your cue level as this will help keep the cue ball from jumping the table. Common mistakes include hitting the point of Side Pocket C and scratching in Pocket B. If this happens, make sure you are applying enough left english or that you are aiming a diamond and a half from Pocket E as shown.

And as a word of caution, be sure no children or breakable objects are near the table as this shot can be dangerous if the cue ball happens to jump the table.

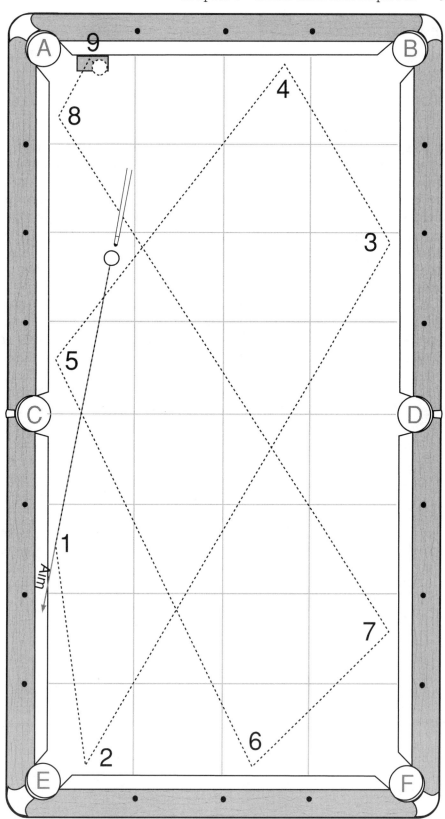

The Traveling Music Shot

SUR: 2.0   AP
EXR: 4.5
MSR: 35 % (to make all three balls)

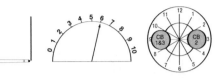

The Traveling Music Shot is made up of three separate shots. The component shots are a lot of fun even though each one is quite challenging. Each shot should be practiced individually. Observe each one carefully to discover the path and to learn how the cushions are playing. Look for a diamond to aim at, or use the diamonds as a point of reference for a contact point nearby. In Artistic Pool you only have four seconds to shoot all three cue balls. I therefore recommend that you use maximum english for each shot as this makes it easier than trying to guess in a split second how much english to apply.

The key is to stay cool and not panic. Work on your rhythm. Four seconds is plenty of time providing you stay relaxed. Use maximum left english at 9:00 on the first shot. Apply maximum right english at 3:00 on the second shot. Finally, use maximum left english at 9:00 for the third shot. Use a medium hard stroke on all three shots as this helps your timing.

The first cue ball must travel five rails before pocketing the 5-ball in Pocket F. The second cue ball goes four cushions on its way to making the 4-ball in Pocket E. The third cue ball then goes three rails before knocking the 3-ball into Pocket A

The first and third cue balls may be adjusted in either direction as long as you keep them on the head string as shown. Consider moving the third cue ball to the right (from the shooters perspective) a few inches if the five rail shot is interfering with the third cue ball.

Most errors come from miscuing on the second shot. This happens as a result of switching from maximum left english to maximum right english in less than two seconds. Try to visualize the shot going before you shoot.

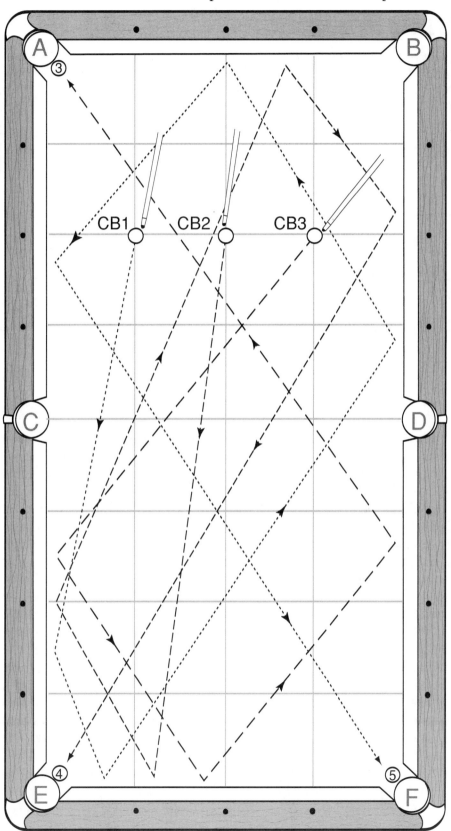

The Lucky Chalk Shot

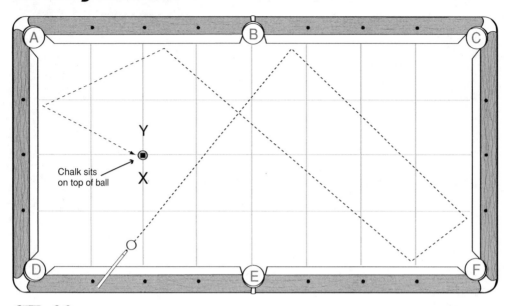

Chalk sits on top of ball

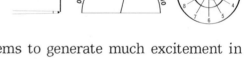

SUR: 2.0
EXR: 5.0
MSR: 20%

This shot, like the one before it, seems to generate much excitement in Artistic Pool competitions. The spectators love to watch the cue ball travel during which they will root enthusiastically for a successful result.

The object of this shot is to bank the cue ball five rails and have it touch the 1-ball placed on the spot so lightly that the chalk mounted on top of the ball does not fall off!! (Note above the 5.0 and MSR:20%.) This shot is probably about 30% skill and 70% luck. I've seen beginners make the shot in just a few tries, and I've witnessed pros shoot the shot ten or more times in a row without success.

The skill is in finding the right spot to hit the first rail. You must be able to adjust to the cushions. And, of course, speed is critical. Begin with a little less than a half tip of english and a medium hard stroke. If the cue ball travels to Side X of the 1-ball, apply the same english and aim to the right of the original spot. If the cue ball reverses too much off the last cushion and comes up short at Side Y, adjust by aiming at the same spot but this time use no english. If that doesn't work, aim a little to the right of your original spot and hit the cue ball a little below center. This will shorten up the cue ball's path so that it will strike high enough up on the fourth cushion.

This shot also can be played with a dime instead of the chalk on top of the 1-ball if you happen to be a masochist.

Four Rail Chalk Shot

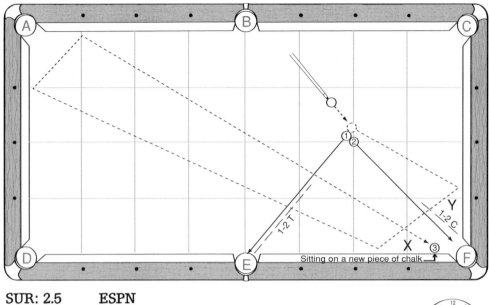

SUR: 2.5   ESPN
EXR: 3.5   AP
MSR: 70%

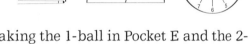

Shoot the cue ball into the 1-ball, making the 1-ball in Pocket E and the 2-ball in Pocket F. The cue ball then travels four rails to pocket the 3-ball.

Place the 2-ball on the spot and the 1-ball as diagrammed. This allows for throw. The 1-ball and 2-ball must be frozen. When the 1-ball and 2-ball are placed correctly with the tangent line pointing at the left edge of Pocket E, the 1-ball will go in this pocket with a thin hit.

The 3-ball is set on top of a piece of chalk. Use a new piece (or one with a shallow worn spot) so the 3-ball will fall off easily when the cue ball hits it. Place the 3-ball close to the pocket. Be sure to allow enough room for the 2-ball to go in cleanly. Place the cue ball as diagrammed and aim to hit the 1-ball thinly with a medium hard stroke. Keep your cue level.

The cue ball should roll in between the 2-ball and the corner when stroked properly. It is possible to make the shot by hitting the 1-ball thicker. With this approach, the 2-ball will get to the pocket before the cue ball crosses its path. However, I think you will be more consistent with the thin hit as it is easier to control.

If the cue ball comes up short at Side X of the 3-ball, you are hitting the 1-ball too thin or you are using too much right english. If you end up long on Side Y, you are probably hitting the 1-ball too thick or are not using enough right english.

10 Stroke Shots

The "trick" shots in this chapter offer you the best of both worlds. You will have the opportunity to master another batch of eye pleasing shots while at the same time building your stroke for your pool games in the real world. Included in this chapter are a number of power draw shots, which happen to be my forte. When they are struck correctly, the cue ball will curve and dance and produce some truly awesome spectacles, much to the delight of your army of admirers. One of my favorites is The Big Circle Draw Shot (which happens to be on my video). In slow motion you can see the cue ball hop to the first rail, bounce back towards the middle of the table, and then curve dramatically as it heads down the table to pocket a ball.

Setting up the stroke shots is not difficult. There are no tangent lines or combos to aim correctly. But you will need a good stroke. You could consider many of these shots as indicators of the smoothness and power of your stroke. If you are unable to execute these shots after much practice, then you should evaluate your technique. In most cases, the reason why players fail at these shots is because they grip the cue too tightly and/or fail to complete their follow through by not dropping their elbow.

The Showoff Spin Shot

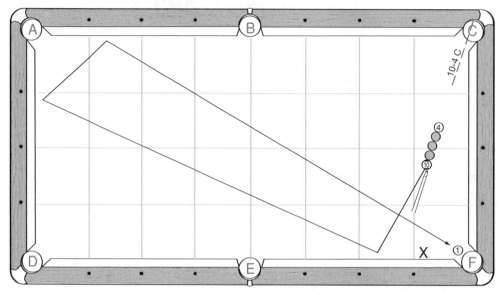

SUR: 2.0   MMS
EXR: 3.5   ESPN
MSR: 85%

This shot offers a vivid demonstration of how much the cue ball spins when extreme spin and draw have been applied to the cue ball.

Place the balls as diagrammed. Use a dark colored striped ball for the first ball (the 10-ball in the diagram). The spinning stripe dramatically demonstrates the spin. Make sure all five balls are frozen and are in a straight line with Pocket C. Strike the cue ball at 4:30 with maximum draw. Aim straight into the line of balls and use a medium hard stroke. The 10-ball should shoot back with a tremendous amount of spin and then travel three cushions before pocketing the 1-ball. If the 10-ball comes up short at Position X, shift your aim to the right a little.

Note: Your chances of making this shot have a lot to do with the table. On new cloth it is a lot more difficult because you get far less "bite" off the cushions.

Triple Reverse

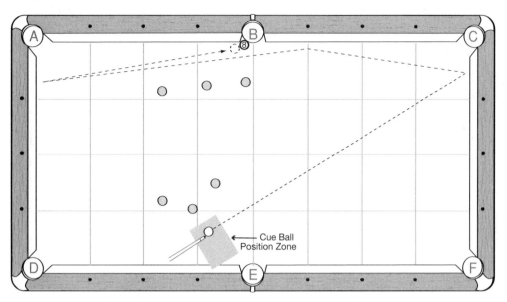

SUR: 2.0   MMS
EXR: 5.0
MSR: 50% - Amateurs: 0-1%

This devilish creation of mine is at times darn near impossible. The set up is easy enough. The 8-ball is on the edge of Pocket B. The cue ball is placed somewhere in the zone. The correct placement depends on the table, and on your stroke. The various object balls spread across the table are blockers that enhance the effect of the shot. The cue ball must follow the path in the diagram and reverse its direction off the third rail. Getting the cue ball to reverse off the third rail is the big challenge to this shot.

Aim at the end rail where shown. Use maximum right english (about as far off center as you can without miscuing) and a hard stroke on most tables.

I suggest that you apply polish to the cue ball every few attempts if the cloth is worn as this will help simulate conditions you would encounter when playing on new cloth.

I was practicing this shot at a tournament in Las Vegas and Francisco Bustamante, one of the best players in the world, was watching. I made the shot and he said, "Darn, what was that?"

The Pelinga Response

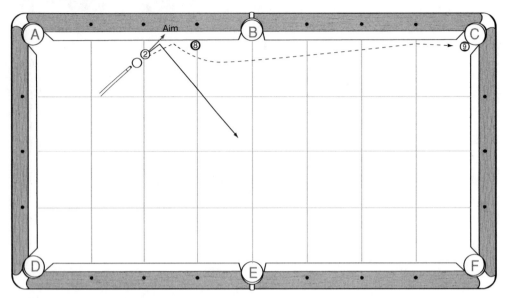

SUR: 2.0   MMS
EXR: 4.0   ESPN
MSR: 80%

25° to 30°

I made this good-looking shot against Stefano Pelinga during the 2000 Trick Shot Magic competition. That rascal then had the nerve to make the shot on his attempt, keeping me from gaining any ground on him.

Place the balls as diagrammed with the 2-ball about a ball's width from the cushion. It should also be an eighth of an inch from the cue ball. Elevate your cue to 25-30 degrees. Aim straight into the 2-ball. Use a half tip of top left english and strike the cue ball with a medium hard stroke.

Circular Draw Shot

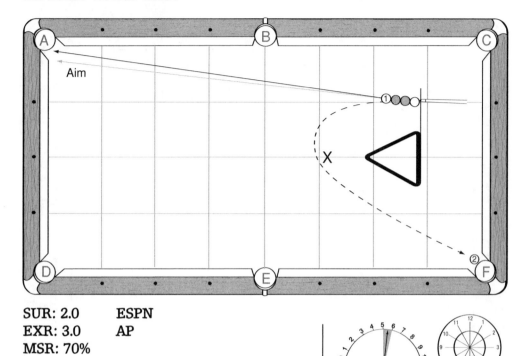

SUR: 2.0   ESPN
EXR: 3.0   AP
MSR: 70%

Use draw at 5:30. This causes the cue ball to deflect out of the way, avoiding a miscue. I recommend a medium to medium hard stroke. Begin by aiming at the left edge of Pocket A. Adjust to the left if needed. The big keys to this shot are a pure stroke and aim. When this shot is executed properly, the cue ball will curve in a very eye pleasing fashion before continuing on to pocket the 2-ball.

Stefano Pelinga placed a little duck statue at Position X to add a little spice to the shot in the Trick Shot Magic 2001 competition on ESPN.

The Jump Draw Shot

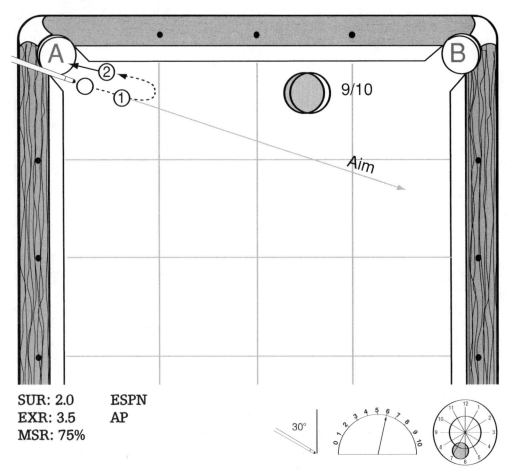

SUR: 2.0   ESPN
EXR: 3.5   AP
MSR: 75%

30°

I suggest you aim to hit the 1-ball 90% full. Be sure to favor the left side of the 1-ball. Elevate your cue to about 30 degrees. Strike the cue ball well below center at about 6:30 with a medium hard stroke and lots of draw. When the shot is hit properly, the cue ball will have enough action after reversing direction to stay with the 2-ball and crowd it into Pocket A.

An Inside Job 3-Railer

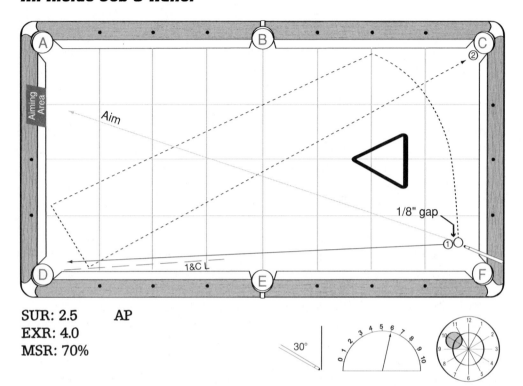

SUR: 2.5   **AP**
EXR: 4.0
MSR: 70%

Align the cue ball and the 1-ball in line with the dashed line as diagrammed. Use an elevated bridge. Elevate your cue to 30 degrees. Cue above center at 10:00. You want to feel like you are stroking over the top of the cue ball. Use a medium hard stroke. You need to put a lot of spin on the cue ball so that it will take sufficiently off the third rail.

Aim at the center of the aiming area and adjust as needed. If the cue ball hits the rack, aim a little more to the right. If the cue ball comes up short, aim a little more to the left.

Mike's Power Draw Shot

SUR: 1.5   MMS
EXR: 4.5   ESPN
MSR: 90%   AP

I devised this shot almost 30 years ago when I first started doing exhibitions. I designed it as a One-Pocket shot. The 8-ball was positioned at W1 with another ball located at W2. The object of the shot was to pocket the 7-ball and send the cue ball around the table and back to the position zone.

At the time this book was written this shot was rated a 10 in Artistic Pool. I think a rating of 11 would be more in line with the difficulty of the shot because very few people can execute it with consistency.

Place the cue ball and object balls as shown. Use a very firm closed bridge. Aim the center of the cue ball at the right edge of the 7-ball. Use an extremely hard stroke (14 miles per hour) and strike the cue ball at 5:15. Let your whole upper arm collapse into the shot on the follow through.

This shot is very difficult on brand new cloth and on a slow table. On brand new cloth the cue ball has a tendency to come off long at Cushion X. To compensate, you will need to draw the cue ball into Cushion Y. If the table is slow, but is taking the english well, you will get better results by relying more on spin and less on draw. Hit the cue ball at 4:30 instead of 5:15.

Mike's Great Improvisation

I was doing an exhibition in Sweden when it came time for this shot. I set up the shot and told the audience I was going to pocket the 7-ball and play position for the 8-ball. I didn't tell them how. I put a real good stroke on the shot but the cue ball hit Point Z. It slid down the rail for perfect position on the 8-ball. Of course they thought that was how I was playing the shot. I didn't dare spoil the moment by telling my true intentions to the crowd!!

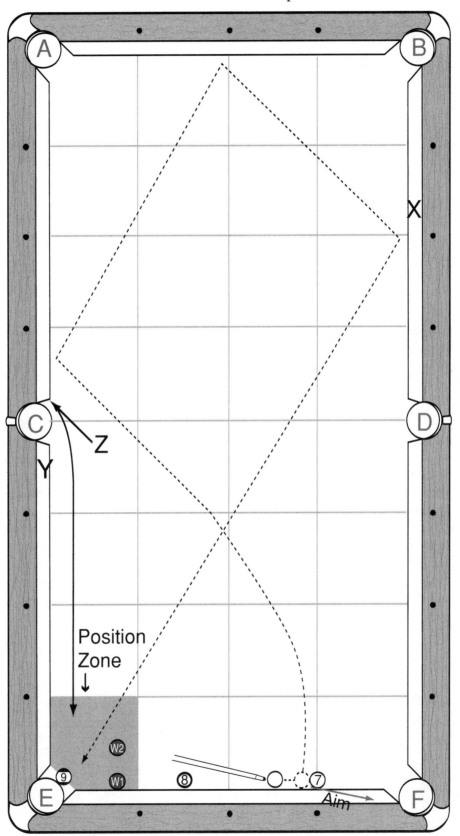

The Jimmy Moore Draw Shot

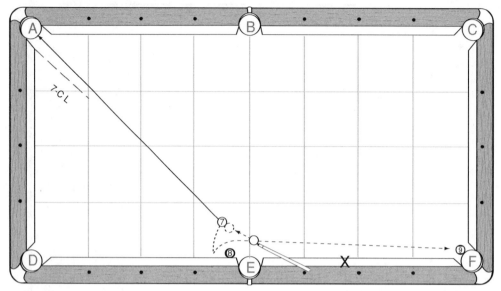

SUR: 2.5   ESPN
EXR: 4.5   AP
MSR: 80%
LMS

A big part of this shot is the set up. Be sure to copy the cut angle shown as closely as possible. This shot will test your draw stroke. Use a medium hard to hard stroke. The correct speed depends on the table. The use of a rail bridge limits the angle on the 7-ball as diagrammed. Be sure to use as little elevation as possible and make sure to grip the cue lightly.

I prefer to use a little left english, although you can make it with straight draw at 6:00. The left english will help lengthen out the cue ball's path should it strike Cushion X first. I can make this shot with two balls out from the rail (the 8-ball plus an additional ball). For this variation there has to be a little more angle on the 7-ball and I use a harder stroke.

Jimmy Moore's Zipppp!

I was doing this shot when I was about 15 without the 8-ball. I discovered it when I was experimenting with my stroke. I'm sure Jimmy Moore was executing the shot well before I was even born. Cowboy Jimmy Moore was a great player who used a slip stroke. In the middle of his final stroke he would repostion his grip hand five to six inches in back of its original location. In all of my years in pool I've only known about four good players who used an extreme slip stroke like his. Jimmy Moore was the best of the group. When he stroked and his hand slipped back it made a neat zipppp sound! Watching him was like poetry in motion. He ran 111 balls in 14.1 on his eightieth birthday.

Tunnel Vision

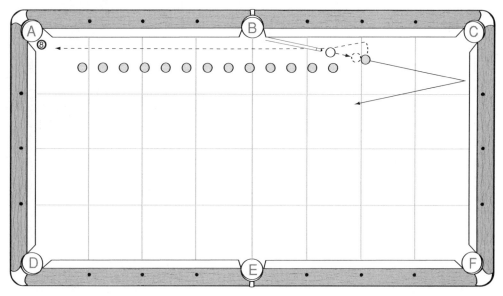

SUR: 2.0   MMS
EXR: 3.5   Video
MSR: 90%
LMS

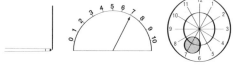

This good looking shot takes an excellent stroke. The stroke is similar to that used for the Jimmy Moore shot, but is not as difficult because there is less of a cut angle. Use low left english. Use a hard stroke and draw the cue ball into the cushion. The cue ball should then go straight up the rail to pocket the 8-ball without hitting any of the balls that form the tunnel.

Sometimes I get a little unlucky when the cue ball catches the point of Pocket B. This shot is especially impressive on a 6′ x 12′ snooker table.

Draw Back 4-Ball Shot

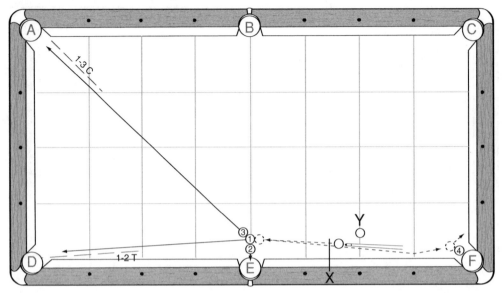

SUR: 2.5   AP
EXR: 2.5
MSR: 90%

This is one of the easiest shots in Artistic Pool. The 2-ball is positioned about an inch from the edge of the pocket drop. Place the cue ball in a straight line with the 1-ball and 4-ball. Make sure the cue ball is behind Line X. In the Artistic Manual, they suggest placing the cue ball at Position Y. I feel that this makes the shot much tougher, so I advise that you stick with my recommended location.

Cue at close to maximum draw with a touch of left english. I like using left english because the natural spin helps to make the 4-ball in case the cue ball hits the rail. The english also is useful under humid conditions. Use a medium hard stroke. The shot can also be made with center draw, so you might try shooting it that way if you have a problem using english.

The Big Circle Draw Shot

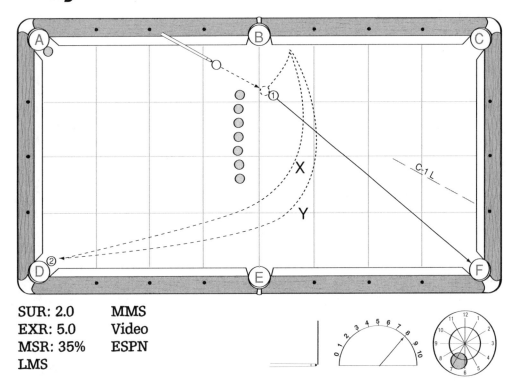

SUR: 2.0   MMS
EXR: 5.0   Video
MSR: 35%   ESPN
LMS

This is one of the most difficult stroke shots so I seldom shoot it during the regular part of an exhibition. However, sometimes after a show some of the better players will ask me to shoot some shots that require a particularly good stroke, and I'll usually play this one.

The Big Circle Draw Shot is similar to the Jimmy Moore Draw Shot on page 144. However, on this shot you must use a very hard stroke. Use low left english. The cue ball normally will follow Path X. But when the cloth is new, it will likely travel down Path Y. For this shot to work, the conditions have to be right. The table must have very good if not brand new cloth.

A common problem is that the cue ball has a tendency to jump over the cushion. This is due to the hard stroke and the downward hit on the cue ball caused by the rail, which is so close to your bridge. You can avoid this disaster by using a rail bridge. Let your cue rest on the rail and slide it between your index and middle fingers. And be sure to hold your cue as level as possible factoring in that you're playing a draw shot.

Mike's Massive Draw Shot

SUR: 1.0   MMS
EXR: 5.0
MSR: 70%
LMS

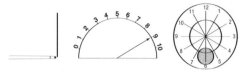

People have asked me forever to explain my technique for drawing the cue ball long distances. Mike's Massive Draw Shot will reveal my secrets and give you an objective test for determining the power of your draw stroke.

The first step is to have excellent equipment. That means a cue you are completely confident in and a tip that it is perfect condition. I recommend a dime radius because it allows a little more of the tip's surface to contact the cue ball. This is critical because you will need to strike the cue ball as close to the miscue zone as possible for maximum draw.

Place an object ball a diamond from Pocket E. (Note: some of you, including lefthanders, may be more comfortable shooting the shot on the opposite side of the table.) Position the cue ball about two inches from the edge of Pocket C. If you find this is too much of a stretch, move the cue ball closer to Pocket A until you feel comfortable.

I use a 12-inch bridge, which is almost exactly the distance between the diamonds. Position your tip as low as possible without entering the miscue zone. Use a firm closed bridge. Make sure your shooting arm is very relaxed. You will need to use an extremely hard stroke. Take several smooth warm up strokes to establish your rhythm. On your final stroke, be sure to let your elbow drop as you accelerate through the shot. This will keep your cue level and prevent it from dipping into the cloth. Make sure to avoid putting any right english on the cue ball as this can greatly alter the cue ball's direction. Let your follow through extend unrestricted.

The diagram shows several possible results. My personal best is 2 3/8 table lengths. The cue ball will stop at or near the end rail (1 7/8 table lengths) when I hit the shot really pure. A good pro will draw about 1 3/8 table lengths while a good amateur will draw about one table length. (Note: all measurements are from the object ball's location.) You should see Larry Nevel play this shot. He might even draw it farther than I do.

The ideal conditions for maximum draw are almost new cloth and high humidity. The almost new cloth works better than new cloth because on new cloth the cue ball spins too much in place and loses much of its energy. The humidity gives the cue ball a boinging action when it bounces off the rails.

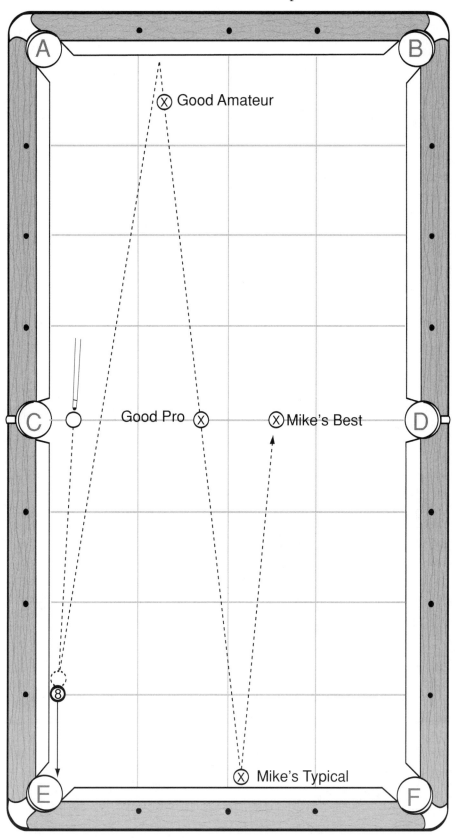

11 *Bank Shots*

The sight of an object ball striking one or more rails before traveling across the table and into a pocket perennially delights both experienced players and novices alike. Bank shots carry an extra element of suspense and luck regarding the outcome, a characteristic that makes them particularly enticing. There is a certain something about bank shots that makes players of all levels want to discover the secrets to pocketing them. During countless clinics I've had complete novices tell me they want to learn bank shots when their most basic fundamentals were in dire need of work.

The eye appeal of most bank shots is way out of proportion to the difficulty of these shots. However, in this chapter you'll discover several banks that will create a stir among onlookers, but that require more than a modest degree of skill. In one shot, for example, the cue ball must jump straight up in the air to avoid a double kiss. In another shot the object ball must travel over 30 feet before finding the pocket. To whet your appetite even further, you will learn the secret to the shot that won Paul Newman a bundle in the opening scene of the movie *The Hustler*. Enjoy!

The Triple Reverse Bank

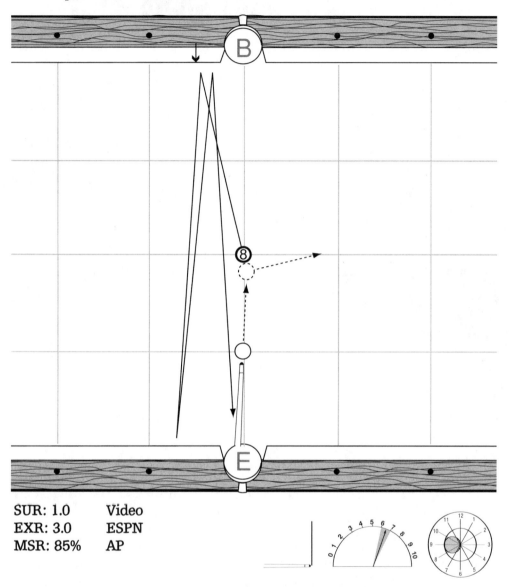

SUR: 1.0   Video
EXR: 3.0   ESPN
MSR: 85%   AP

This shot is not difficult on most tables. However, I have tried it on tables where it was impossible. Aim to have the 8-ball hit about a third of the distance from the point of the side pocket to the nearest diamond. The contact point on the first cushion is one of the big keys to this shot. You only need about a half tip of left english. When you cut the 8-ball to the left, the cut will put right english on the 8-ball. Use a medium hard to hard stroke. The correct speed of stroke depends on the conditions. Be sure to guard against using too much english as this could lead to overcutting the 8-ball. This type of miss is a result of deflection caused by excessive english.

"The Hustler" Bank Shot

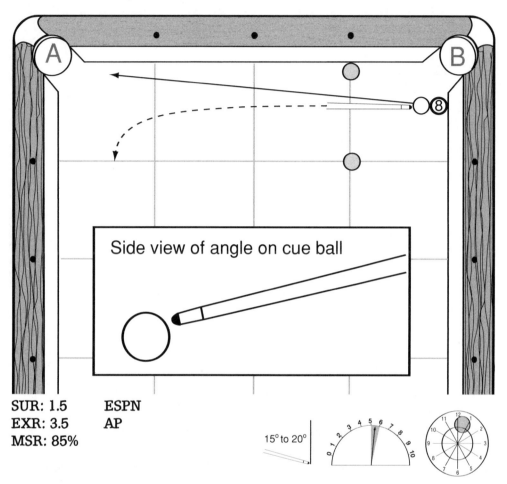

SUR: 1.5   ESPN
EXR: 3.5   AP
MSR: 85%

15° to 20°

This is the bank shot that Paul Newman made in the opening scene of the movie *The Hustler*. The only difference was that the two gray balls weren't there.

Aim straight into the 8-ball (be sure not to cut the shot) and apply a touch of right english so the 8-ball will come off the cushion at a slight angle to your left and across the table into Pocket A. Use an open and elevated bridge with a medium to medium hard stroke. The open bridge allows your cue to deflect up and out of the way, thus avoiding a double hit on the cue ball.

The Golf Ball Bank Shot

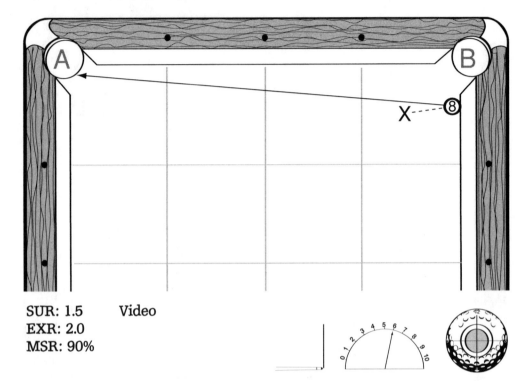

SUR: 1.5   Video
EXR: 2.0
MSR: 90%

When I first started doing exhibitions I always played this shot, which I learned from watching Hall of Fame member Jimmy Caras in a demonstration at the 1970 Tulsa State Fair. They also held a 9-Ball tournament as part of the fair. I emerged as the winner, beating Randy Wallace, who was a very good young player, in the finals. At that time I was mostly hustling and played in very few tournaments. After observing my play, Mr. Caras said I should play in more tournaments. I never forgot that and he turned out to be a very positive influence in my life.

When Caras performed the shot, he would place the 8-ball as shown and then ask for a volunteer. His pigeon was supposed to bank the 8-ball into Pocket A. He told them they would have to place their toy (the cue ball) at Location X. No one could make the shot because they could not avoid the kiss. After the volunteer failed on a couple of attempts, Caras would take a golf ball out of his pocket and say, "You used your toy, now I'm going to use mine."

Naturally he had no trouble making the shot with a golf ball in place of the cue ball. To make The Golf Ball Bank Shot, just make sure to hit the golf ball with a firm stroke. Use center golf ball (no english)! This simple shot will earn you a lot of laughs when you pull out the golf ball and pocket the 8-ball.

Mike's Jump Bank

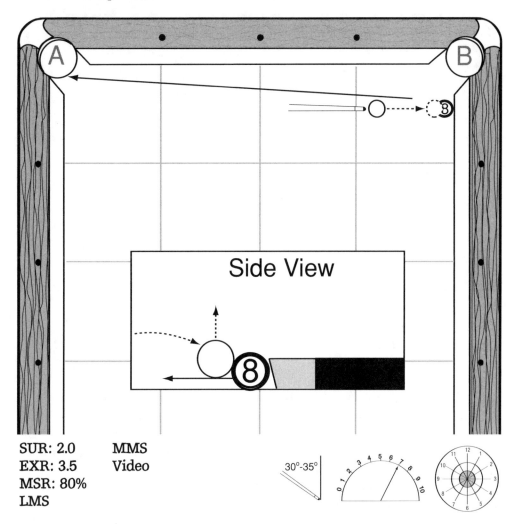

SUR: 2.0   MMS
EXR: 3.5   Video
MSR: 80%
LMS

30°-35°

I eventually figured out how to make the bank in the previous shot with the cue ball. The trick is to hit the 8-ball a little above center as shown in the inset. Elevate your cue about 30-35 degrees for a jump shot. If the cue ball hits too high on the 8-ball, the cue ball will fly off the table. Use a hard stroke. The cue ball will jump almost straight up, about 12-18 inches depending on how hard you hit the shot. The 8-ball will travel under the flying cue ball and into the opposite corner pocket. Once you've perfected this bank, you can add to it by catching the cue ball with your left hand. Lefties will naturally be better off catching it in their right hand unless they don't mind first throwing their cue aside after shooting the shot. I'm just joking. Lefties should play the shot into Pocket B from the opposite side of the table.

Three-Rail Long Rail Bank

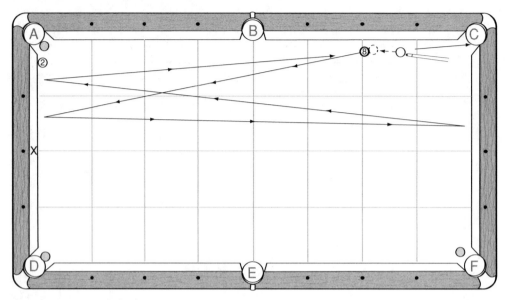

SUR: 1.5   MMS
EXR: 4.5   Video
MSR: 60%   ESPN

Your objective is to bank the 8-ball off three cushions and into Pocket C. This shot is similar to the Triple Reverse Bank, which is in the World Artistic Program, only this one is played up and down the length of the table. This shot could some day come up in a game of One-Pocket or Eight-Ball, so you should definitely give it a try.

Notice that Pockets A, D and F have blockers in front of them, and the 2-ball near Pocket A is blocking the path of a one rail reverse bank. Try aiming a little less than one and a half diamonds below Pocket A. On some tables I've played on, however, I've had to aim clear over at Position X. Apply a little left english (it doesn't take much). In fact, on some tables, you may be able to make the shot using centerball. The spin (or turning of the object ball) is caused mostly by cutting it to the left use a very hard stroke.

You can make this shot on almost any table. The only problems would be encountered on a very worn or slow cloth, or on brand new cloth that's too slick for the english to bite properly.

12 *Jump Shots*

The cue ball leaves the cloth on virtually every shot that is hit hard, especially after contacting the object ball. The altitude it obtains, however, is so slight as to be undetectable to the eye. Jump shots, however, provide a whole new dimension to the game because the cue ball's flight is clearly visible. Spectators just love the sight of a cue ball flying through the air. In addition, jump shots tend to be among the noisiest shots in pool.

Like so many other shots we've covered, there is an element of danger inherent in these shots. Take for example one of my favorites, the Evel Knievel Shot, which appeared for a long time on ESPN. The cue ball must jump several busses and cars (okay, a series of object balls) on its way to the pocket. If the shot fails, the cue ball could wind up rolling across the poolroom floor. In another crowd pleaser the cue ball jumps over two different sets of obstacles.

Jump shots don't require you to slam into the ball as many players have a tendency to do. Technique is vital. The keys are proper elevation, correct speed of stroke, and cuing. When your cue is elevated, remember to view the clock and the proper point of contact from your elevated point of view. Many players also own cues made exclusively for jump shots.

Jump shots are very entertaining and quite practical. In normal play you will regularly be confronted with jump shots, so skill at the shots in this chapter will transfer over to your regular pool game. Practice these trick shots and you'll be working on your game at the same time. You can't beat that!

The Evel Knievel Shot

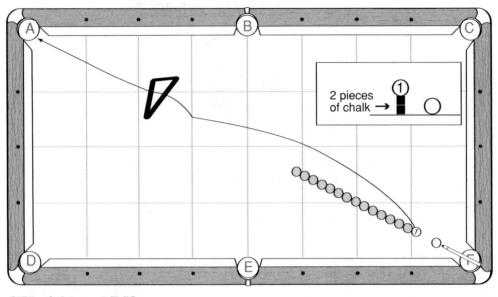

2 pieces of chalk →

SUR: 2.5   MMS
EXR: 3.0   Video
MSR: 75%   ESPN

35° - 40°

I devised this shot as a tribute to the exploits of legendary motorcycle daredevil Evel Knievel. Despite this shot's great eye appeal, it is not a very difficult shot providing it is set up correctly. Make sure all 15 object balls are in a straight line from Pocket A to Pocket F. Then place the 1-ball (the first ball in the line up) on top of two pieces of chalk. Place the cue ball about three inches from the 1-ball. Aim straight for Pocket A. Elevate your cue about 35-40 degrees. Hit the cue ball a little less than a half tip above center. Use a medium hard stroke. You will jump into the 1-ball and send it airborne, propelling it over the 14 balls.

The rack is placed where shown. Oftentimes, the 1-ball will jump the table if it hits the rack or doesn't hit the center of the pocket. In this case you should; 1) adjust the position of the rack forward or back a little, 2) make up some line for the crowd about a crash landing. Remember, even the great Evel Knievel did not land perfectly on every jump.

Mike's ESPN Shoot

I came up with this shot when I first started doing exhibitions. For a few years it was a highlight shot for ESPN. David Howard made the shot for them and they would show it at the beginning of all of their 9-Ball matches. It really looked cool on TV when shown in slow motion. When I play this shot I tell the audience the 1-ball is Evel Knievel, the other object balls are buses, and the chalk is the ramp.

The Jump Draw Shot

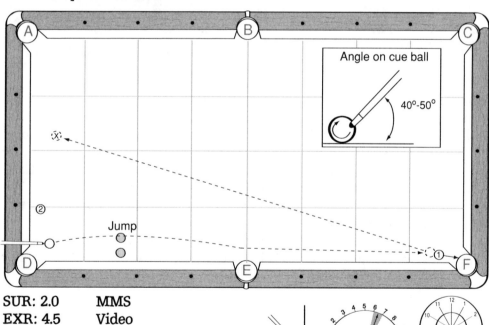

SUR: 2.0   MMS
EXR: 4.5   Video
MSR: 70%

40°-50°

The object of this shot is to jump over the two object balls, pocket the 1-ball, and draw back for position on the 2-ball. No sweat. Elevate your cue to about 40-50 degrees. Strike the cue ball a little less than a half tip above center. Use a medium hard to hard stroke.

Although you make contact a little above center, you can still impart backspin to the cue ball because of the elevation and the angle.

The Double Jump Shot

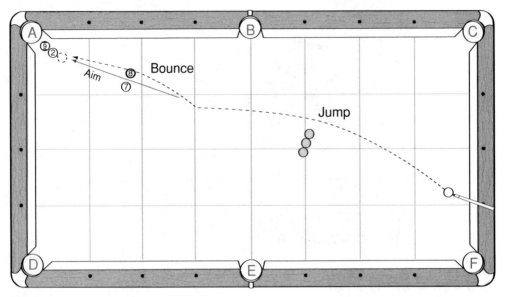

SUR: 3.0   MMS
EXR: 4.0   ESPN
MSR: 70%

Even though there are two clusters between the cue ball and the 2-9 combo, you can win this game by playing a double jump shot. Set up the balls as diagrammed. The 7-ball and 8-ball should be about an inch and a half apart. I suggest that you use a jump cue for this shot. The key is to aim for the center of the gap between these two balls. Elevate your cue to 45 degrees. Strike the cue ball a half tip above center with a hard stroke. The cue ball will soar over the first row of blockers and then bounce just enough to clear the 7-ball and 8-ball when played successfully

I suggest that you practice this shot using four or five pieces of chalk in a line in place of the 7-ball and 8-ball because the cue ball has a tendency to jump the table when either ball is hit.

The Shrinking Cue Ball

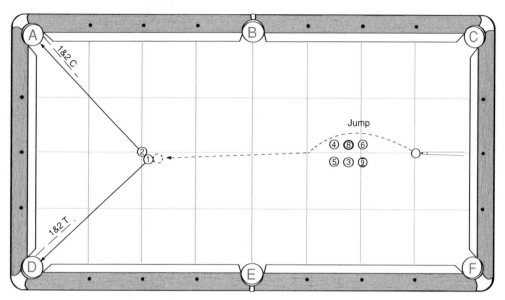

SUR: 1.5   ESPN
EXR: 2.0
MSR: 98%

Place six balls on the right side of the table close enough together so the cue ball cannot quite fit between them. Position the 2-ball on the spot with the 1-ball frozen to it. Elevate your cue to about 15 degrees. Strike the cue ball a half tip above center. Use a hard stroke. The cue ball will jump just enough to go between the balls while appearing to have shrunk to fit through the tunnel.

I used to tell people the cue ball was made of a material called Shrinkaflex. When you hit the cue ball hard enough it will shrink momentarily in size. You might try this line and see what your fans have to say. If they go for it, perhaps you can then sell them some beachfront property outside Tucson, Arizona.

No Scratch City

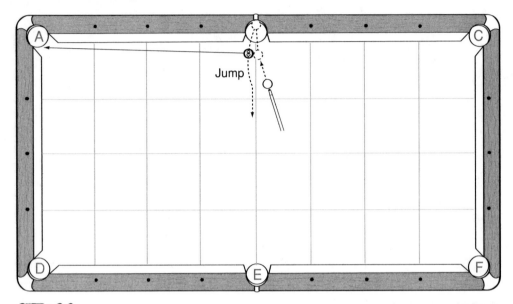

SUR: 2.0
EXR: 3.5
MSR: 70%

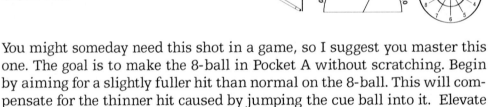

You might someday need this shot in a game, so I suggest you master this one. The goal is to make the 8-ball in Pocket A without scratching. Begin by aiming for a slightly fuller hit than normal on the 8-ball. This will compensate for the thinner hit caused by jumping the cue ball into it. Elevate your cue to about 30 degrees. Use a hard stroke. The cue ball will jump into the 8-ball, hit the back of the pocket near the top, and rebound back out onto the playing surface.

My good friend and Pool School in Paradise partner, Paul Potier, shoots this shot very well.

Escape from Jail

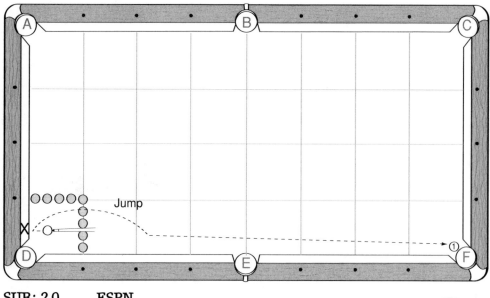

SUR: 2.0   ESPN
EXR: 3.0   AP
MSR: 85%
LMS

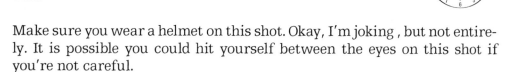

Make sure you wear a helmet on this shot. Okay, I'm joking , but not entire-ly. It is possible you could hit yourself between the eyes on this shot if you're not careful.

Place the cue ball about four inches from Cushion X. Elevate your bridge slightly. If you elevate too much, the cue ball will jump too high, making control difficult (and the helmet necessary). Use a medium stroke and hit very high on the cue ball. Aim like you would for a normal kick shot.

The Flying 8-Ball Bank Shot

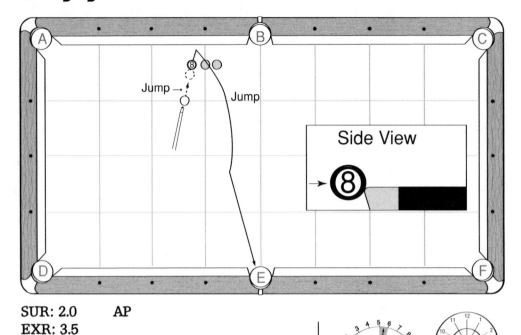

SUR: 2.0   AP
EXR: 3.5
MSR: 60%

The idea is to make the 8-ball strike the cushion while in midair a little above it's equator. Aim straight into the 8-ball with about 20 degrees of elevation. If you use any more than this, the 8-ball will jump too high and you will likely lose control of the shot. Use a medium to medium hard stroke while hitting the cue ball in the center. If the 8-ball doesn't jump high enough, try elevating the cue a little more. The less the 8-ball jumps, the straighter the shot will go.

On, Over and Around

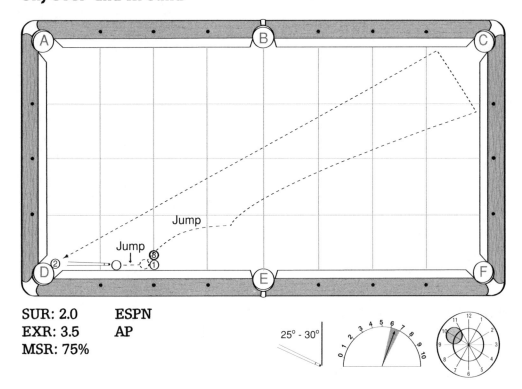

SUR: 2.0   ESPN
EXR: 3.5   AP
MSR: 75%

25° - 30°

The cue ball is supposed to jump into the 1-ball and then over the 8-ball before traveling two rails into the 2-ball in front of Pocket D. Aim for a full ball hit on the 1-ball. Since the cue ball is frozen to the cushion, it will veer to the left a little when struck with your cue elevated.

Use about 25-30 degrees of elevation and use a medium hard to hard stroke. You should hit the cue ball at 10:00 with a lot of left english.

The Over and Under Shot

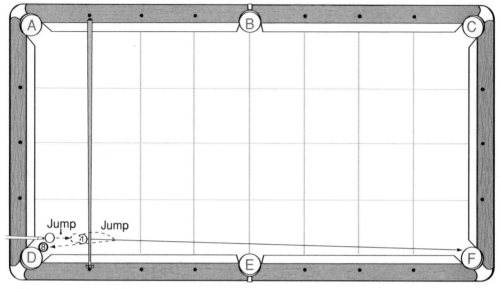

SUR: 2.0   Video
EXR: 3.5   ESPN
MSR: 80%   AP

The object is to make the 1-ball in Pocket F and have the cue ball jump over the bridge, and then draw back under the bridge and pocket the 8-ball. Elevate your cue to about 30 degrees. Aim to shoot the 1-ball straight into the corner pocket and hit the cue ball slightly above center with 5:30 english. Make sure you allow for deflection by aiming a little to the right. Use a medium hard to hard stroke.

Massey's Over, Around and Under Shot

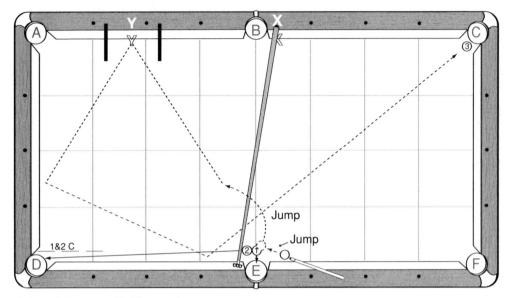

SUR: 2.5	MMS
EXR: 3.5	Video
MSR: 90%	ESPN
	AP

30°-40°

After I'd been doing exhibitions for a short time I became very familiar with The Over and Under Shot. I wanted another shot that would make use of the bridge so I created this version of The Over and Under Shot many years ago in Chattanooga, Tennessee. It was selected for Artistic Pool even though I didn't submit it to the shot selection committee.

Set up the shot as diagrammed. Make sure the cue ball has enough room to go under the bridge. If the bridge is not high enough, place a piece of chalk under the handle at Position X. The 1-ball is about one inch from the edge of Pocket E and is frozen to the 2-ball. The balls are aligned towards the right edge Pocket D.

Elevate your cue to about 30-40 degrees. Aim for a half ball hit on the 1-ball. Use a medium hard stroke and a tip of left english. The cue ball will fly over the bridge and continue to the upper side rail at Zone Y. If the cue ball hits to the left of Zone Y you are either 1) hitting the 1-ball too thin or 2) jumping the cue ball too high. To correct either error, aim for a thicker hit or lower the elevation of your cue. You could also try moving the cue ball a half inch to an inch closer to the 1-ball. If the cue ball jumps the table, you are shooting too hard. In this case, use less speed.

The Great Race

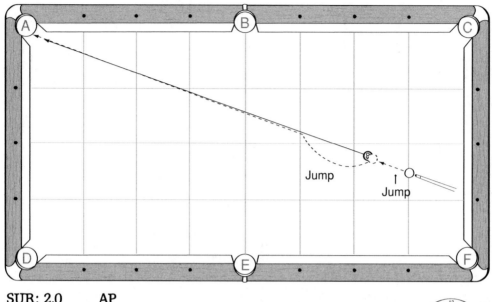

SUR: 2.0   AP
EXR: 4.5
MSR: 35%

The first objective is to jump the cue ball into the top of the 8-ball. The cue ball is then supposed to scurry into Pocket A first followed by the 8-ball.

Place the cue ball about 10 inches from the 8-ball. Aim straight at the 8-ball with your cue elevated to 30 degrees. Use a medium hard stroke. I use my jump cue for this shot.

Accurate aiming, speed control, and skill at jump shots are all required on this shot. If your aim is off a millimeter you'll miss. If you shoot too hard, the cue ball will likely jump the table. And if the cue ball jumps too high, it could fly right over the 8-ball. If the cue ball doesn't jump high enough, the 8-ball will beat it to the pocket.

13   *Massés*

Willie Mosconi, who executed massé shots in all of his exhibitions, was a master of these shots. Mosconi performed one in the movie *The Hustler*, which is in this chapter. Viewers, of course, are supposed to believe that Fast Eddie played it. I had the honor of doing a few exhibitions with Mosconi before he passed away, and I also recreated the shots on a DVD of *The Hustler*.

I get many requests for masse shots, which are among the most beautiful and feared shots in pool. Massés are executed with the cue in a vertical or near vertical position. A sharp downward blow on the cue ball can produce feats of sheer magic. On a typical massé, the cue ball will start down the table away from the object ball, and then reverse course all by itself and return to knock in a pocket hanger.

Poolroom owners fear massé shots because there is always the chance that novices will rip the cloth when practicing them, and rightly so. Since the cue ball will be long gone before the tip hits the table, it might save some wear and tear (literally) if you place a small piece of cloth where the tip will be striking the cloth. When you have mastered the massé stroke, the cue ball should absorb the brunt of the impact. The only damage to the table will be a small pit mark, which will usually disappear in a short while.

Massés are all about technique. You've got to assume a completely different stance than normal. On many of them you will need to sit on the rail. Most massés require that you hold the cue at anywhere from a 70-90 degree angle to the table. Make sure to hit the cue ball on the correct spot on the clock while taking into account the increased elevation.

Massés seldom come up in a game, so your practice time on these is mostly to improve your show. But there will come a time when you'll face one in a game. If you can pull one off in competition, you might completely unnerve your opponent.

Kiss Back Massé

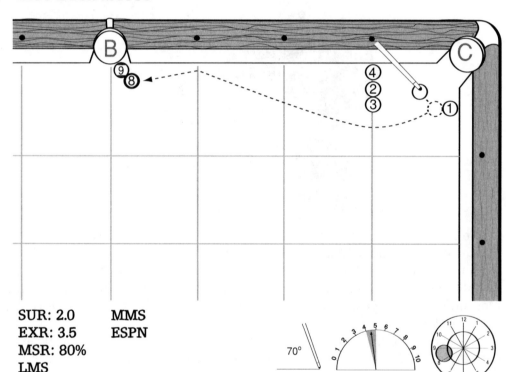

SUR: 2.0   MMS
EXR: 3.5   ESPN
MSR: 80%
LMS

70°

With a little practice you will find yourself making this rather impressive shot. Aim for about a half ball hit on the 1-ball. Elevate your cue to 70 degrees. Use maximum english at 8:30 and a medium soft to medium massé stroke.

Yo-Yo Massé

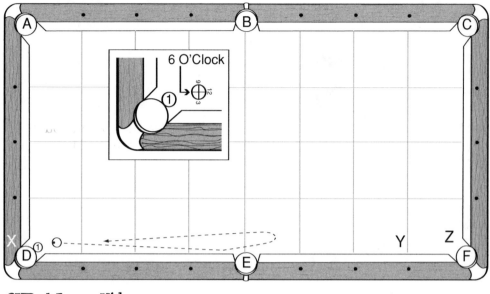

SUR: 1.5   Video
EXR: 4.5
MSR: 60%
LMS

85°-90°

I use the Yo-Yo Massé as my warm up massé shot. I sit on the edge of the table at Location X and brace my bridge hand up against my thigh while using a closed bridge. Elevate to 85-90 degrees. Hit sharply down on the cue ball at about 5:45 extreme. The inset shows another view of where 6:00 is in relation to the table.

When properly executed, the cue ball will scurry up table past the side pocket, reverse course, and come back to pocket the 1-ball. In my video the cue ball traveled all the way to Location Y before turning around.

Fantastic Surprises

Once during an exhibition with Minnesota Fats at a shopping center in Huntsville, Alabama the cue ball went all the way to Location Z, about three inches from the end rail. The cue ball stopped for a second, then came back to pocket the 1-ball. The cloth and balls were brand new so there was very little friction.

This is but another example of the things that make trick shots so fascinating: sometimes things happen that make the shot more fantastic than planned.

Machine Gun Massé

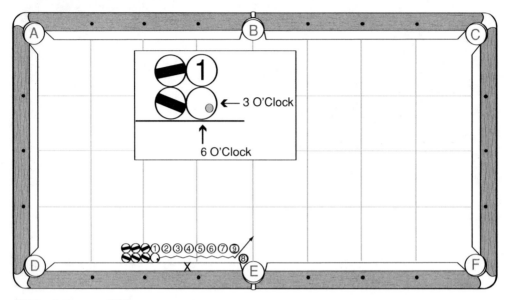

SUR: 2.5   Video
EXR: 4.0   ESPN
MSR: 80%

This crowd pleaser is also one of my favorite massé shots. Place the balls as diagrammed. The row of balls should be a ball's width from the cushion. Leave a quarter inch gap between the balls. Place the 8-ball on the edge of the side pocket as shown. The six striped balls to the left of the 1-ball should be frozen together. The cue ball is frozen to the 1-ball, the ball to its left, and to the rail.

Use a massé stroke with the cue in a totally vertical position. Strike the cue ball over a tip from the center at 4:00. Hit sharply down on the cue ball. The cue ball will make contact with the row of balls before pocketing the 8-ball into Pocket E.

Sometimes the cue ball will actually hesitate momentarily near or at Location X before resuming its journey to the 8-ball. When this happens, you will receive an added bonus to what is already a spectacular shot.

Massey's Massé 9-Ball Shot

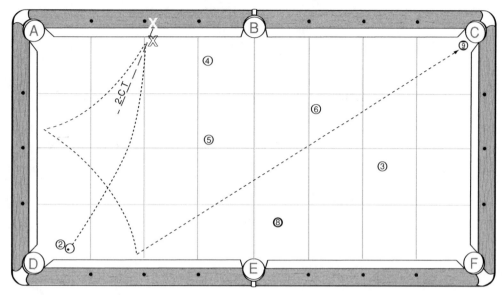

SUR: 2.0   MMS
EXR: 4.5
MSR: 50%

80°

This is a very attractive massé that I've made into a situation shot playing 9-Ball. Place the cue ball and 2-ball as diagrammed. They should be about an eighth of an inch apart. The tangent line between the balls should be pointing at Position X.

Use a vertical massé. Tilt the top of your cue inward slightly away from the intended target (the first cushion). Cue a full tip from center at 8:00. Stroke down sharply and cross your fingers.

The Rocket Massé

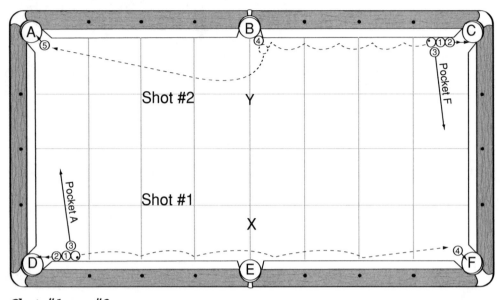

Shot #1	#2	
SUR: 2.5	2.5	Video
EXR: 4.0	5.0	
MSR: 75%	35%	
LMS	LMS	

90°

I call Shot #1 The Rocket Massé or Long Massé. The object is to make the 1, 2, 3, and 4-balls. Play the shot with a vertical massé stroke. Hit down sharply on the cue ball at about 4:30. As a point of reference, the cue ball should touch the rail at 6:00. The cue ball will force the 2-ball and 1-ball into Pocket D and the 3-ball into Pocket A. It will then rocket up table to pocket the 4-ball. Sometimes when the conditions are right the cue ball will start off slowly and then pick up speed. By the time it strikes the 4-ball it will be traveling very fast. In my video the cue ball made contact with the long rail six times.

Shot #2 is one of the most gratifying and beautiful shots I've ever made for TV. The shot is played exactly the same as the one in Shot #1. This time, however, you have to doctor up the cue ball. Apply furniture wax, car wax or silicon spray to the cue ball. The spin will stay on the slicker cue ball longer because there is less friction.

In Shot #2, the cue ball will carom out toward the center after pocketing the 4-ball. The tremendous spin on the cue ball enables it to come back towards the rail to pocket the 5-ball in Pocket A. This shot also played a prominent role in the Carom Christmas TV show in Barcelona.

The Rocket Massé Version 2

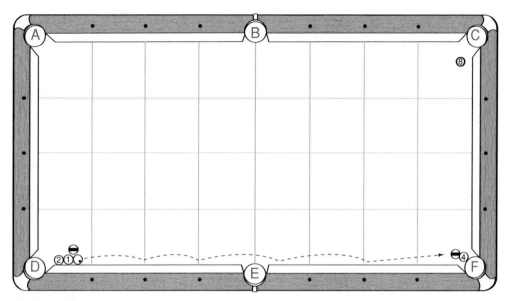

SUR: 2.5
EXR: 4.0
MSR: 75%
LMS

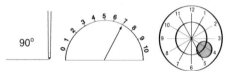

The 3-ball in Shot #1 on the previous page can be most troublesome, espe-cially on a slow table. If you are having trouble making the 3-ball, you might want to turn The Rocket Massé a situation shot as shown.

Tell your friends or spectators you are in a tough spot in a game of Eight-Ball. You can make the 1-ball and 2-ball, but it's impossible to play position for the 4-ball since the striped ball is in the way. Now you've transformed the shot into one that could come up in a game of Eight-Ball.

Use a striped ball instead of the 3-ball. In addition, place a stripe frozen to the 4-ball. Then place the 8-ball near a pocket on the other side of the table. When you make the shot, you will have position for the 8-ball.

Gerni Brings Down the House Shot

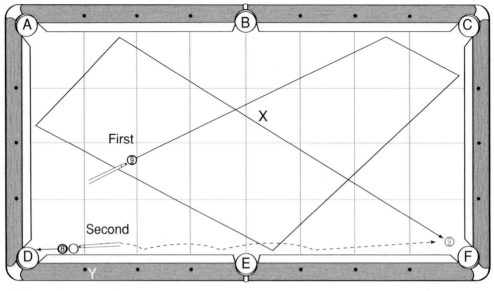

SUR: 2.0   ESPN
EXR: 5.0
MSR: 5-7%
LMS

The next time you take a month long vacation and want to spend a good portion of it learning a superb shot, this is the one for you. If you are an excellent pupil, you might even make it before you have to go back to work. I might make it on my first attempt, or maybe not until the 50th. Now remember that I shoot this kind of shot for a living, so that should give you some additional perspective on the challenge this shot presents.

Place the balls as diagrammed with the cue ball and 8-ball about an eighth of an inch from the cushion. Shoot the 9-ball five rails on the path shown. Use a medium hard stroke so the 9-ball is not rolling too fast when it gets near the intended pocket.

Now comes the hard part. As soon as you shoot the five-railer, immediately step over to Location Y and get in position for a massé shot. When you see or feel the 9-ball is near Position X, execute a rocket massé. Excellent peripheral vision is a big plus for this shot. Use a vertical massé stroke and hit down sharply on the cue ball. This shot takes a lot of skill and luck. Good luck!

Perhaps the best at this shot is fellow trick shot shooter Paul Gerni. He had the nerve to make this against me in the 2001 Trick Shot Magic Competition. Even though I ended up winning the competition, it was Paul who brought down the house when he made this incredible shot.

Scratching with Style

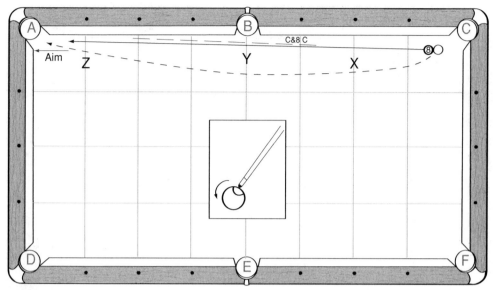

SUR: 2.0 Video
EXR: 4.0 ESPN
MSR: 80% AP

40°-50°

This is one of my most requested shots. While most people call this The Passing Shot, I like to call it Scratching With Style. The first person I saw execute this shot was George Middleditch in Sacramento, CA. He played the shot with a harder stroke than I do. His method makes the cue ball zip around the 8-ball at the area marked Z. George's way is more difficult, but he nevertheless is able to consistently make the shot. Tom Rossman does the opposite. He uses a softer stroke than I do. Tom's approach makes the cue ball pass the 8-ball at the area marked X. I shoot with a medium hard stroke. The cue ball usually passes the 8-ball at the area marked Y.

You can execute the passing shot using a medium, medium hard, or hard stroke! I elevate to about 40-50 degrees and stroke down over the top of the cue ball at 1:30. I aim down the aiming line and adjust if need be. Try to visualize the cue ball curving around an object ball sitting near Pocket B.

"The Hustler" Massé Shot

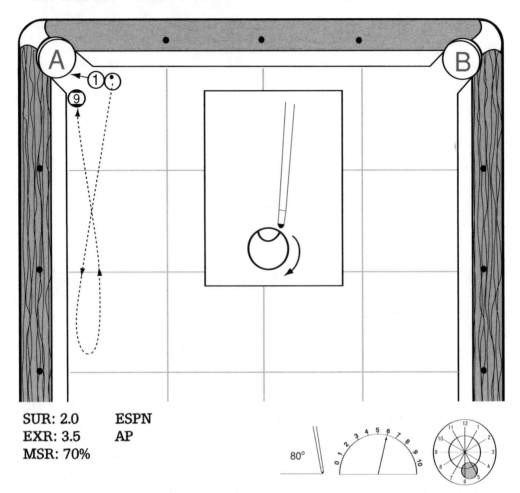

SUR: 2.0   ESPN
EXR: 3.5   AP
MSR: 70%

80°

Willie Mosconi made this shot in the movie *The Hustler*. Of course, the audience didn't see Mosconi as they were tricked into believing that either Fast Eddie or Minnesota Fats played it.

Place the 9-ball about a quarter inch from the cushion. Shoot this massé with an almost vertical stroke. Hit down on the cue ball with a medium hard stroke. I am successful on this shot using either a light or heavy cue. However, the heavier cue makes the cue ball travel farther down the rail before it comes back towards the 9-ball. The heavier cue also requires less effort.

A European Massé Shot

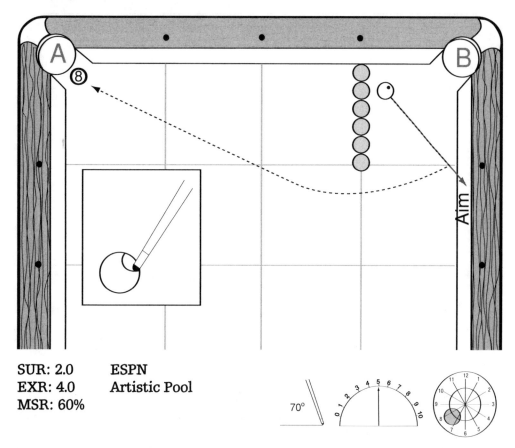

SUR: 2.0   **ESPN**
EXR: 4.0   **Artistic Pool**
MSR: 60%

70°

This rather impressive looking shot is not nearly as difficult as it appears. In the 2001 North American Championships at Hard Times in California, six of the eight players were successful at it.

There are several ways to play this shot. In fact, I've changed the way I shoot it three times now. I now believe the best way is to employ a European style massé stroke. Elevate about 70 degrees and shoot with a medium stroke. Cue at 7:30.

The European Massé stroke is when you hold the cue with your thumb and first two fingers sort of like you would when holding a dart. The stroke uses more wrist action than a normal stroke.

Changing Direction

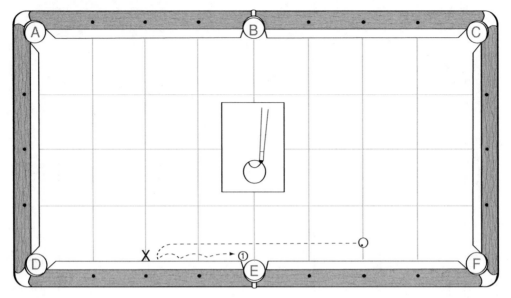

SUR: 1.5   AP
EXR: 4.0
MSR: 40%
LMS

80°

This shot helped me to lock up the 2002 World Championship in Willingen, Germany. After executing this massé, I had an insurmountable 20 point lead going into the last shot.

I recommend a near vertical massé stroke on this shot. Use a medium hard to hard stroke. When I hit it good, the cue ball will travel to Point X and then shoot back up the rail at a rapid clip. My massé cue weighs 27 ounces and is about 40 inches long. I use it for this shot most of the time unless the cloth is really slick and fast, in which case I would use my normal cue, which weighs 18.5 ounces. Aim out past the 1-ball a little. The left english will make the cue ball turn back to the rail before it reverses course and comes back to pocket the 1-ball.

Exit Stage Right

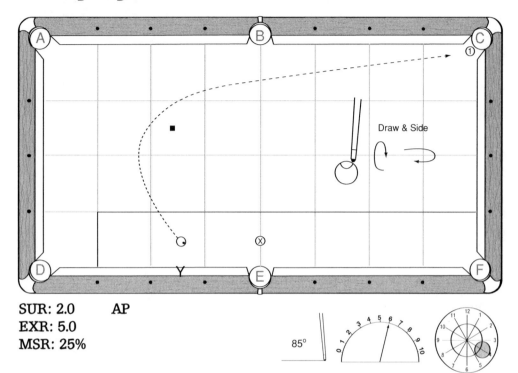

SUR: 2.0   AP
EXR: 5.0
MSR: 25%

Draw & Side

85°

I've made this incredible looking shot many times, but never in competition. The first year of the Artistic Pool Championships (2000) against Yoshikazu Kimura I missed it by about a half-inch. I had already won the tournament so there was no pressure to pocket this extremely challenging shot. Charlie Darling made the shot in the 2002 World Championships with the cue ball at Point X. The shot helped him jump to third place and a bronze medal. On a billiard table there's a similar shot, but it is much easier because of the bigger and heavier balls and two inch thick slate.

I prefer my heavy cue because it takes less effort and it gives me a better feel for the shot. Elevate your cue to about 85 degrees. Use a medium hard stroke. Tilt your cue back toward Rail Y about five degrees. This will cause the cue ball to squirt a little more out past the chalk. The backspin causes the cue ball to slow up before it reaches the cushion. The sidespin then takes over, propelling the cue ball up table and into the 1-ball.

The Level Cue Massé

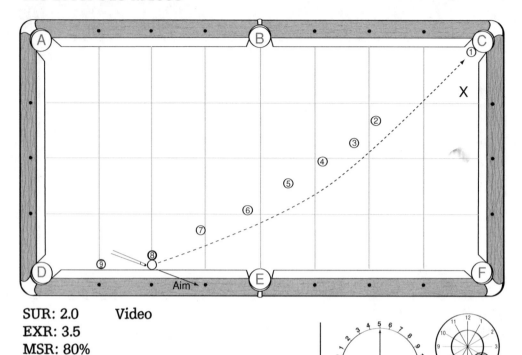

SUR: 2.0   Video
EXR: 3.5
MSR: 80%

The Level Cue Massé is not too difficult once you learn the correct speed for this shot. Aim at the third diamond as shown. Shoot directly into the cushion. Use low right english with a draw stroke. Try using medium speed. If the cue ball hits to the right of Pocket C at Position X, use a softer stroke. Should the cue ball run into the obstructers, try shooting a little harder. Knowing the principle behind this shot could be very valuable in a real game when you are hooked and must play a kick shot.

14 A Few of Mike's Favorite Creations

I love fooling around with the balls trying to see what I can come up with next. The shots in this chapter are just a few of the results of my experiments with variations of existing shots, and brand new shots as well. Throughout the book are several more shots that I've devised over the years.

While you are practicing and performing the shots in this book you may perhaps have a brainstorm and come up with a trick shot that amuses and amazes your friends. If so, I would like to hear about it. I might even use it in one of my shows or put it in a future edition of the book. And I'll give you credit and maybe name it after you, the inventor. You can write me at the address in the back of the book. Happy experimenting!

Time the 9 Shot

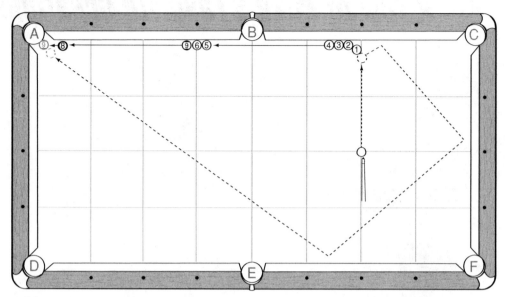

SUR: 3.0   MMS
EXR: 3.5   Video
MSR: 70%

This shot hasn't come up yet in a game of 9-Ball, but in case it does, I'll be ready for it and so will you. The 1-ball is the lead ball in a four ball combination. The first objective is to hit the 1-ball in the correct spot. The 4-ball, which is the last ball of the combo, will then proceed into the 5-ball. The 5-ball will then send the 9-ball into the 8-ball. The 9-ball will continue on to the ghost ball location shown in the diagram. In the meantime, the cue ball will have traveled three rails towards Pocket A on its way to pocketing the 9-ball, thus completing this beautiful time shot.

When setting up the shot, make sure the two clusters are frozen to the rail and that each ball is frozen to its neighbor. The 1-ball is not frozen to the cushion but is placed a half a ball away. The 8-ball is about a sixteenth of an inch from the cushion. Aim for a half ball hit. Use a full tip of right english with a medium stroke.

Collision Drawback 9-Ball Shot

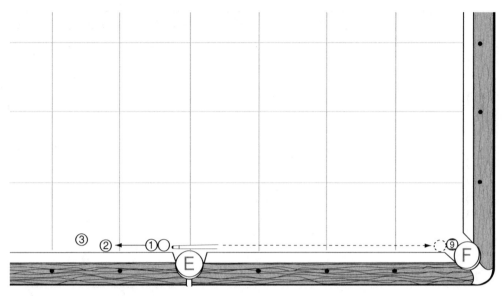

SUR: 2.0   MMS
EXR: 3.5   Video
MSR: 80%
LMS

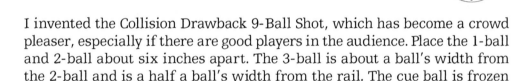

I invented the Collision Drawback 9-Ball Shot, which has become a crowd pleaser, especially if there are good players in the audience. Place the 1-ball and 2-ball about six inches apart. The 3-ball is about a ball's width from the 2-ball and is a half a ball's width from the rail. The cue ball is frozen to the 1-ball and is about an inch from the point of the side pocket.

Use low left english and a medium soft stroke. When you play this shot, be sure your cue is parallel with the cushion. This will help prevent the tendency to aim into the rail. If you do aim slightly into the rail, the cue ball will come back at an angle, leave the rail, and miss the 9-ball. The reason the cue ball comes back is that it stays with the 1-ball until the collision with the 2-ball. At that moment, the draw spin propels the cue ball toward the 9-ball.

The Inquisitive 7

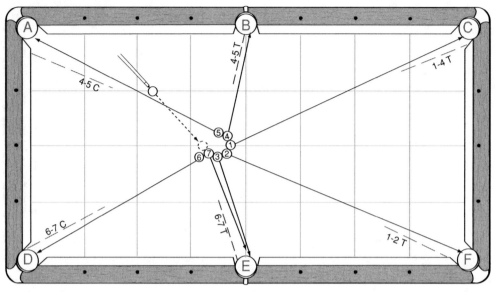

SUR: 4.0   MMS
EXR: 3.5
MSR: 90%

The Inquisitive 7 is my variation of the Slam Dunk (see page 116). The set up for the first five balls is exactly the same. The 7-ball is frozen to the 3-ball. There is about an eighth of an inch gap between the 6-ball and 7-ball. The cue ball is about a half diamond closer to the rail than with the Slam Dunk.

Aim for a full hit on the 7-ball. Hit the cue ball dead center with a very hard stroke. Make sure not to apply any draw spin to the cue ball. If you commit this error, the cue ball will run into the 5-ball.

Inspired 4 Ball Shot

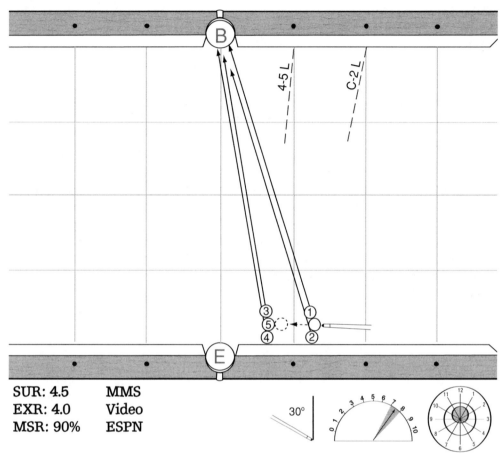

SUR: 4.5	MMS
EXR: 4.0	Video
MSR: 90%	ESPN

I came up with the Inspired 4 Ball Shot while Ewa Laurance and I were performing in Youngstown, Ohio several years ago. It has now become one of my favorite set up shots

The object is to make the 1, 2, 3, and 4-balls in rotation in Pocket B. Place the balls as diagrammed. You want everyone's attention on Pocket B. Therefore, I recommend that you substitute another cue ball for the 5-ball if one is available. The second cue ball helps to focus the crowd's attention properly.

Use an open bridge so your cue will glance up and out of the way. Aim for a 90% hit on the right side of the 5-ball. Elevate your cue to about 30 degrees. Hit the cue ball about a quarter tip above center. Use a hard or very hard stroke. When the cue ball hits the 5-ball it will jump up out of the way making room for the 4-ball to bank into Pocket B.

If the 1-ball hits the 3-ball while they are racing for Pocket B, move the cluster containing the 1-ball, 2-ball, and cue ball a little further to the right or move the 3, 5, and 4-balls to the left. Align the cue ball and 1-ball with the right side of Pocket B. Do the same with the 3-ball and 5-ball to allow for throw.

Giz and Hum Mess

SUR: 5.0   MMS
EXR: 3.0   Video
MSR: 90%

I'm afraid I must take the credit or blame for this challenging set up shot. The set up component rates a 5.0 on my 5 Scale, which makes this the toughest shot to set up in the book. This work of art was concocted at Giz and Hum Billiards in San Angelo, Texas, hence the name Giz and Hum Mess. This shot, which I've played on ESPN, is very impressive, especially with good players because they have no idea where the balls are going to go.

Try to be as precise as possible when setting up this shot, paying special attention to the set up lines. There is an eighth on an inch gap between the 6-ball and 7-ball. All of the other balls are frozen to one another. Hit maximum draw with a medium hard stroke. When practicing this shot it helps to have a friend watch. Ask them to tell you where the ball(s) that miss struck the rail(s). Then make any necessary adjustments.

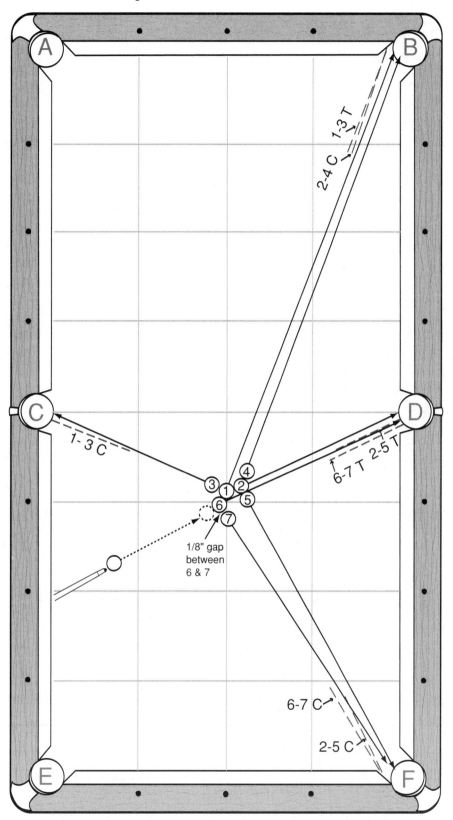

Pocket Seven for the 8-Ball

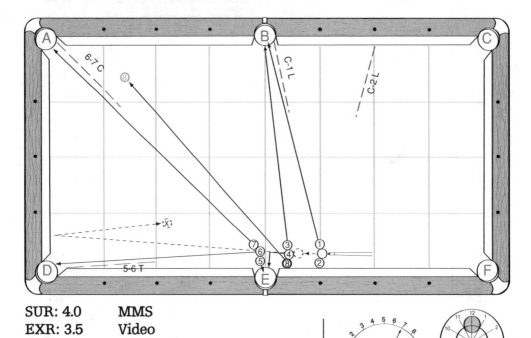

SUR: 4.0	MMS	
EXR: 3.5	Video	
MSR: 90%	ESPN	

This creation of mine has been a crowd favorite since its inception, and is heavily requested. The object is to pocket all seven solids and play position for the 8-ball. You don't have to allow for much throw on the 7-ball, especially if the balls are clean.

Aim for about a 90% hit on the right side of the 4-ball. Cue at least one full tip above center. Use an open bridge and a hard stroke. Make sure when you stroke the shot that your cue glances upward after contact. This will keep it from hitting the 2-ball. Hold your cue level to keep the cue ball from jumping.

If you play this shot enough you will notice you don't always get good position for the 8-ball. If this happens, just rake the 8-ball into a pocket and tell your audience that your opponent knew that if you could make seven balls in one shot, you could make the 8-ball no matter where it ended up. So he just conceded the 8-ball.

15 Pure Skill Shots

When your gathering consists largely of knowledgeable players who you are dying to impress, and you have put in the requisite hours honing your skills, then its Showtime for the shots in this chapter. In addition to impressing your knowledgeable fans, you could also wind up facing some of these shots or variations of them in competition. I certainly hope these twin objectives will motivate you to work long and hard on these shots.

The most practical of the bunch is Pitching a Curve Ball. This shot will teach you to control the curve and speed on angled draw shots. The 92 Degree Cut Shot will certainly win you many games over the course of your career. At the other end of the practicality spectrum are Rapid Fire Wing Shots. To date I know of no pool game that requires you to shoot at a ball while its racing down the table. They do, however, insist that you master wing shots in the world of Artistic Pool.

Technique rules on the shots in this chapter. You will need superb fundamentals and possibly a sharp eye to make four of them. For the Rapid Fire Wing Shots and the Jack Up Spot Shot you will need to master two new and very challenging shooting techniques. If you are successful, you will have added to your repertoire a couple of shots that could win you a gourmet meal some day. You will have earned a five star meal, and your victim should not mind paying for your display of otherworldly hand-eye coordination.

Jack Up Spot Shot

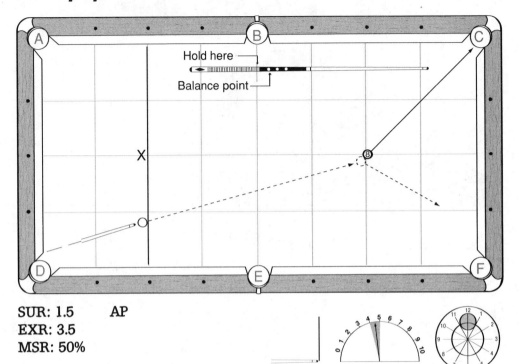

SUR: 1.5   AP
EXR: 3.5
MSR: 50%

This exacting skill shot requires that you to be able to keep your arm steady under pressure. The object is to pocket the 8-ball in Pocket C while shooting one handed and jacked-up. Jacked up means you are not allowed to rest your cue on the rail. The cue ball must be placed behind Line X.

When I shoot one handed jacked up, I normally hold the cue about 3-4 inches behind the balance point. I place the cue ball as shown. From this location a half ball hit on the 8-ball will send it into the pocket. A half ball hit is one of the easiest shots because you have a distinct point to aim at. I recommend a high center hit on the cue ball. Aim your tip at the right edge of the 8-ball.

You must rely on your instincts on this shot because you don't have a bridge to steady your cue. Hold your cue as steady as possible. When you feel it's right, stroke straight through the cue ball using a medium soft to medium speed.

I prefer to shoot this shot into Pocket C. However, you can play the shot into Pocket F if you find it easier from the opposite side of the table.

Pitching a Curve Ball

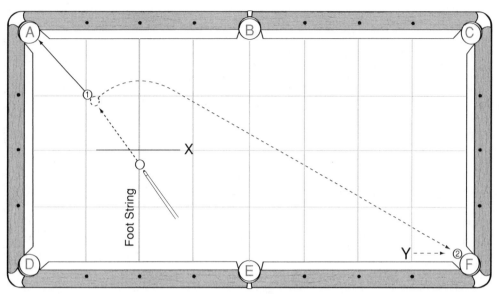

SUR: 1.5   AP
EXR: 4.0
MSR: 50%

Even though this shot only rates seven points in Artistic Pool for a successful first attempt, it is not nearly as easy as it appears. It takes expert cue ball control to pocket the 2-ball. The 1-ball is placed at the intersection of the first diamonds. The cue ball is placed on the foot string behind Line X. Placing the cue ball one ball's width from Line X should provide sufficient cut angle.

Strike the cue ball well below center at 7:00. English will help to make the 2-ball should the cue ball strike the cushion around Point Y or below. Use a medium hard stroke.

You must shoot very accurately. Make sure to aim for the center of the pocket. This will help you to adjust your stroke following any misses. It also helps to know the condition of the table. When you are shooting on old cloth, you will probably need to move the cue ball a little farther from the center line. This will help you to compensate for the draw, which takes quicker on old cloth.

Slice N' Draw Shot

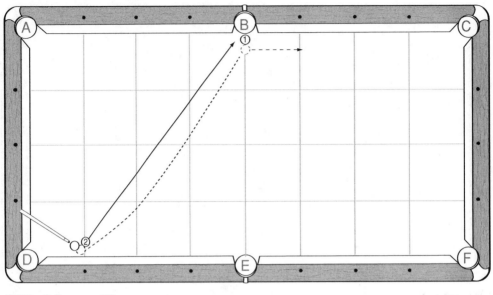

SUR: 3.0   AP
EXR: 4.5
MSR: 30

On this shot you must be even more accurate than the previous one for two reasons. First, you've got to play a difficult cut shot on the 2-ball. In addition, the cue ball must hit the 1-ball and then move out of the way for the onrushing 2-ball.

Place the cue ball an inch from the 2-ball and about one and a half inches from the cushion. Use a medium speed stroke.

Finding the correct location for the cue ball is a big challenge. When you practice this shot, start with the cue ball at my recommended location. If you have a problem making the shot, make some minor adjustments. Try moving the cue ball a little farther from the 2-ball. Also consider adjusting your speed of stroke and where you strike the cue ball. If you are getting a double kiss on the 2-ball, you are using too much draw, or you are not cutting the 2-ball enough.

The 92 Degree Cut Shot

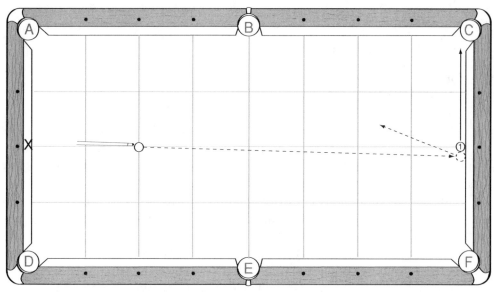

SUR: 1.0   AP
EXR: 4.0
MSR: 60%

The 92 Degree Cut Shot is a skill shot that tests your aim and use of english. You need to know how your cue plays because of the amount of english required. Position the balls exactly as diagrammed. The cue ball is placed on the head spot and the object ball is frozen to the end rail opposite the middle diamond.

Use maximum left english. Keep your cue as level as possible to minimize curve. Cueing at 9:00 also helps to virtually eliminate curve as a consideration in aiming. Be sure not to hit below center as this will cause the cue ball to curve. Use a medium speed stroke. Practice by aiming your tip at a certain location on the 1-ball. You may have to aim your tip at the left edge of the 1-ball because of the squirt caused by the maximum english.

The cue ball must hit the cushion first very close to the object ball. The spin will bring the cue ball back into the 1-ball, causing it to roll along the cushion and into the pocket.

I prefer to shoot this shot into Pocket C. However, you can play the shot into Pocket F. In this case you would aim to the left of the 1-ball and use right english.

When I was hustling I used this as a proposition shot. I placed the cue ball on top of Rail X and shot it one handed jacked up. I could make it about 10% of the time. So as long as my intended victim gave me a sufficient number of attempts, I could walk away a winner.

Rapid Fire Wing Shots

SUR: N/A   AP
EXR: 4.0 *1
EXR: 5.0*2
MSR: 60% (for one)
1 - (for one)
2 - (all seven balls)

When preparing for this shot, place six additional object balls where shown. You must roll the object ball into the target zone by hand and shoot it into Pocket F while it is rolling down the table. The cue ball must be shot from behind Line X. I prefer to place the cue ball after letting go of the object ball because I feel this improves my rhythm. You can, however, have the cue ball in place prior to rolling the object ball or you can place it after letting go of the object ball.

These so called Wing Shots are mostly timing and instinct. What makes the Artistic Pool version more difficult than the "normal" version is the cube of chalk on the foot spot. It can throw off your rhythm, which is crucial on a shot that requires such precision.

I hold the cue ball and object ball in my left hand. I roll the object ball and place the cue ball in a smooth and continuous motion. Most good wing shot shooters shoot medium hard because they don't have much time before the object ball reaches the zone. In competition we have to shoot seven shots in succession. The key is to stay cool and acquire a good rhythm. Plan on spending a lot of time practicing these shots if you intend to master them.

Tom Rossman and Earl Strickland are excellent at wing shots. Minnesota Fats was also pretty good. Don Willis was great at wings shots. In fact, I heard that he once made 30 in succession. In exhibitions I shoot one handed jacked up, while rolling the cue ball and object ball at the same time. I also shoot them one handed jacked up under my leg!

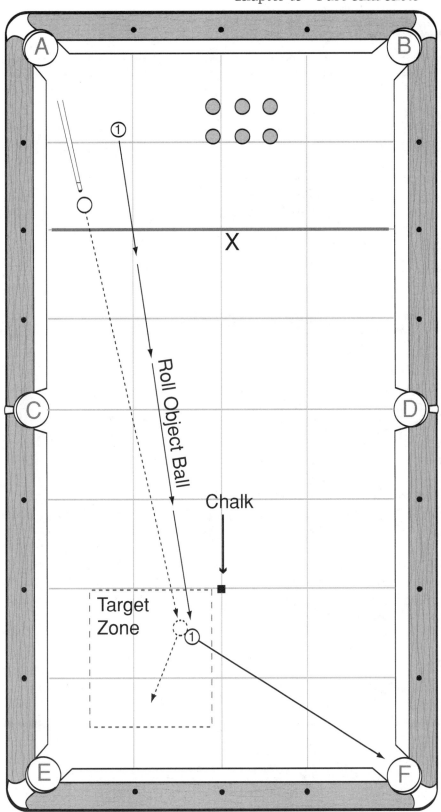

X

Roll Object Ball

Chalk

Target
Zone

Inside Spinner

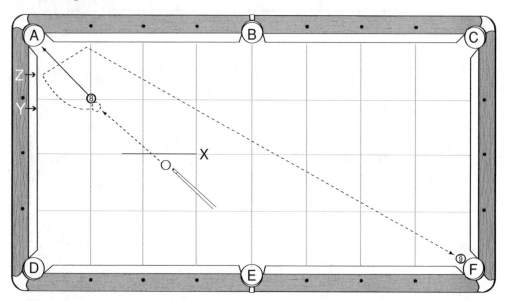

SUR: 2.0   AP
EXR: 3.0-4.5 *1
MSR: 30-80% *2
1&2 - depends on the conditions

This shot only rates a 7 in Artistic Pool, but on new cloth it plays like an 11 because the english doesn't take very well off the second cushion. In the first year of Artistic Pool, the shot was only rated 6. However, because of the new cloth only one person could make it.

Strike the cue ball very high at 1:30. Hold your cue as level as possible. Use a medium to medium hard stroke (it depends on the conditions). On worn cloth strike the cue ball at 2:00 as this will put more spin on the cue ball. You want the cue ball to hit the rail at Point Z and let the spin generate the required speed off the second cushion. If the cue ball strikes Point Y, you are cutting the 8-ball too much or shooting too hard. This is the most common fault.

16 Mike's Famous Finger Pool

I'm showing you these "shots", which have become known as Finger Pool, because I receive requests for them at almost all of my exhibitions. You don't even need a cue for Finger Pool. And you don't have to worry about cutting in balls or concern yourself with intricate set up procedures. You've simply got to flick your fingers just so, and the cue ball will curve in ways that will simply dazzle your fans. I swear to you that the diagrams you are about to study are completely accurate. It is possible to make the cue ball curve and dance as shown. You will, however, need to acquire expert technique.

Before you spend endless hours trying to perfect Finger Pool, I should warn you that my teaching you these shots is akin to Nolan Ryan instructing you on how to throw a 100MPH fastball. You were either born for this or you weren't. Since I make my living largely as an entertainer, I feel blessed that I have several advantages when it comes to Finger Pool. I am 6' 4" and have large and very strong hands and fingers, which I inherited from my father. My hands became even stronger when I worked as a brick and block mason for a few years before I started doing exhibitions. My hands allow me to flick the cue ball and impart tremendous spin with ease. My physical advantage is a lot like a basketball player who finds it easy to dunk because they are 6' 9" and can palm the basketball. In addition, I've been performing Finger Pool for over 30 years.

Some of you may be born with the talent and desire to perfect these shots. If so, great. If you attend one of my shows, I would love to see you demonstrate your skills. But you've got to promise to tell the audience that you learned the "shots" in this book or from my video. I perform all of these "shots" in my exhibitions, and they are on my video as well.

It wasn't long after I started doing exhibitions before I began to fool around rolling the balls down the table. I tried holding the cue ball between my thumb and middle finger. I then snapped my fingers like you would to music. The snap is also similar to the way Europeans snap their fingers when they applaud a good shot. So to my fellow Americans, you have just learned a new way to show your appreciation for a well played shot.

To continue, I snapped my fingers and threw the ball down the table at a good speed. About three quarters of the way down, the cue ball came to a dead stop. I thought wow, this is neat. So I started experimenting. I threw a ball and snapped my fingers a little harder and used a slightly different release. Lo and behold, the cue ball went about half way down the table and, like a yo-yo, came right back towards me. This, my friends, is how I discovered Finger Pool. Robert Byrne has done research on numerous trick shots and on Finger Pool and found out people were doing it over a 100 years ago.

Some other people I know who do Finger Pool are Reid Smith and Smiley. Reid Smith has a nice selection of Finger Pool shots. Reid also has some neat skill shots for One-Pocket. I've seen Johnny Archer do some Finger Pool a few times. He has the technique down, so I'm sure if he practiced he would be very good at it. But he's been too busy winning 9-Ball tournaments.

Finger Pool Draw Shot

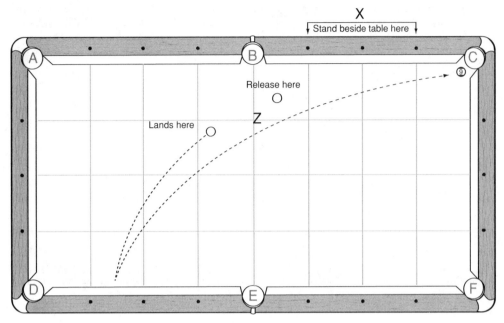

Video
LMS

Now I'll try to explain some of my Finger Pool "shots". Take the ball between your thumb and middle finger. Try snapping them together. Try to spin an object ball in place by holding your palm down and directly over the table.

To make the Finger Pool Draw Shot, the Finger Pool Hook Shot, and the extreme version of The Limbo, you will need to be able to make the cue ball spin in place for about 15-20 seconds. This should give you an idea of how much power you will need.

I stand at Position X and roll a ball with a throwing motion into or near Position Z. I always snap my fingers just when I release the ball. I turn my wrist so I'm looking directly at the back of my hand. Throwing the ball into the cushion causes it to bounce back out toward the middle of the table. Then the friction causes the back spin to take, making the cue ball come back up table to pocket the ball in front of Pocket C.

This shot takes very good feel. You must learn how hard to throw the ball into the cushion. If you throw the ball too hard, it will bounce across the table too far. Should you toss the ball too easily, it will arc too quickly.

Finger Pool Hook Shot

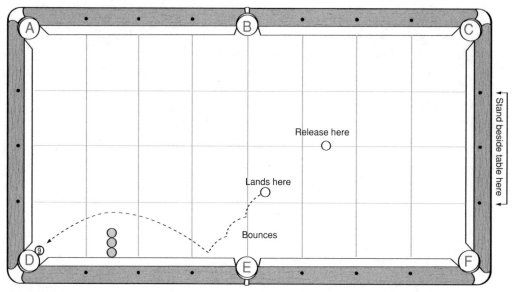

Video
LMS

Stand where indicated. Snap your fingers with your thumb aiming straight up and your palm facing you and throw the ball into the cushion. To "play" this shot, you have to be on a table with very good if not new cloth, or on a table with Simonis cloth. When I'm really pumped up and the conditions are right I will place five balls instead of three as shown.

The Dragster

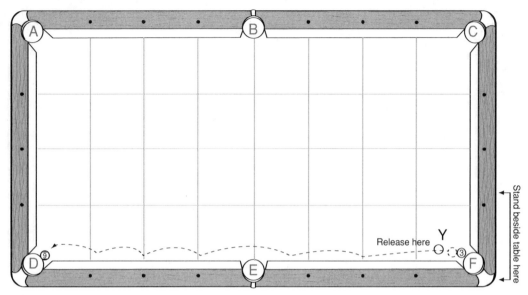

Video
LMS

I really have a lot of fun with this shot. Almost anyone can perfect this shot with enough practice. Just stand where shown. Hold the ball out in front of you over Location Y. Throw the ball into the object ball in front of Pocket F. It should hit the slate slightly before the ball. You want your palm facing up. This shot doesn't take a lot of power. However, it is more impressive with a powerful release because then the tremendous spin will make the cue ball change gears and accelerate about half way up the table, kind of like a drag racer.

The Limbo

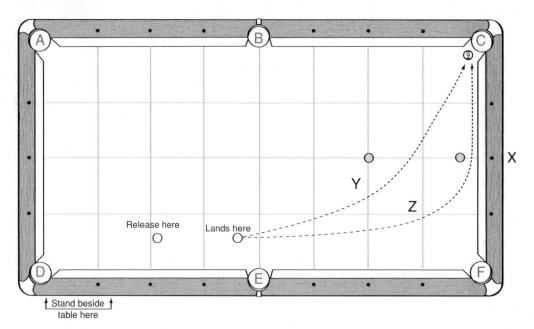

Video
LMS

I start off with a ball on the spot and a ball in front of Pocket C as diagrammed. I stand where indicated. I throw the ball and make it curve around the ball to pocket the 9-ball in the corner. Then I have someone stand at Location X. Their job is to pull the gray ball back six inches each time after I make the shot. Path Y shows my typical first toss. My last toss will follow Path Z, which requires that the cue ball make a nearly 90 degree left turn. I usually end up with the last gray ball about a ball and half or two ball widths from the rail.

This one's hard to explain but I'll make an attempt. I stand where shown and face the table with my right hand in front of my chest. I sling the ball out to my right and snap my fingers. My thumb faces down and my knuckles are angled anywhere from 50-80 degrees. My knuckles are angled to the right 80 degrees when the cue ball must go around the ball that's closest to the cushion.

Mike the Standby Star

In Las Vegas a few years ago the World 9-Ball Championships was being shown live on ESPN. Earl Strickland played Efren Reyes in the finals. If you know Earl's style of play, then you know that when he's on his game, he's the only one at the table and he plays very fast. The match was scheduled for an hour but Earl beat him in about 20 minutes. I was on stand by just in case something like that happened, so I demonstrated Finger Pool. When I did the Limbo, Francine was caddying for me. Would you believe that she started with the obstacle closest to the end rail. She must have been mad at me about something. And this was on live TV! She said, "Honey I have faith in you. Faith can move mountains so surely you can move that little ball around the other little ball." Well, I made it on my first attempt.

The Dedicated Student

The best way to practice the limbo is in a room with nothing but a table and no windows. I could tell you few horror stories about people who went home after my exhibitions and tried it. I saw one man a few days after he came to one of my shows and his hand was covered with bandages. He had practice so long he had worn blisters that had burst into sores. Another thing is that it really hurts when the ball goes out the wrong way. I've had that happen to me a few times. Good luck!

Mike Wants a Rematch

I know a black player named Smiley. He could spin the ball as long as I can. To this day, he's the only one I've seen do that. I don't know his full name cause everyone calls him Smiley. Even on the tournament board where I met him, they just wrote Smiley. I remember him very well because I played him in the tournament in Nine-Ball. I had him 8 to 1 going to 9 and he ended up beating me. I don't forget things like that. I wish I could, but I can't. Smiley, wherever you are, I want a rematch.

17 *You're the Star*

Why Become a Trick Shot Artist

Mastering a fair number of the shots in the previous 16 chapters is all well and good. The shots are, after all, fun to execute. And each carries with it an element of suspense. Will it work or won't it? Now, you may be comfortable not having your failures be witnessed by others. But on the other hand, there's nothing like the adulation that will be showered upon you from an appreciative audience following a successful effort.

At this point I'm going to make the assumption you are reading this chapter because you have a sincere desire to impress people with your skill at trick shots. But in case you're still not yet sure about your future in showbiz, let's look at a few reasons why you may wish to give your career as a trick shot artist some further consideration.

You should become a trick shot entertainer if:
• You like to be the center of attention.
• You are a ham, a natural born showoff.
• You want to impress people.
• You have a romantic interest you'd like to woo with your charisma.
• You like to be the life of any pool party.
• You like to have fun.
• You are looking for a fantastic new hobby.
• You want an excuse to hold a party to show off your new pool table.
• Your therapist says becoming a trick shot artist is the perfect antidote for shyness.
• You just love to see people smile around a pool table.

12 Components of a Trick Shot Artist

The rest of this chapter will help to prepare you for your career as an entertainer. The list below provides you with a capsule summary of the necessary attributes of a trick shot artist. After that we'll move on to a detailed discussion of how to prepare for and give your show.

Attitudes

Personality – It helps if you are outgoing, like to show off, or if you are a natural born ham who loves to be the center of attention.

Desire – You must want to be a star, to be the life of the party, or you love to see people have a good time around a pool table.

Preparation

Practice – Some of these shots take practice setting up, some in execution, and many require that you master both components. So plan on spending the necessary time at the table.

Props – Assemble a bag of tricks, just like a skilled magician. Audiences love prop shots well out of proportion to their degree of difficulty.

Shot Selection – Learn to select shots that will: 1) make you look good, 2) generate a response from the audience. There are over 170 shots in this book. An exhibition usually consists of 10-20. Choose wisely.

Variety – You must be able to pick shots that are high in skill and/or entertainment value. This means mixing up your show.

Know Your Equipment – The table and the balls can make a big difference in the set up and/or execution of a good percentage of the shots in the book. Study, test and learn the equipment you will be performing on. Learn to make the necessary adjustments.

Your Show

Conversation – Your value as an entertainer will rise dramatically with your skill in the conversational arts.

Know Your Audience – You can and should tailor your shots to your audience. The show you give to knowledgeable pool players may differ greatly from the one that you might, for example, give to a gathering of novices on your home table.

An Eye for Talent – Audience participation is a part of any worthwhile show. Get'em into the act. Remember: everybody wants to be a star.

Escape Lines – You will make some shots on nearly every attempt, once you get the hang of them. To truly impress audiences composed of knowledgeable pool players, you will have to go out on a limb and play some shots that are not guaranteed. It will help to short-circuit any hecklers if you have a humorous escape line or two handy.

Abandoning a Shot – You must know when to give up on a shot that just doesn't seem to want to cooperate. This may be due to the conditions or to a temporary decline in your skills. I recommend 1-3 tries. Be sure to have a good reason why you are going to move on to the next shot. A humorous escape line is much better than a weak excuse.

Your Approach to Showmanship

Your approach to how you present your show should take into account your personality and your audience. If you are supremely skilled or if you will only be shooting shots you can make virtually every time, you may wish to adopt the demeanor of the competent professional. The great Willie Mosconi chose this approach for his trick shot shows. His pride would simply not allow him to play the role of a fool for even one shot. You may also wish to select the sure shots if you are easily embarrassed or hate to fail in front of others.

Some entertainers love the spotlight so much they find it difficult to share the stage with members of the crowd. If this describes you, then you will probably want to limit audience participation. However, I've found that some of my best moments have come when a member of the crowd has gotten into the act.

If the audience is composed of close friends, most will probably be supportive, but some will undoubtedly engage in some good-natured heckling. If you are still learning many of the shots and/or if you are willing to go out on a limb and play shots that carry an element of risk, you should be prepared for some laughter or even mild hostility from the crowd. There's nothing wrong with that. In merry old England they had court jesters, whose job was to make people laugh, often at the jester's expense. So if you fail on a few shots but the crowd revels in your misery, consider those shots a success of sorts.

Your approach can also be based on the role you wish to play. Do you prefer to be a hero or villain? With skillful showmanship you can have the crowd rooting for or against you. You might be one of those people who loves to come through when the crowd is rooting against you. With skill you could engineer a situation where the crowd is rooting for a volunteer to make a shot that you have failed at. With some mental dexterity, you could even win the crowd back, perhaps by turning an audience member into a hero.

Just remember, your show is supposed to be fun, and fun can come in all different sizes and shapes.

Some Techniques of Showmanship
- Base your show on your audience.
- Adopt the demeanor of the skilled professional.
- Keep the spotlight for yourself if you must.
- Share the spotlight with a member of the audience.
- Try a few risky shots.
- Play the role of the court jester.
- Be a hero.
- Play the villain's role.
- Fail miserably on purpose.
- Make comebacks.

The Length of Your Show

There are about a zillion ways to structure your show. Primary in importance, however, is how much time you have for your show. You will need to become familiar with how long it takes to set up and execute each shot. And you also need to factor in the possibility of failure and the time required to set up and play a shot over again.

Below are some ideas on the length of shows that will satisfy any gathering and that will enable you to avoid the dreaded walk out syndrome. Factors for individual shot selection and time:
• How long the set up takes.
• How long the conversation that accompanies the shot takes.
• How much time will it take to secure a volunteer for audience participation shots.
• Will you play the shot more than once in the event of a miss?

5 Shot Quickie Shows -15-20 Minutes

If your time is limited, five well chosen crowd pleasers can work wonders. You might also consider giving several short shows spread throughout the evening. This is especially true if you can only:
• Fit so many people around the table.
• The party will last a long time.
• The guests will be arriving at different times.

10 Shot Mini Show - 25-35 Minutes

A show with 10 shots may be perfect for a party where there are numerous activities competing for people's attention, or when the crowd has a short attention span or a limited interest in pool. It might also be ideal for the aspiring entertainer whose act needs some work and who may be straining the audience's patience by giving a longer show.

20-25 Shots - A Complete Show - 45 Minutes to 1 Hour

Once you have gotten your act down and you can't wait to dazzle your guests with your cuemanship, then it's time to give them a complete show. Give your guests the full treatment when:
• Your act is polished.
• There is little going on that will compete with the show.
• Your show is a (the) focal point of the party.
• Your guests, or at least a fair percentage, are pool enthusiasts.

Two Shows

Once you have mastered enough shots and you can present them in groups of 5- 10 or more, you might consider giving a couple of different shows throughout the evening. One show might be geared to the novices, while the other is for knowledgeable pool people.

Shot Selection

Picking the right mix of shots plays a big part in the success of your show. Below are a few guidelines that will help you make an excellent selection. Pick shots that:
- Have entertainment value – visually and orally.
- Make you look good, that you can make almost every time.
- Are not a sure thing. This builds suspense and appreciation for your skills.
- Involve the audience.
- Allow you to make the most of your time.
- Fit the crowd.

The Right Shots for the Crowd

The ability of the crowd to appreciate most shots is directly proportional to their skill and knowledge. Shots that will have novices in hysterics might bore knowledgeable players to sleep. And shots requiring great skill may not posses the pizzazz that the beginner craves and may thus go unappreciated. And then there are shots that have crossover appeal to both groups. As general rules of thumb:
- Novices are entertained by flashy trick shots – things happening, props.
- Knowledgeable players like to see shots that require skill.
- There is a definite crossover between the two audiences. Some shots have universal appeal.

Eye Pleasers

Beauty is indeed in the eye of the beholder. There is oftentimes no correlation between the difficulty of a shot and it's ability to generate the desired response from the crowd. Some of the easiest shots may result in a thunderous ovation while the subtleties of a stroke shot may generate no more than a mild applause from all but the most knowledgeable of spectators.

You should use the revelations above in structuring your show. Pick shots that are most pleasing to the eye or that have some element that is highly amusing. These shots do not have to be difficult to execute. In fact, many of them may rate a 2.0 or below on my five point scale.

Audience Participation

Just because it is your show and you are the star doesn't mean you should do all of the shooting. Be sure to include at least a few shots that require audience participation. Your volunteer might play the shot, shoot with you in a double shot, or even become a prop for a shot. The crowd loves it when you involve one of them because now they are a part of the show. All of a sudden they have a rooting interest in the success (or maybe even failure) of one of their peers.

The audience may also participate by voicing opinions and by asking questions.

Preparing for the Show

Shot List

Make a list of the shots you're going to use.

Shot Diagrams

You may have the set up for some if not all shots committed to memory. And some shots are so easy to set up that you will have no trouble remembering them. But for some shots it will help to have a diagram handy, or even a template.

Make copies of the shots you have trouble remembering. You can fit four diagrams to a page. So if you make two sided copies, you can fit a 20 show on three pieces of 8.5" x 11" paper.

Props

Make sure you have your props with you for prop shots.

Prep the Table Owner

If the table is at your home or is owned by a person who knows pool, there should be no problem. You might, however, need to counsel the owner that you need to tap the balls lightly to get them positioned correctly, but that this will do no permanent damage to their table. Tell the owner you can rub out the marks afterward. If you plan to execute some masse shots, you should have the ability to make them without damaging the cloth.

Test the Table

Test the table before your guests arrive. Set up the shots you're going to play. Tap down the balls. Test them and make any necessary adjustments.

Rehearse Your Lines

Know what you're going to say about each shot unless, of course, you have a gift of gab and the ability to improvise. The best entertainers combine rehearsed lines with spontaneous bursts of conversational genius.

The Room

Make sure there will be adequate visibility for the number of people you expect at the show. Move furniture out of the way or make any other necessary alterations.

A Final Touch

If your ego is large and/or your show is actually quite polished, you may wish to make a poster of yourself with a caption that says something serious or funny. Examples:
- Joe Smith – Voted the World's #1 Trick Shot Artist by Joe Smith
- The Amazing Joe Smith – World's Finest Trick Shot Artist.

The Flow of Your Show

You know your audience and the length of your show. Now it's time to structure your show. This will enable you to make the best use of your time, achieve a variety of goals, and arrange your shots in a sequence that maximizes their effect and your skill as an entertainer. When the crowd disperses after their final ovation, you want them to be talking about the incredible roller coaster ride you've just put them through. You want them to have experienced the thrill and spills of a journey into the land of the trick shot artist, the world of the consummate showman.

How Many Attempts

Ideally you will make most of your shots on the first attempt, especially those that take a long time to set up. But nobody's perfect, not even me. So you must be prepared for the inevitable failures. When a shot fails you can:
• Abandon it with a clever line and quickly move to the next shot.
• Give it a second try and maybe a third if it takes little time to set up.
• Let someone from the audience shoot the second (or third) attempt if you missed on purpose and want to make someone's day.

What to Say While Preparing for a Second Attempt
After a narrow miss:
"Can you believe how much skill it takes to almost make that shot. I'll bet you thought I was going to showoff and make it on the first attempt."
After a disaster:
"Folks, you were lucky enough to see that shot played worse than any other time in pool history. Let's try it again. It can only get better."

What to Say While Preparing for a Third Attempt
"Well folks, here goes strike three. Wish me luck."
"Here goes one more try for the Gipper."

When Abandoning a Shot
It is useful to have some exit lines ready in the event of failure.
After one attempt:
"Well you get the idea. Close sometimes counts in this game."
After two tries:
"In this game it's two strikes and you're out."
"I guess I'm as good at that as Shaq is at free throws."
After three tries:
"Like baseball it's three strikes and yer out."
"I guess it wasn't in the stars."
"Man, I knew the odds were only 1 in a 1,000, but I thought we'd give it a whirl."
"That shot's impossible. Let's try another one."
"That shot went in my dream last night. Now it's turning into a nightmare."

Start to Finish

The sequence of your shots plays a big part in their overall effect on the crowd. You want to mix things up. Follow up hard shots with easy ones and vice versa. Put your audience on a roller coaster. Get them confident in your ability and showmanship in the beginning, then start to work the crowd. Let them participate. Have them cheer you on, then boo a failure. Make miraculous comebacks. Amaze and amuse them. It's showbiz. Create the flow. Go with the flow. Orchestrate your show correctly and you'll have the crowd eating out of the palm of your hand.

The Introduction - Welcome the Crowd

"You are about to witness exquisite displays of success and failure. The thrill of a well played shot and the agony of a miss. Over the next 30 minutes or so we'll go on a roller coaster ride together as I play for you some of pool's most entertaining and challenging trick shots. So let's get started." If you are a pro, you might have an MC do the introduction.

Starting Shot

You want to get off to a good start, build credibility, and capture the crowds attention. So start off with an impressive shot that demonstrates your skills, and that you can make almost every time. Or consider something humorous to warm up the crowd.

Audience Participation

Make a friend(s) in the audience quickly. They will cheer for you and be supportive. Win them over.
Trick: Set up a shot wrong and then miss it on purpose.
Then set it up correctly and have a member of the audience make it.

Tough Shots

Tell the crowd what a challenge the shot presents. This can even be the truth. Prep them for failure so you have an out if you miss. You are also prepping them for a big applause should you succeed.
Trick: This can be a ruse. You are setting them up to applaud you when the shot is not so tough at all.

Intermission

Use a shot that takes a long time to set up correctly. The Chattanooga Choo Choo, The Titanic, and the Giz and Hum are three perfect intermission shots.

After Missing a Tough Shot

Follow an unsuccessful tough shot with a sure thing. You don't want to ever (or almost ever) miss two in a row. You might try a humorous shot as this will quickly make the crowd forget your previous disaster.

After Making a Tough Shot

Follow a successful tough shot with another. This is your chance to push the envelope and to make an incredible impression.

The Grand Finale

End on a high note. Tell them what a great crowd they've been. Finish with a shot that you can make almost every time and that has that certain something that appeals to the crowd's senses.

Some lines you might use to introduce the final shot include:
- "I picked this shot just for you."
- "This shot is a special request." (You might name the person.)
- "In honor of our hosts, I'm going to play the ____shot."
- "This is the most requested shot in pool."
- "We're going to make pool history with the shot you are about to see."

Acquiring an Audience

When Showtime nears you will need to get your audience assembled around the table.

Making an Announcement

You can beckon them to the table yourself or better yet, have the host or someone with a loud and commanding voice call out to your fans.
- "Gather 'round for the greatest show on slate."
- "I've got some outrageous shots to show you."
- "Time to grab your wallets."
- "In five minutes the show will begin in the gameroom."

Refreshments

You may be wise to bribe potential attendees by placing (or moving) refreshments into the immediate vicinity of the show.

Invite the Guests In

Have someone go around and ask people to go to the gameroom.

The sight of a pretty girl or two entering the room with the table may also draw an audience.

Applause

You will naturally want to be rewarded with at least a polite, if not downright thunderous applause for your demonstrations of cue wizardry. While your audience may know when to clap and cheer, it doesn't hurt to prompt their efforts. Applause also makes the person doing it feel better who is clapping and it loosens the crowd up and makes them feel more together. After all, even TV shows use signs and other gimmicks to elicit the appropriate response. Once you get your fans used to applauding, they may keep it up shot after shot. Here are a few methods to generate crowd appreciation:

The Right Crowd

Plan to have some friends and admirers in the audience who know enough about pool and have enough respect for your skills that they will clap for even your most modest successes.

Enlist the Aide of a Shill

If you suspect that you will be performing for a tough crowd, the kind that is silent when comedians tell jokes, plan on enlisting the aid of a shill. Your shill will applaud immediately at the conclusion of each successful shot. This should fire up the crowd for a similar show of appreciation.

"Let's hear it for ____."

Lead the Applause

In the worst case scenario you may have to train your spectators to demonstrate their enthusiasm for your expertise and showmanship. If you are particularly bold, you may even start by clapping for yourself. Or you may wish to deliver a clever line or two.

• "Folks I just made one of the greatest shots in the history of pool."
• "Applause is free and I guarantee it won't hurt your hands too much."

Wagering

This chapter is supposed to teach you how to give an entertaining show to your friends, family, and guests. I am against you using the shots in this book to hustle a living or to win your friends' paychecks.

Keep it Friendly

I see nothing wrong with you wagering modest amounts such as a beverage or a burger on the outcome of these shots. This is all meant to be in fun. But by all means don't let somebody ruin the festivities by trying to turn your show into a spectacle for gambling large amounts.

Having a Shill Bet

You may loosen up the crowd and prepare them to be a part of the hustle (note: they might just hustle you) by having a shill place the first bet, perhaps a Big Mac and fries. This will warm up the crowd to the idea.

Prizes

You may wish to give a prize during or at the end of the show to a volunteer who makes a shot or participates in some fashion or another.

What to Give

I'm going to suggest what I feel is the perfect gift for your participants: A copy of *Mike Massey's World of Trick Shots*. If they already own the book, a copy of one of Phil Capelle's other books would also work just fine, or a video on trick shots.

Possible Awards

• Best Shot
• Worst Attempt (as a joke, of course)
• Best Sport
• Gutsiest Volunteer

Dedicating Shots

Dedicating shots is an easy and effective way to personalize any shot and to bond with your audience. You can dedicate shots through pure inspiration. Also consider the list below before your show so you can make a truly meaningful (or humorous) dedication to the perfect person or people.

Dedicate a Shot to the Hosts

"I want to dedicate this shot to our gracious hosts who have shown us such a great time."

Dedicate a Shot to Yourself

"I want to dedicate this shot to our gracious host, me, for having the intelligence to invite such a great group of people. Thank you all for coming."

Dedicate to a Member of the Crowd

- To someone who is a special guest.
- To a prominent member of the audience.
- To someone who is going on a long trip, or has just come back from one.
- To new friends.
- To someone who has recovered from a health problem.
- To proud new parents.
- To a pool player who has accomplished something special.
- To someone who is going to be playing in a big tournament.
- To someone who loves pool and is down in the dumps.

Personalizing a Dedication

Once you have your list of shots, you may wish to select one or more that you can use for a personalized dedication. Here are a few samples:
- "Robert (name the person) is going on a train trip cross country, so I'm going to play *The Chattanooga Choo Choo Shot* in his honor."
- "Mary (name a person) loves country western music so I'm going to play *The Johnny Cash Shot* in her honor."
- "I'm going to dedicate *The Disappearing Shot* to Frank (name the person) in recognition of his ability to vanish into thin air, especially when his wife wants him to wash the dishes or change a diaper."

Intermissions

People's attention spans have been known to wander. And the last thing you want is to have people desert your show. So if your show is going to last over 30-40 minutes you might wish to schedule an intermission. The most natural point is prior to a shot at the mid way point that requires a long time to set up. It might even be a set up shot that you will have to repeat to get right. Typical examples include: the Butterfly, Titanic and Giz and Hum.

After setting up a spectacular shot, you may wish to cover the balls with light paper napkins. When the spectators return, the sight of the covered balls will add to the suspense.

Announce the Intermission

Tell your audience the shot you are about to set up is one of the most spectacular in pool, but that it takes a while. So if they need to take a break, now is the time. This line will hopefully ensure that they return.

Be a Storyteller

It helps if you can tell a story while you are setting up the balls. You might even tell them one or two from this book, some other with colorful anecdotes on pool, or possibly a nice clean joke.

Lines for All Seasons

A big part of your skill as an entertainer is the ability to charm and provoke the crowd with your conversation. Below are a few ideas that can be used on numerous shots in the book. These ideas and the ones that follow for the three shows will give you some food for thought. You will no doubt soon find yourself spouting off totally original material that will have your onlookers rolling on the floor.

An Easy Shot that Appears Difficult

"This is a tough shot, so I ask you for your patience. Hopefully I'll make it in less than a 100 tries."

When to use it: On an impressive shot you usually make in one or two tries.

Purpose: It makes the crowd think you are going to attempt the nearly impossible. When you make the shot, they will heartily applaud your success.

Suggest the Impossible

"After the cue ball makes this ball it is going to ___ (suggest some outrageous stunt). "

When you get over the shot, then say that:

"You don't think I'm serious do you?" Then tell them what you're really going to do.

Tell Whoppers to the Crowd

Lies in everyday life are bad, but in the world of trick shots, they're all part of the show. Be sure to tell stories that add shine to your performance, that transport the crowd into the make believe world of showbiz, into the domain of the trick shot artist. These examples should get your creative juices flowing.

• "While I was on the road hustling pool back in 1974 I earned my motel money (bought a new car, etc.) with the shot you are about to witness."

• "In a personal session with Mike Massey (or some other trick shot artist) the master showed me the incredible shot you're lucky enough to now witness."

• "The ovation I got for this shot when I performed it at the Waldorf-Astoria brought the house down."

Miss on Purpose

The idea: To make a hero out of someone in the audience. This will really get the crowd buzzing, and your volunteer will have something to talk about for months to come. Follow these steps:
• Set up a shot with a ball lined up to miss.
• Shoot the shot and it will of course fail.
• Set it up correctly, then choose a volunteer.
"I've had trouble with this shot lately. Maybe you (a volunteer) can make it."
Your volunteer will then make it, much to the delight of the crowd.

Priming Them for an Eruption

"Now I want to warn you that the noise level could reach airport levels after I make this shot. So please try to contain yourself."
Use this as a joke on a simple shot, and you might expect complete silence. Use this on a tough shot and you may very well earn an earsplitting response. Whether you get one or not is another matter.

Audience Instructions

Unless your gameroom is outfitted like a TV studio, your audience will not benefit from instant replays of your heroic deeds. This means they must get the full effect of a shot on your first successful attempt. This will raise both their appreciation and the subsequent level of their applause.

To achieve these sought after objectives you should make it a habit of directing their attention. There may be one focal point of interest in a trick shot that is obvious to all. In this case, the audience needs no instructions. On some shots, however, you will need to direct their attention to a specific part of the shot. And on some shots, they may be required to shift their attention from one part of the shot to the next and so on.

When preparing for a shot, consider what is going to take place. Then instruct the audience on the eye candy they'll soon be privileged to witness. On each shot ask questions like these:
• Is the cue ball the star?
      Example: **The Twelve Rail Kick Shot**
• Is a particular object ball the single biggest attraction?
      Example: **The Flying 8-Ball Shot**
• Is there a sequence of events that must be watched in a certain order?
      Example: **Three and Three Shot** – (Two balls go in, then the cue ball makes the 3-ball.)
• When multiple objectives are going to be met, is there one that stands out as the "can't miss" feature of the shot.
      Example: **The Bottle Shot** – (Landing on the bottle.)
• Will the audience need to exercise their peripheral vision and look at the table as a whole?
      Example: **The Butterfly Shot**

- Will the cue ball be jumping or curving in a certain manner?
    Example: **Through the Great Wall**
- Is there something completely unique or magical about the shot?
    Example: **Connected Balls**

Dealing with Hecklers

The odds are good that there will be a heckler or two in a group of any size or when your "friends" are gathered around the table. You could try to pre-empt a strike by warning the crowd in a jovial manner that you have taken your anti-heckler pill and are ready. It is also helpful to have your anti-heckler tactics ready just in case the proverbial bad apple makes his presence felt. You can adopt any number of strategies:

Make Him Into A Hero

My favorite approach is to have the heckler play a shot. I usually make it one that he can make with little trouble. I've found that most hecklers are really dying for attention. Here are a couple of lines you can use to get him into the act.
- "You look like you are probably a pretty good pool player. Why don't you come down and try this shot?"
- "Who would like to have Joe shoot a shot or two? Let's hear it for our surprise guest, Joe the pool shark."

Standard Old Lines

"Who let this guy in." "How did he get through security?" "He proves there's one in every crowd."

Turn the Crowd Against Him

Peer pressure and looks of disgust could silence him quickly. You could instruct the audience thusly:
"Okay everyone, get the most disgusted look on your face possible. Now look at Joe."

When Your Show Is Over

You may wish to master a few shots for a once in a lifetime show. But if you are planning on giving shows at least once a year, you would be wise to evaluate your performance. There are several questions to ask yourself:
- What shots did the crowd love?
- Which generated little enthusiasm, even when executed successfully?
- Was the audience participation successful?
- Did I receive a positive response from the crowd?
- Did they think my lines were funny? Did laughter fill the air?
- Did the crowd stay with me till the end? Any walk outs?
- Was I able to deal with any heckling?
- Did I establish and maintain a rapport with the crowd?

Three Truly Big Shows

The following sections provide you with three completely different shows. The first show is for novices and newer players. The second show is for experienced players who have a well-developed stroke. The final show is for gluttons for punishment and those who don't mind embarrassing themselves in front of others. It is also for those people who have thousands of hours available to perfect the shots in this program.

Throughout the book I've given you Execution Ratings for each shot. They range from 1.0 (the easiest) to 5.0 (the very most difficult). The average shot in the book is 3.35. The average difficulty of the three programs should be helpful in choosing the right one for you.

Program	*Executing Rating*
1 - You're the Star	2.00
2 - The Greatest Show on Slate	3.38
3 - Mike's Extreme Pool	4.45

The shots are in the order in which they appeared in the book. Feel free to change the order or to edit shots or to adapt the program in any way you see fit.

Below is a sample listing of a shot:

The Great Deceiver -7 CP   1.5 / 2.5

The information includes in order:
• The Name.
• The page in the book where the shot appears.
• CP stands for crowd participation (if any).
• The first number is the SUR.
• The second number is the EXR.

Show #1
You're the Star

20 Shots Anyone Can Master
Average Set Up: 2.00
Average execution: 2.00
Mike's %: 93.9
9 are audience participation

The 20 shots in this show have been selected for their low ratings in degree of difficulty and for their entertainment value. These shots are particularly suited to new players and novices. The shots in You're the Star will allow you to realize your goals as an entertainer for those of you who wish to impress your friends, who are natural born hams, and who like to be the life of the party.

About half of the shots encourage audience participation. Their contributions should help to make you look even better. The end result is that you will, at the end of your show, be steeped in glory just like any superstar entertainer.

The setup and execution of these shots appears throughout the book. Below you will find some recommended lines that will add entertainment value to your show. Perhaps you will come up with some lines of your own that you prefer to mine. If so, I would love to hear them. You can e-mail me in care of BilliardsPress.com.

1 Hustler's Specials

Jar the Table - 2 CP   1.0 / 1.0

• "I know it looks like there's no way I can hit the 1-ball first with the cue ball here (point to its location) but I'm going to give it a try. Any takers?"
• Wait to see if anyone takes you up on the wager.

You have a taker. "I don't blame you. It sure looks like easy money." Play the shot. "It is easy money (pause) for me!"

You don't have any takers: "You guys think I'm trying to hustle you? We'll you were right." Play the shot.

It's Your Choice 8-Ball Shot - 6 CP   3.5 / 1.5

• "Normally in 8-Ball you have to hit the 8-ball first and choose your pocket. On this shot, I'm going to let one of you choose the pocket, but in return I get to place the cue ball where I want and I can hit one of your balls first. Who wants to call the pocket?"
• A member of the crowd calls the pocket.
• "You're not trying to trip me up here are you? Okay, 8-ball in the corner (or side)."
• "How did you know that was the most difficult pocket?"

The Great Deceiver - 7 CP   1.5 / 2.5

• "I wager any of you a beverage I can make this shot before any three of you can. Pick three volunteers and you get to go first."
• The three volunteers will most likely fail.
• "This is a tricky little rascal. To make this you've got to approach the problem from an angle." Shoot the shot. "Nothing to it."

Ball Out of the Rack (2) - 17 CP   1.0 / 1.0

• "I am going to do the impossible by making the 8-ball in the side. Can anyone guess the secret before I play the shot?"
• Wait for their replies.

Somebody guesses correctly: "How the heck did you know that? Are you a professional?"

Nobody knows what you're going to do: Play the shot. "Sometimes the obvious is not so obvious after all."

2 Three for the Price of One
Gerni's ESPN 3 Ball Shot - 24   2.5 / 2.5
- "I'm going to make these three balls in one shot. If I'm successful, I'll duplicate a feat accomplished by World Champion Mike Massey, who won an important point on this shot on his way to winning the Trick Shot Magic competition on ESPN."

The Disappearing Shot - 28   1.5 / 2.5
- "If you are like me then you probably scratch far more often than you'd like to. I was thrilled when I discovered this shot because it is perfect for those of us who can't seem to keep whitey on the table. On this shot I actually want to scratch on purpose. So come now cue ball, after the zillions of scratches I suffered through, don't fail me now."

3 Prop Shots
Connected Balls (Shot #1) - 30   1.0 / 2.0
- "As most of you may know, english can be a very useful tool in making balls and controlling the cue ball. After years and years of practice I've come up with a very special kind of english. I call it adhering english. I think you'll be amazed at what it can do. I want you to watch very carefully to what happens as you might need this special english sometime in a game."

Coin Wrapper Shot - 34   2.0 / 1.5
- "Perhaps you've known somebody who rubs you the wrong way and you can't wait to get away from them? Well, that's the problem with the 2-ball and 3-ball. They can't stand the sight of each other so I'm going to help them to swiftly part company."

The Moving Cue Shot - 40   2.0 / 2.5
- "Yesterday I was playing Eight Ball with this rather argumentative sort. He claimed that it was his turn after he'd turned his back and failed to see me make my last two balls. The jerk had the nerve to block my shot on the 8-ball by laying his cue on the table. I showed that wise guy not to fool with me."

The Chattanooga Choo Choo Shot - 42 CP   3.5 / 3.0
- "One of the most popular shots in pool is called the Chattanooga Choo Choo Shot. The 5-ball's going to embark on a long journey around the table (point to it's path). When it boards the railroad about here (point at the spot where the 5-ball enters between the cues) it would be nice to hear some sound effects from you kind folks. The five balls are going to go in rotation. I want you to go whooo, whooo, whooo like a train! Okay, let's get this cue ball on the road. And if you know the song Chattanooga Choo Choo, let's hear it!"

Roy's Psychic Energy Shot – 47 CP   2.0 / 1.0
• "We're going to attempt to make pool history with a shot that has until now been impossible. You're such good friends that I think if we put our minds to it, we can make the 8-ball. Gather around and concentrate fully on making the 8-ball bend around the 10-ball. Are you all giving the 8-ball your complete psychic energy? Good. I think we're ready. Here goes. Total concentration. On the count of one. 5-4-3-2-1." Shoot.

4 Crowd Pleasers
The Butterfly - 54   3.5 / 2.0
• "This shot is called The Butterfly because the layout looks like a butterfly's wings. This shot is really cool because we're going to make six balls in six pockets. The 5-ball and 6-ball are actually going to go backwards into these (point to Pockets A and C) two pockets. Since the balls are going to be flying all over the table, you're going to have to really exercise your peripheral vision. Time for the butterfly to spread her wings."

Flying 8-Ball Shot - 72   2.5 / 2.5
• "The 8-ball is going to take to the airways here. Hopefully we'll have a safe flight and a smooth landing into the pocket (point to Pocket A). But just in case, I would like for those of you behind the pocket to move a little to the side. Okay, its time for takeoff."

5 Great Escapes & Gamewinners
The Johnny Cash Special - 81   CP   2.0 / 2.5
• "Johnny Cash made this shot on his first take while on the set of *The Baron and the Kid*. I'm going to try to recreate that historic moment. The game is Nine-Ball and my opponent has me in a bad spot. Would anyone care to wager against me on this shot?"

There is a taker: "No way. I was just testing to see who of you likes to jump on such easy money."

There are no takers: "I don't blame you for not wagering when you consider my great skills. 9-ball in the side pocket" (Said with supreme confidence providing, of course, that you have mastered this shot).

6 Mystery Shots
Which Goes First – 94 CP   2.0 / 2.0
• "We're going to have a pop quiz. I want each of you to pay special attention to this shot. I need to know which of the three balls enters the pocket first. I'll give you a clue: the 1-ball has to travel about 50% farther than the 2-ball and 3-ball to reach its pocket." (This is intended to mislead your audience into an incorrect guess.)

The crowd will voice their opinions. Play the shot.

• "The same cameramen used at the Kentucky Derby studied this shot and he determined that this photo finish is too close to call. So the correct answer is that it is a three way tie."

8 Lots of Balls In Action

Jesse Cue Shot - 110   CP   1.5 / 1.5

• "I need a daredevil for this shot."

• Look over the crowd and pick someone out, preferably a lady with a nice curve in her back for the cue ball to pass under.

• "You look like you have nerves of steel."

Once the balls are set up and the "volunteer' is in the position of the dog in the diagram, it's time to announce the shot.

• "Okay, the 1-ball and 2-ball go in the side pockets, the 3-ball and 4-ball go in the corners." (This is said with authority, because this is an easy shot that you can play with tons of confidence.)

4 Balls in 4 Pockets - 112   2.5 / 2.5

• "For my next shot I'm going to consult with the Pool Gods. This will take a moment." Close your eyes and lower your head to consider the possibilities.

• "I've got it. It's time for the 4 Balls in 4 Pockets shot, an old favorite that's one of the most requested shots in pool. You're going to have to exercise your peripheral vision again to see all of the balls go in cause they are going to go in these four pockets." Point to the four pockets.

• "The 1-ball goes here (point to Pocket E), the 2-ball goes here (point to Pocket C), the 4-ball goes here (point to Pocket B). The 3-ball goes to this rail (point to the rail between Pockets A and D) and back in this pocket (point to Pocket F). Here we go."

9-Multi Rail Masterpieces

Three and Three Shot - 126   1.5 / 2.0

• "There is a game called Three Cushion Billiards that's played on a table without pockets. One way to score a point is to send the cue ball into another ball. Then the cue ball's got to hit at least three rails before hitting a third ball. On the shot I'm about to play the cue ball's going to hit these three rails (point at the rails) before making the 3-ball. On top of this amazing three-cushion billiard I'm going to pocket the 1-ball and 2-ball. You could call this shot a Super Billiard. Wish me luck!"

11 Bank Shots

The Golf Ball Bank Shot – 154   CP   1.5 / 2.0

• "I need a volunteer for this shot."

Get someone who you don't mind casting in the role of a fall guy for this shot.

• Set up the bank shot with the cue ball. Let your victim try it. They will fail.

• "Okay, you got to use your toy. Now I get to use my toy."

Set it up with the golf ball. You will then, of course make the shot.

• "Now that wasn't so hard was it? You've just got to have the right equipment to do the job." A big smirk helps to heighten the effect of the con.

12 Jump Shots

The Shrinking Cue Ball - 161   1.5 / 2.0

• "I'd like to make both the 1-ball and 2-ball, but it looks like these balls (wave your hand over the 3-ball and 9-ball) are in the way."

• Demonstrate that the balls are in the way by putting the cue ball on the table at each entrance to the channel. Show that it won't fit.

• "What I'm going to have to do is make the cue ball shrink so it will pass through this corridor."

Play the shot.

• "It's pure magic!" Exclaim with glee.

You're the Star

Show #2
The Greatest Show on Slate
20 Advanced Shots for the Serious Practitioner
Average Set Up: 2.63
Average execution: 3.38
Mike's %: 80.3
5 are audience participation

This program offers you great variety as the shots were chosen from 14 of the 15 shot chapters. The 20 shots in this program are definitely up a couple of notches in difficulty compared to the first program. The average execution rating for The Greatest Show on Slate is 3.38 compared to an average of 2.0 for You're the Star. This average tells you this is a more challenging program.

You will have to spend quite a bit more practice time to fully master this group. The investment will be well worth it, however, as you will now command an arsenal of shots that will delight both novices and knowledgeable players alike.

1 Hustler's Specials (Betting Shots)
Christopher Walken Take One - 8 CP   2.5 / 4.0
• "The game is Eight Ball and it's my shot on the 8-ball. The corner pocket is blocked (point at the most logical pocket). I know it looks hopeless, but I'm going to figure out some way out of this mess. Anyone care to wager on my chances?"
• Wait for an answer.
• **There is a taker**: "I guess you know a fool when you see one. Well let's see what I can come up with." Play the shot.
• **No takers**: "Before I shoot I would like to congratulate you on your intelligence. You obviously know a con job when you see one."

Ball Out of the Rack (Shot #1) - 14   2.0 / 3.5
• "If you are ever in a game of Eight-Ball and your opponent puts the rack over the 8-ball to argue some completely groundless point, you will know what to do in just a moment. Tell him you'll double the wager if he'll allow you to shoot with the 8-ball and rack just where they are. He'll most certainly jump at the opportunity. Then it's time for you to jump as well."

2 Three for the Price of One
One Pocket Run Out - 21   3.5 / 2.5
• "Those who like One-Pocket and who also prefer to play quickly will appreciate this shot. For those of you who are not familiar with the game, the first one to make eight balls in their pocket wins. I was trailing 5-7 when I came across this shot. The balls were in this position (wave your hand over the cluster) and this was my pocket (point to the pocket). I was able to pull this game out of the fire by making the three balls I needed in just one amazing shot."

3 Prop Shots
Mid Air Collision Special - 31   3.0 / 3.5
• "You are about to witness a spectacular mid-air collision. In it's aftermath, none of the balls will remain on the table. There is a lot going on in this shot. First I want you to pay special attention to the 5-ball and 6-ball. Then shift your glance over here (point to Pocket F). If you listen carefully you will hear a big thud when the balls land on the table."

4 Crowd Pleasers
Football Shot – 58 CP   4.0 / 3.0
• "I need someone to tell me who is their favorite running back in football and who does he play for."
Wait for the answer.
• "And who are the XX Teams chief rivals?"
Wait for the second answer.
• "On this shot Joe Runningback (insert his name) is going to score a touchdown against the XX Team (point to the balls that are defensemen) by running clear into the end zone (point at the side pocket). I need a quarterback to call signals. 1-2-3."
• Play the shot. "Touchdown!!"

Bachnine 10-Cent Special - 64 CP   3.5 / 3.5
• "I'm going to make all three object balls. The cue ball normally is the center of attention but this time it is going to do absolutely nothing but sit still. The dime you see perched on the rail is going to fly into the glass. When it comes to rest in the bottom of the glass, it will be either heads or tails. Anyone care to guess which."
Wait for their answer.
• "Okay, you're on. Let's see if you guessed correctly. Loser buys."
• Play the shot.

5 Great Escapes & Gamewinners
Off the Point Three Railer - 79   1.5 / 3.5
• "Any of you who have played Nine Ball long enough know that the balls can end up in the weirdest positions after the break. Why just last week, my opponent broke the balls and left me in this predicament. Now you may be thinking there is no way the balls could end up like this, but I'm simply going to ignore the doubting Thomases. As Magic Johnson used to say, "It's winning time.""

6 Mystery Shots
The 8-Ball Riddle Shot – 90 CP   3.5 / 2.5
• "I know you're going to think I'm a little off my rocker, but I swear the 8-ball can be made on this shot. Would any of you care to venture a guess where? And how?
• Wait for replies.
If they guessed correctly, comment on the person's intelligence: "You're a pretty sharp fellow."
If they failed to get it right: "Don't feel too bad cause it's a real brain teaser."
• Now explain it real fast like this:
"The 2-ball moves out of the way. The 1-ball hits the 3-ball, moving the 4-ball out of the way. The 3-ball hits the 5-ball, sending the 7-6 combo into the 9-ball, which makes the 8-ball go straight up the rail into a kiss off the 10-ball and into the side pocket."
NOTE: This is the best shot to begin this show with.

7 Curve Balls
Long Distance Curve Ball - 98   1.5 / 3.5
• "You can win at Nine-Ball any time you make the 9-ball, as long as you hit the lowest numbered ball first. Whenever the 9-ball is close to a pocket, you may have a chance for a quick win. As luck would have it, I happen to have such an opportunity. I'm going to make the cue ball curve around all of these blockers (wave your hand over the blockers) and pocket the 9-ball."

8 Lots of Balls In Action
What Happened Shot - 106   2.0 / 2.5
• "I swear that the story I'm about to tell you is true. But before I begin, I want to inform you I'll be selling my swampland in Florida when the show is over. Now I like to feel that I can grasp an opportunity when one present's itself. When I broke the balls recently in a Nine-Ball game, I was faced with this impossible looking layout. I put my computer like mind to work and came up with a game winning shot that had my opponent shaking his head and wondering 'What happened'."

The Scatter Gun - 107   4.0 / 3.5

• "This shot is called the Scatter Gun because balls are going to go flying into pockets all over the table. The 1-ball and 2 ball are going to go in these pockets (point at Pockets A and D). The other four balls are going to go in these two pockets (point at Pockets C and F). This shot is just as much a test of your peripheral vision as it is my skills as a trick shot artist. You'll have to have the vision of the great quarterback Johnny Unitas if you hope to see them all go in."

9 Multi-Rail Masterpieces

12-Rail Kick Shot - 120   1.0 / 3.5

• "After I get the cue ball started, I've got to hit it three more times while its moving across the table in front of me. I can't blame Mike for this one, and he won't tell who devised such a ridiculous shot, but I hope you enjoy it. It's my responsibility to warn you that you might get dizzy watching this shot cause the cue ball's going to go around the table four times before I get exhausted and permit the little white rascal to do its job and pocket the 8-ball. Time to get the show on the road."

10 Stroke Shots

Circular Draw Shot - 139   2.0 / 3.0

• "You lucky folks just happened to be in the right place at the right time if sweeping curve balls happen to be one of your favorite treats. I'm going to make the 1-ball in that pocket (point at Pocket A). But I don't want that to divert your attention from the cue ball, which plays the starring role in this shot. It is going to make a complete about face and pocket the 2-ball. Now due to the incredibly spectacular sight you are about to witness, I'm going to ask that you hold the applause down to a mild roar." Now that's putting your backside on the line!

The Jimmy Moore Draw Shot - 144   2.5 / 4.5

• "Cowboy Jimmy Moore was one of the best and unluckiest pool players in history as he happened to be in his prime when Willie Mosconi, the best straight pool player in history, was also at his peak. Nonetheless, Cowboy Jimmy Moore had one of the most powerful strokes in the game. The shot I'm about to play shows one of his favorite tricks. Keep your eyes glued to the cue ball."

11 Bank Shots

"The Hustler" Bank Shot - 153 CP   1.5 / 3.5

• "This shot comes from the best movie ever made on pool, *The Hustler*, which starred Paul Newman and Jackie Gleason. Newman made a big score in the opening scene by making this bank. I'm going to recreate pool history. Before I do, anybody want in on the action? I accept all beverage bets, one per customer."

• Wait for their response.

No takers: "Come on now, just cause Paul Newman made it doesn't mean I will. It might have taken him 50 takes. Now does anyone care to wager?"

There is a taker: "So you're after some easy action just like the bartender in the movie. Right? We'll just see about that."

12 Jump Shots

Evel Knievel - 158   2.5 / 3.0

• "Evel Knievel was the ultimate daredevil. He was truly a man with 9 or was it 29 or 109 lives? Anyway, he managed to survive numerous spills while providing countless thrills for his millions of fans. Please let's have a moment of silence before Evel (point at the 1-ball) jumps over these busses and cars (point at the row of balls)."

• Play the shot.

If it is successful: "Great. No broken bones this time."

If not tell them: "Well as you know even the great Knievel did not always land perfectly either." The shot has the perfect escape line.

Massey's Over, Around, and Under Shot - 167   2.5 / 3.5

• "Chattanooga, Tennessee is a city that derives a great deal of its notoriety for having the Chattanooga Choo Choo Shot named after it. There must be something about Chattanooga that stirs a trick shot artist's imagination because, while giving an exhibition there, Mike came up with the spectacular jump shot you are about to witness. The cue ball is going to jump over the bridge and travel three rails around the table and back under the bridge before making the 3-ball."

13 Massés

Machine Gun Masse - 172   2.5 / 4.0

• "On this spectacular massé shot the cue ball is going to contact every one of these balls (wave your hand over the line of balls) before it pockets the 8-ball. Now I'm going to ask everyone to be real quiet (turn off the music if it's playing) so you can hear the chatter of the machine gun like those gangsters on *The Untouchables*. Ready? Here goes."

14 A Few of Mike's Favorite Creations

Time the 9 Shot - 184   3.0 / 3.5

• "It is said in life that timing is everything. Well, that old adage certainly holds true in pool, as you are about to see. The game is Nine Ball and it's my shot. I suppose I should be thinking about a safety, but hidden within this mess is an eye-popping time shot on the 9-ball. I suggest that you watch the action along the rail (wave your hand over the two lines of balls). The cue ball will enter the picture again after traveling three rails. Remember, timing is everything!"

Pocket Seven for the 8-Ball - 190   4.0 / 3.5

• "In a game of Eight-Ball last year at the National Championships in Las Vegas my opponent ran all of his stripes and left me with this mess. I took a timeout and studied the layout. I could feel the eyeballs of hundreds of spectators as they waited to see what I'd come up with. My response was, in all modesty, the greatest shot in the history of pool."

In fiction the reader is asked to suspend belief for the sake of the story. Similarly your audience's ability to swallow your conversation will be put to the ultimate test on this shot. You're going to tell them a whopper, but it's showbiz, so anything goes.

The Greatest Show on Slate

	SUR/EXR	Ch./Page
Christopher Walken Take One - 8 CP	2.5 / 4.0	1-8
Ball Out of the Rack (Shot #1) (1) – 14	2.0 / 3.5	1-14
One-Pocket Run Out - 21	3.5 / 2.5	2-21
Mid Air Collision Special - 31	3.0 / 3.5	3-31
Football Shot – 58 CP	4.0 / 3.0	4-58
Bachnine 10-Cent Special - 67 CP	3.5 / 3.5	4-64
Off the Point Three Railer - 79	1.5 / 3.5	5-79
The 8-Ball Riddle Shot – 90 CP	3.5 / 2.5	6-90
Long Distance Curve Ball - 98	1.5 / 3.5	7-98
What Happened Shot - 106	2.0 / 2.5	8-106
The Scatter Gun - 107	4.0 / 3.5	8-107
12 Rail Kick Shot - 120	1.0 / 3.5	9-120
Circular Draw Shot - 139	2.0 / 3.0	10-139
The Jimmy Moore Draw Shot - 144	2.5 / 4.5	10-144
"The Hustler" Bank Shot - 153 CP	1.5 / 3.5	11-153
Evel Knievel - 158	2.5 / 3.0	12-158
Massey's Over, Around & Under Shot - 167	2.5 / 3.5	12-167
Machine Gun Massé - 172	2.5 / 4.0	13-172
Time the 9 Shot - 184	3.0 / 3.5	14-184
Pocket Seven for the 8-Ball - 190	4.0 / 3.5	14-190

Show #3
Mike's Extreme Pool
A 20 Shot PHD Course in Trick Shots and Artistic Pool
Average Set Up: 2.29
Average execution: 4.45
Mike's %: 46.3
8 audience participation shots

The 20 shots in Mike's Extreme Pool average a hefty 4.45 on my 5.0 scale for difficulty. If you can make a majority of these shots, you'll earn a standing ovation from any crowd. While you are mastering these shots, as an added bonus, you will be developing skills that could be used in a big match some day. If you plan on shooting these shots in public, you must either: 1) put in hundreds of hours of practice, 2) have a very thick skin and a high tolerance for failure. Don't say I didn't warn you. But remember, no guts, no glory.

If any member of the audience doubts your skills or the difficulty of these shots, invite them to give the shots a try. Unless they get extremely lucky or have read this book and practiced long hours, they won't have a chance. Their complete and utter failure will, of course, make you look all the better!

There are a couple of extra pieces of information on the shots in this section. Let's take the first shot below as an example. Above the shot's name is a description of the shot. The 1-2-3 Proposition Shot is also "The Slickest Hustle". At the end of the line after the shots SUR and EXR is my percentage. My success ratio will hopefully spur you on to greater heights. Perhaps you can learn to shoot like Mike on some of these shots. Best of luck!

1 Hustler's Specials
The Slickest Hustle
1-2-3 Proposition Shot - 11   CP   2.5 / 4.5   40
• "The idea is to make the 1, 2 and 3-balls in order. Any volunteers?"
Wait to see if anyone dares to attempt the shot.
They will fail (unless they've read this book and practiced the shot).
• "I might be a little off my rocker but I think I can make this rascal. Anyone care to give me 5-1 before I make a complete fool of myself? Here goes."

3 Prop Shots
The Toughest Field Goal
The Silver Dollar Proposition Shot – 48   CP   3.0 / 5.0   15
• "The object of this shot is to bank the silver dollar off the rail way down there (point to the distant end rail) and have it bounce back between these two pieces of chalk. Mike says his odds of making this field goal are about 1 in 7. I only want 1 in 50. Anyone care to win a beverage?"

4 Crowd Pleasers
Most Balls in One Shot (Solo)
Titanic Shot - 56   5.0 / 4.0 75
• "Mike calls this shot the Titanic. I'm going to shoot 14 balls and use every pocket on the table. Now you skeptics in the crowd may doubt my ability to execute this shot, but trust me, I've come prepared for this voyage."

The outcomes:

You make all the balls and accept your richly deserved applause,

If some balls miss, say, "Even the Titanic had some survivors."

Fast Shooting Required
Speed Demon - 60   2.0 / 4.5 70
• "I'm going to demonstrate the speed, reflexes and timing of Michael Jordan in his prime by shooting this ball (point at the solitary object ball) slowly into the corner pocket. While it's crawling across the table I'm going to fire all of these balls into the same pocket before it gets there. Now don't blink or you'll miss all of the fun."

5 Great Escapes & Gamewinners
The Greatest Escape
Corner Hook (Shot #2) - 74 CP   1.0 / 4.0 60
• "Those of you who play Eight-Ball no doubt have come across this shot many times."

The crowd will probably not agree with your proclamation.

"You haven't? Well I did just the other night. I told my opponent I'd double the wager and the fool took me up on my offer."

• You are inviting hecklers from the crowd if you fail, so you better come through. Hey, no potential pain, no gain.

9 Multi-Rail Masterpieces
The Toughest Shot of All
George Middleditch's Relay Shot - 125 CP   2.5 / 5.0 5
• "For the life of me I can't imagine why anyone would think this is the toughest shot in Mike Massey's book. Why all I've got to do is clobber the cue ball with a ton of english and send the 8-ball three rails back into the cue ball which should be spinning like a top. Then the cue ball's got to travel three rails into the 9-ball (show it's path with your hand). No problemo. Mike's odds are 1 in 20. So you should give me 1,000 to 1. Any taker's? "

Wait for their response: They will probably refuse, but only because of the outrageous odds.

• "Okay, here goes nothing, and I mean, most likely nothing."

The reason for giving them those ridiculously high odds is so the crowd will fully understand that if you do make the shot, they will have witnessed one of the greatest shots in the history of the game.

The Hardest Stroke (15 MPH)
Dollar Bill 9-Railer - 128   2.0 / 3.5   70
• "I get a kick out of those pictures of golf holes where you've got to shoot to a green on the edge of Niagara Falls. This shot is sort of like that. In this case the cue ball's going to travel 33 feet and stop on this (point to the dollar) bill. I'm going to have to really smash into this one, so I want you all to get your catcher's mitts ready just in case."

Most Distance Covered
The Traveling Music Shot – 130 CP   2.0 / 4.5   35
• "On this beauty you get three shots for the price of one. The first cue ball is going to travel 5 rails and make this ball (point to Pocket C). The second cue ball is going to hit 4 rails before making this ball (point to Pocket F). The last cue ball is going 3 rails into this ball (point to Pocket D) and I'm going to shoot all 3 in less than 4 seconds. I'm going to ask those of you who are musically inclined to hum a little traveling music for our long trip ahead. Ready?"

10 Stroke Shots
Super Stroke Shot
Triple Reverse - 137   2.0 / 5.0   50
• "If you play Eight-Ball long enough you're going to eventually encounter this shot. After what I'm about to show you, you'll be prepared to win the game, or to throw your hands up in despair. Mike calls this his triple reverse. I hope when I'm done you won't be calling me names."

Most Extreme Cue Ball Curve (Non-Massé)
The Big Circle Draw Shot - 147   2.0 / 5.0   35
• "I've got to give this one my very best stroke. If all goes well, the cue ball will actually stay on the table and you'll see it curve far more than Koufax's curve ball ever did. The curve takes place here (point to the table). And if all does not go well? We don't want to think about that."

Draw Like Mike
Mike's Massive Draw Shot - 148   1.0 / 5.0   40
• "Mike uses this shot to test his power draw. The cue ball will usually stop about here (point to a spot on the table) under normal conditions. Tonight I'm going to make pool history by outdrawing the master."
Play the shot. If you do beat Mike's effort, graciously accept the crowd's applause.
• If the cue ball comes up a few diamonds short of Mike's effort, as it most likely will, just say, "You didn't think I was really going to beat Mike's best, did you?"

11 Bank Shots
Power and Precision
Three Rail Long Rail Bank - 156   1.5 / 4.5   60

• "Mike says this is another of those shots that could come up in a game of Eight Ball, One Pocket, or for that matter, Bank Pool. I took his word for it and put in a hundred hours perfecting this gem. The object ball is going to go back and forth three times before disappearing into that (point at Pocket C) pocket. Now I want to hear an explosion when I pocket this monster. Ready?"

12 Jump Shots
An Extreme Draw Shot
Jump Draw Table Length - 159   2.0 / 4.5   70

• "I've got to merely jump over these (point at the obstructers) balls, pocket the 1-ball, and draw back to here (point at the position zone for the 2-ball) for position on the two ball. Yeah right. Even I, your great trick shot artist, know my limitations. But Mike can do it, so I'm forced by the Trick Shot Artists Code to give it a try."

• Of course, you know you are a cinch to make it after long hours of practice, right?

Precision Jumping
The Great Race – 168 CP   2.0 / 4.5   35

• "I'm going to pocket the 8-ball and cue ball in that (point at Pocket A) pocket. The 8-ball is in front of the cue ball, so it certainly seems obvious that the 8-ball will reach the pocket first. Would you agree with that assessment?"

Wait for their answer.

They agree. "Things are not always as they appear to be."

They think the cue ball will get there first. "You're absolutely correct. Smart crowd."

• Then play the shot.

13 Massés
Fastest Moving Cue Ball After Contact
The Rocket Massé (Shot #2) - 174   2.5 / 5.0   35

• "Mike taught me a couple of versions of this shot, which he calls the Rocket Massé for reasons that will soon become obvious. I of course chose to master the more difficult of the two. He made this gorgeous shot on TV. I'm going to try to duplicate his efforts."

Crowd reaction: Your humbleness will earn you the crowd's sympathy, which could be quite welcome in a few moments.

• "4-ball in the side, 5 in the corner (said with authority)."

Toughest to Time Correctly
Gerni Brings Down the House - 176   2.0 / 5.0   5-7
• "All I've got to do is shoot the 9-ball five rails and then run over here and execute a perfect massé that happens to arrive at this pocket (point at Pocket F) just as the 9-ball does. Mike's nickname for this shot is the Vacation Shot cause he figures it will take at least a month long vacation for mere mortals like myself to make this demon. I hope he's wrong, but none of you have any other plans for the next few weeks. Right?"

The Most Extreme Massé
Exit Stage Right - 181   2.0 / 5.0   25
• "Mike won the 2003 World Artistic Championship after his opponent missed his final attempt on this shot by a half an inch. I'm going to attempt to show you what the shot that would have beaten Mike looks like when perfectly executed. The cue ball is going to make a right turn around the chalk (point to the place where it turns) and pocket the 1-ball. Wish me luck. (Hesitate for a moment.) Come to think of it, wish me lots of luck."

14 A Few of Mike's Favorite Creations
Biggest Mystery & Toughest Set Up
Giz and Hum Mess - 188 CP   5.0 / 3.0   90
• "You can never tell when moments of great inspiration may strike. While deep in the heart of Texas, San Angelo to be precise, Mike concocted this beauty, which he calls the Giz and Hum Mess. I'm going to confess that making this shot is not too difficult. Setting it up is a whole other matter."
Set up the shot.
• "Would any of you care to guess which pocket the 6-ball is going into?"
Listen for their replies.
• "Let's see if you're right."

15 Pure Skill Shots
Shooting Jacked Up
Jack Up Spot Shot - 192 CP   1.5 / 3.5   50
• "We've been doing trick shots which may have some element of deception to them. Not so with this one. I've got to simply make the 1-ball way down there while holding my cue in the air with one hand."
Take a stance like you're going to shoot the shot. Let them see how your hand shakes (you're hopefully faking the shaking).
• "Darn it, sometimes my hand won't stop shaking. Any one care to wager a beverage before I take a stab at this."
Wait for their replies.
They take you up on your wager. "So you would take advantage of old Shaky Jake? Nice guy."
They refuse. "I don't blame you. After all people also are lucky enough to win the lotto."

Hitting a Moving Target
Rapid Fire Wing Shots - 196   NA/ 4.0 for 1/5.0 for 7   60 (for 1)

• "Its not as if pool isn't hard enough when you consider that we must make a round ball strike another round ball within a millimeter or two of perfection to drive it into a pocket. Then one day some fool invented what's called a Wing Shot. The deal is I've got to toss the object ball down the table and make it while its moving. Is that crazy or what? Once again the Trick Shot Artists Code forces me to try this tomfoolery. I'm going to shoot seven of these demons. Don't boo too loud if they don't all go in. Come to think of it, don't boo if none go in."

Crowd control: You are inviting a negative reaction, but that's okay because you know that crowds love to boo, and they'll have a good time, even if it's at your expense!

Mike's Extreme Pool

	SUR/EXR/MSR		Ch./Page
1-2-3 Proposition Shot - 11 CP	2.5 / 4.5	40	1- 11
The Silver Dollar Proposition Shot – 48 CP	3.0 / 5.0	15	3-48
Titanic Shot - 56	5.0 / 4.0	75	4-56
Speed Demon - 60	2.0 / 4.5	70	4-60
Corner Hook (Shot #2) - 74 CP	1.0 / 4.0	60	5-74
George Middleditch's Relay Shot – 125 CP	2.5 / 5.0	5	9-125
Dollar Bill 9-Railer - 128	2.0 / 3.5	70	9-128
The Traveling Music Shot – 130 CP	2.0 / 4.5	35	9-130
Triple Reverse - 137	2.0 / 5.0	50	10-137
The Big Circle Draw Shot - 147	2.0 / 5.0	35	10-147
Mike's Massive Draw Shot - 148	1.0 / 5.0	40	10-148
Three Rail Long Rail Bank - 156	1.5 / 4.5	60	11-156
Jump Draw Table Length - 159	2.0 / 4.5	70	12-159
The Great Race – 168 CP	2.0 / 4.5	35	12-168
The Rocket Massé (Shot #2) - 174	2.5 / 5.0	35	13-174
Gerni Brings Down the House - 176	2.0 / 5.0	5-7	13-176
Exit Stage Right - 181	2.0 / 5.0	25	13-181
Giz and Hum Mess - 188 CP	5.0 / 3.0	90	14-188
Jack Up Spot Shot - 192 CP	1.5 / 3.5	50	15-192
Rapid Fire Wing Shots - 196	NA/ 4.0 for 1-5.0 for 7	60*	15-196

*For one successful attempt.

18 *Trick Shot Listmania*

NO PROBLEM

You see lists everywhere. The top 25 college football teams. Golf's leading money winners. Baseball's 50 all-time best players. Lists of five star restaurants in New York or the top 10 hotels in the world. Anything and everything is categorized into lists, some useful, and some just for our amusement.

Since listmania has indeed swept the country, I decided to give in to this cultural phenomena by presenting you with lists that should help with your enjoyment of trick shots and the book. In the pages that follow are a dozen lists which will undoubtedly answer many of your most nagging questions. Things like what are the 10 toughest shots? The 10 easiest shots? And how about the five shots in the book that are named after big time celebrities? Got to include that list.

Some lists should prove useful in deciding which shots to learn now, and which can wait till later. The lists, along with the three in Chapter 17, can also serve as a starting point towards selecting shots for your show.

If you're a fan of sports, particularly baseball, then you know how lists of a player's accomplishments can run amuck. And so it goes with trick shots. While this chapter undoubtedly presents, to date, more different kinds of lists than any other book on trick shots, I still have only scratched the surface. Numerous trick shots are not included in this book. They could be merged into these lists. Or you might make up your own lists. They could include the 10 Shots I Impressed My Friends With at My Birthday Party or the Five Toughest Shots I've Mastered. Indeed, the possibilities are endless.

I invite you create your own lists. Let your imagination run wild. And I also invite you to e-mail your creations to me at billiardspress.com. If your list passes my intense scrutiny, it will be published on the site.

The 10 Easiest Shots to Execute

The shots below are like gimme putts in golf. You should expect to make them nearly every time, and yet there is always the chance of a miss despite their relative simplicity. Even though these shots are quite easy, all have some characteristic that makes them a worthwhile entry into the book. Roy's Psychic Energy Shot is very entertaining thanks to the conversation that accompanies it. Meanwhile, the mystery of It's Your Choice 8-Ball shot has befuddled audiences for decades. If you are a novice who wishes to experience some success in the early going of your career as a trick shot artist, this list is a good place to start.

		SUR/EXR	MM%	Ch.- Page
1	Ball Out of the Rack (2)	1.0 / 1.0	100	1- 17
2	Connected Balls (#2)	1.0 / 1.0	100	3-30
3	Roy's Psychic Energy Shot	1.0 / 1.0	100	3-47
4	Jar the Table	1.0 / 1.0	99.9	1-2
5	A Dab Will Do You	1.0 / 1.0	99	1-9
6	Jesse Cue Shot	1.5 / 1.5	100	8- 110
7	Coin Wrapper Shot	2.0 / 1.5	95	3-34
8	It's Your Choice 8-Ball Shot	3.5 / 1.5	95	1-6
9	Hit Your Hand on the Table (#1)	1.0 / 2.0	90	1-23
10	Connected Balls (#1)	1.0 / 2.0	90	3-30

Average Player's 10 Toughest Shots to Execute

These shots are the most difficult ones for the average player to make. All rate 5.0, the highest rating on the difficulty scale. The shots below in most cases require great skill, such as The Big Circle Draw Shot and The Rocket Massé (Shot#2). With a little practice anyone might make On the Rebound or The Silver Dollar Proposition Shot even though the odds would be heavily stacked against them.

		SUR/EXR	MM%	Ch.- Page
1	George Middleditch Relay	2.5 / 5.0	5	9- 125
2	Gerni Brings Down the House	2.0 / 5.0	5-7	13- 176
3	The Silver Dollar Proposition Shot	3.0 / 5.0	15	3-48
4	The Lucky Chalk Shot	2.0 / 5.0	20	9- 132
5	On the Rebound	2.0 / 5.0	25	5-86
6	Exit Stage Right	2.0 / 5.0	25	13- 181
7	The Big Circle Draw Shot	2.0 / 5.0	35	10- 147
8	The Rocket Massé (Shot #2)	2.5 / 5.0	35	13- 174
9	Triple Reverse	2.0 / 5.0	50	10- 137
10	Mike's Massive Draw Shot	1.0 / 5.0	70	10- 148

Mike's 11 Toughest Shots

This is a list of the shots that give me the most trouble Their difficulty aris- es from a unique blend of skill and luck that is required to make most of them. The George Middleditch Relay, for example, requires the ability to hit the cue ball very precisely with a hard stroke while applying tons of english. Even so, you must be somewhat lucky to make it. The Lucky Chalk Shot takes more luck than skill. Even novices can make it if luck is on their side. Finally, Exit Stage Right is 100% skill.

	SUR/EXR	MM%	Ch.- Page
1 George Middleditch Relay	2.5 / 5.0	5	9- 125
2 Gerni Brings Down the House	2.0 / 5.0	5- 7	13- 176
3 The Silver Dollar Proposition Shot	3.0 / 5.0	15	3- 48
4 The Lucky Chalk Shot	2.0 / 5.0	20	9- 132
5 On the Rebound	2.0 / 5.0	25	5- 86
6 Exit Stage Right	2.0 / 5.0	25	13- 181
7 Slice N' Draw Shot	3.0 / 4.5	30	15- 194
8 The Rocket Massé (Shot #2)	2.5 / 5.0	35	13- 174
9 The Big Circle Draw Shot	2.0 / 5.0	35	10- 147
10 The Traveling Music Shot	2.0 / 4.5	35	9- 130
11 The Great Race	2.0 / 4.5	35	12- 168

Mike's 12 Shot Supershow

My shows usually have 25-30 shots. If time was limited and I wanted to give the audience, especially one that has never seen my show, a dozen shots that are guaranteed to generate the best response, I would perform the shots on this list. There is great variety among these shots. Better yet, they almost always lead to generous applause, and on many occasions I've been treated to thunderous ovations and exclamations of glee and won- derment. The show number refers to the three shows in Chapter 17.

	SUR/EXR	MM%	Ch.- Pg.	Show
1 Ball Out of the Rack (1) (#1)	2.0 / 3.5	80	1- 14	2
2 Bottle Shot	3.0 / 4.0	75	3- 33	-
3 The Chattanooga Choo Choo Shot	3.5 / 3.0	95	3- 42	1
4 Bachnine 10-Cent Special	3.5 / 3.5	80	4- 64	2
5 Titanic Shot	5.0 / 4.0	75	4- 56	3
6 Football Shot	4.0 / 3.0	90	4- 58	2
7 The 8-Ball Riddle Shot	3.5 / 2.5	90	6- 90	2
8 What Happened Shot	2.0 / 2.5	95	8- 106	2
9 The Jimmy Moore Draw Shot	2.5 / 4.5	80	10- 144	2
10 Machine Gun Massé	2.5 / 4.0	80	13- 172	2
11 Scratching with Style	2.0 / 4.0	80	13- 177	-
12 Giz and Hum Mess	5.0 / 3.0	90	14- 188	3

Toughest 10 Shots to Set Up

The Toughest 10 Shots to Set Up obviously time and patience to position the balls correctly. But they are all well worth it as you'll discover by the ovations you will undoubtedly receive upon their successful execution. Five of the shots come from Chapter 4, Crowd Pleasers. One is in Chapter 8, Lots of Balls in Action. And it seems many of my creations wound up on this list as it includes four shots from Chapter 14.

	SUR/EXR	MM%	Ch.- Page
1 Titanic Shot	5.0 / 4.0	75	4-56
2 Giz and Hum Mess	5.0 / 3.0	90	14-188
3 Inspired 4 Ball Shot	4.5 / 4.0	90	14-187
4 Rempe Eight Balls in One Shot	4.5 / 3.0	90	4-52
5 Air Raid	4.5 / 3.0	90	4-61
6 Mike & Earl's Bjg. 14-ball Shot	4.0 / 4.5	60	4-66
7 The Scatter Gun	4.0 / 3.5	70	8-107
8 The Inquisitive 7	4.0 / 3.5	90	14-186
9 Pocket Seven for the 8-Ball	4.0 / 3.5	90	14-190
10 Football Shot	4.0 / 3.0	90	4-58

15 Best Named Shots

A colorfully named shot can inspire an aura of mystery and anticipation prior to its execution. As you peruse the list below, just imagine what kind of magic or mayhem could possibly be associated with shots like The Great Deceiver or the Slam Dunk. When you give your show, emphasize the names of the shots below and others in the book that did not make the top 15, but that which you feel will especially appeal to the crowd. Perhaps you can construct a story around the name of the shot that will whip your fans into a frenzy.

	SUR/EXR	MM%	Ch.- Page
1 The Great Deceiver	1.5 / 2.5	95	1-7
2 The Chattanooga Choo Choo Shot	3.5 / 3.0	95	3-42
3 The Butterfly	3.5 / 2.0	95	4-54
4 Titanic Shot	5.0 / 4.0	75	4-56
5 Bachnine 10-Cent Special	3.5 / 3.5	80	4-64
6 Just Showing Off Shot	3.5 / 3.5	90	4-62
7 The Machine Gun Shot	3.5 / 3.5	90	4-71
8 The Boomerang Shot	1.0 / 2.5	90	5-83
9 The Koufax Curve Ball	2.5 / 4.0	75	7-104
10 Slam Dunk (aka Smiley Face)	3.5 / 2.5	95	8-116
11 Going for the Cheese	2.0 / 4.0	85	9-122
12 The Rocket Massé (Shot #1)	2.5 / 4.0	75	13-174
13 Exit Stage Right	2.0 / 5.0	25	13-181
14 The Inquisitive 7	4.0 / 3.5	90	14-186
15 Giz and Hum Mess	5.0 / 3.0	90	14-188

21 Ageless Classics

The 21 shots on this list have amused and entertained audiences for decades with some going back over a hundred years. These shots have stood the test of time and will doubtless still be played long after we're giving our exhibitions in the sky.

A fair percentage of trick shots most likely originated to give their creators a means of hustling a buck or two. So the list is heavily tilted in favor of the Hustler's Specials in Chapter 1. The Jar the Table shot and A Dab Will Do You are outright con jobs. If you are out to win a modest wager with Christopher Walken Take One you will first have to put in some practice time.

There are five shots from the Chapter 4, Crowd Pleasers, giving proof that popular shots like the Butterfly, Titanic and the Football Shot never seem to wear out their welcome.

When you play a shot from this group, perhaps you can give your audience a little history lesson on the shot. Once again, I give you full permission to exercise your artistic license.

	SUR/EXR	MM%	Ch.- Page
1 Jar the Table	1.0 / 1.0	99.9	1-2
2 Cue Is Quicker than the Eye	2.5 / 3.0	90	1-5
3 It's Your Choice 8-Ball Shot	3.5 / 1.5	95	1-6
4 The Great Deceiver	1.5 / 2.5	95	1-7
5 Christopher Walken Take One	2.5 / 4.0	50	1-8
6 A Dab Will Do You	1.0 / 1.0	99	1-9
7 Ball Out of the Rack (1) (Shot #1)	2.0 / 3.5	80	1-14
8 6 Balls in One Shot	1.5 / 2.0	99	1-18
9 The Chattanooga Choo Choo Shot	3.5 / 3.0	95	3-42
10 The Butterfly	3.5 / 2.0	95	4-54
11 Titanic Shot	5.0 / 4.0	75	4-56
12 Just Showing Off Shot	3.5 / 3.5	90	4-62
13 Football Shot	4.0 / 3.0	90	4-58
14 The Machine Gun Shot	3.5 / 3.5	90	4-71
15 The 8-Ball Riddle Shot	3.5 / 2.5	90	6-90
16 Topspin Curveball	1.0 / 3.0	75	7-100
17 4 Balls in 4 Pockets	2.5 / 2.5	90	8-112
18 "The Hustler" Bank Shot	1.5 / 3.5	85	11-153
19 The Golf Ball Bank Shot	1.5 / 2.0	90	11-154
20 The Over and Under Shot	2.0 / 3.5	80	12-166
21 Rapid Fire Wing Shots	NA/ 4.0 one. 5.0 for 7	60	15-196

5 Celebrity Shots

The five shots on this list all are named after celebrities other than pool players who are household names in America. When you play these shots for your friends, be sure to do a little name dropping as you will be in excellent company.

	SUR/EXR	MM%	Ch.- Page
1 Christopher Walken Take One	2.5 / 4.0	50	1-8
2 Jerry Orbach's 3 Ball Shot	2.0 / 2.5	95	2-26
3 The Johnny Cash Special	2.0 / 2.5	95	5-81
4 The Koufax Curve Ball	2.5 / 4.0	75	7-104
5 Evel Knievel	2.5 / 3.0	75	12-158

20 Player's Shots

The shots below will certainly earn you a nice round of applause from a crowd of novices. When they are played in front of a group of pool aficionados, however, they will typically result in a much more enthusiastic response. Experienced players especially appreciate the subtle nuances, situations, and special strokes contained within these shots. They may stare in disbelief, wondering how did he do that? Or they could be thinking how they could use the shot in a game. Quite often, experienced players will ask me to play these shots over again so they can learn the big secret.

Most of these shots have some practical application. By practicing them you will learn a special skill and/or prepare yourself for situations that could come up in a real game.

	SUR/EXR	MM%	Ch.- Page
1 Snake Shot	1.5 / 4.0	90	5-75
2 The Jerry Briesath Karate Chop	2.5 / 3.5	90	5-82
3 Kiss Back to Win	3.0 / 4.0	75	5-85
4 Ultimate Trap Shot	2.0 / 4.0	80	6-88
5 The Jimmy Reid Sneaky 8-Ball Shot	2.0 / 3.0	90	6-92
6 The Jeff Carter Showed Me Shot	1.5 / 3.0	90	8-108
7 Going for the Cheese	2.0 / 4.0	85	9-122
8 Triple Reverse	2.0 / 5.0	50	10-137
9 The Jump Draw Shot	2.0 / 3.5	75	10-140
10 Mike's Power Draw Shot	1.5 / 4.5	90	10-142
11 The Jimmy Moore Draw Shot	2.5 / 4.5	80	10-144
12 The Big Circle Draw Shot	2.0 / 5.0	35	10-147
13 Three Rail Long Rail Bank	1.5 / 4.5	60	11-156
14 Mike's Jump Bank	2.0 / 3.5	80	11-155
15 Jump Draw Table Length	2.0 / 4.5	70	12-159
16 A European Massé Shot	2.0 / 4.0	60	13-179
17 Scratching with Style	2.0 / 4.0	80	13-177
18 Machine Gun Massé	2.5 / 4.0	80	13-172
19 Giz and Hum Mess	5.0 / 3.0	90	14-188
20 Inspired 4 Ball Shot	4.5 / 4.0	90	14-187

Mike Massey's 43 World Famous Creations

The shots below are my creations. Some are complete originals while others are variations of existing shots. I hope you have a great time studying and performing them.

	SUR/EXR	MM%	Ch.- Page
Massey's Proposition Shot #2	3.0 / 3.0	90	1-4
Straight and Narrow Three Ball Shot	2.5 / 3.0	90	2-25
Time Will Tell 9-Ball Shot	2.0 / 5.0	80	3-38
The Flying Three Ball Shot	2.5 / 3.0	90	3-39
Mike's Three Ball Railroad Shot	2.5 / 2.5	95	3-43
Bar Table Railroad Shot	3.0 / 2.5	95	3-44
4-Balls In Rotation -Bank and Kick	3.0 / 4.0	85	3-45
Bachnine 10-Cent Special	3.5 / 3.5	80	4-64
Mike and Earl's Beijing 14-ball Shot	4.0 / 4.5	60	4-66
Snake Shot	1.5 / 4.0	90	5-75
The Corner Hooked 3-Railer	2.0 / 3.0	90	5-77
The Mysterious 9-Ball Shot	3.0 / 3.5	85	6-89
The Magical Helper Shot	2.0 / 3.5	80	6-91
It Almost Looks Legal	2.0 / 3.5	70	6-93
What Happened Shot	2.0 / 2.5	95	8-106
Jesse Cue Shot	1.5 / 1.5	100	8-110
The Double Double	3.0 / 2.0	95	8-111
4 Plus 4 (or 5) with Rack	3.0 / 4.0	70	8-113
3-4-5 Shot	3.5 / 4.0	65	8-114
Going for the Cheese	2.0 / 4.0	85	9-122
The Lose Your Opponent Shot	2.5 / 4.0	75	9-123
Position Wizard Shot	3.0 / 3.0	95	9-124
The Showoff Spin Shot	2.0 / 3.5	85	10-136
Triple Reverse	2.0 / 5.0	50	10-137
The Pelinga Response	2.0 / 4.0	80	10-138
Mike's Power Draw Shot	1.5 / 4.5	90	10-142
Tunnel Vision	2.0 / 3.5	90	10-145
The Big Circle Draw Shot	2.0 / 5.0	35	10-147
Mike's Massive Draw Shot	1.0 / 5.0	70	10-148
Mike's Jump Bank	2.0 / 3.5	80	11-155
Three Rail Long Rail Bank	1.5 / 4.5	60	11-156
Evel Knievel	2.5 / 3.0	75	12-158
Jump Draw Table Length	2.0 / 4.5	70	12-159
Double Jump	3.0 / 4.0	70	12-160
Massey's Around, Over & Under Shot	2.5 / 3.5	90	12-167
Kiss Back Massé	2.0 / 3.5	80	13-171
Massey's Massé 9-Ball Shot	2.0 / 4.5	50	13-173
Time the 9 Shot	3.0 / 3.5	70	14-184
Collision Drawback 9-Ball Shot	2.0 / 3.5	80	14-185
The Inquisitive 7	4.0 / 3.5	90	14-186
Inspired 4 Ball Shot	4.5 / 4.0	90	14-187
Giz and Hum Mess	5.0 / 3.0	90	14-188
Pocket Seven for the 8-Ball	4.0 / 3.5	90	14-190

Shot Ratings

The list below ranks every shot in the book in order of their difficulty. The list starts with the sure things and ends with the nearly impossible shots. The list can help you to pick the shots that are within you current level of skill.

If you are extraordinarily ambitious, you may wish to make a copy of the list. Start at the top and forge right through the entire lot. You who are gluttons for punishment and/or those looking for the supreme shotmaking challenges this sport has to offer have 24 shots rated 4.5-5.0 in execution to choose from.

The average difficulty rating is 3.35. The list is divided in quartiles so you can easily find the 25% that are the easiest, toughest and so forth. Enjoy!

1.0's

	SUR/EXR	MM%	Ch.- Page
Ball Out of the Rack (2)	1.0 / 1.0	100	1-17
Connected Balls (#2)	1.0 / 1.0	100	3-30
Roy's Psychic Energy Shot	1.0 / 1.0	100	3-47
Jar the Table	1.0 / 1.0	99.9	1-2
A Dab Will Do You	1.0 / 1.0	99	1-9

1.5's

Jesse Cue Shot	1.5 / 1.5	100	8-110
Coin Wrapper Shot	2.0 / 1.5	95	3-34
It's Your Choice 8-Ball Shot	3.5 / 1.5	95	1-6

2.0's

Hit Your Hand on the Table (#1)	1.0 / 2.0	90	1-23
Connected Balls (#1)	1.0 / 2.0	90	3-30
6 Balls in One Shot	1.5 / 2.0	99	1-18
The Shrinking Cue Ball	1.5 / 2.0	98	12-161
Three and Three Shot	1.5 / 2.0	95	9-126
The Golf Ball Bank Shot	1.5 / 2.0	90	11-154
Three In One Shot	2.0 / 2.0	95	2-20
Which Goes First	2.0 / 2.0	95	6-94
Three for the Price of One	2.0 / 2.0	90	2-22
The Skyscraper Stop Shot	2.5 / 2.0	98	3-36
Massey's Proposition Shot (#1)	2.5 / 2.0	95	1-4
The Double Double	3.0 / 2.0	95	8-111
The Butterfly	3.5 / 2.0	95	4-54
The Four in Three Shot	3.5 / 2.0	90	8-109

2.5's

Intentional Miscue	1.0 / 2.5	90	1-3
Corner Hook (#1)	1.0 / 2.5	90	5-74
The Boomerang Shot	1.0 / 2.5	90	5-83
Nine-Rail Kick Shot	1.0 / 2.5	90	9-120
The Great Deceiver	1.5 / 2.5	95	1-7

	SUR/EXR	MM%	Ch.- Page
Disappearing Shot	1.5 / 2.5	90	2- 28
Sarge's Astounding 8-Ball Shot	1.5 / 2.5	80	6- 96
Three's Company	2.0 / 2.5	95	2- 23
Jerry Orbach's 3 Ball Shot	2.0 / 2.5	95	2- 26
The Johnny Cash Special	2.0 / 2.5	95	5- 81
Air Bridge Position Shot	2.0 / 2.5	95	6- 95
What Happened Shot	2.0 / 2.5	95	8- 106
Three Off the Spot	2.0 / 2.5	90	2- 27
The Moving Cue Shot	2.0 / 2.5	90	3- 41
Coin in the Glass	2.0 / 2.5	80	1- 12
Walking the Dog (#1)	2.0 / 2.5	80	7- 101
Mike's Three Ball Railroad Shot	2.5 / 2.5	95	3- 43
Curving Silver Dollar Shot	2.5 / 2.5	90	3- 49
Flying 8-Ball Shot	2.5 / 2.5	90	4- 72
4 Balls in 4 Pockets	2.5 / 2.5	90	8- 112
Draw Back 4-Ball Shot	2.5 / 2.5	90	10- 146

• **One Quarter**

	SUR/EXR	MM%	Ch.- Page
Gerni's ESPN 3 Ball Shot	2.5 / 2.5	80	2- 24
Bar Table Railroad Shot	3.0 / 2.5	95	3- 44
Slam Dunk (aka Smiley Face)	3.5 / 2.5	95	8- 116
The 8-Ball Riddle Shot	3.5 / 2.5	90	6- 90
The Mysterious Flying 8-Ball Shot	3.5 / 2.5	85	3- 39
One-Pocket Run Out	3.5 / 2.5	75	2- 21

3.0's

	SUR/EXR	MM%	Ch.- Page
Pocket the X-Ball Three Ways (#2)	1.0 / 3.0	90	5- 80
The Triple Reverse Bank	1.0 / 3.0	85	11- 152
Topspin Curveball	1.0 / 3.0	75	7- 100
The Double Kiss 8-Ball Shot	1.5 / 3.0	95	5- 84
Magical Four Rail Kick	1.5 / 3.0	90	5- 78
The Jeff Carter Showed Me (#1)	1.5 / 3.0	90	8- 108
The Corner Hooked 3-Railer	2.0 / 3.0	90	5- 77
The Jimmy Reid Sneaky 8-Ball Shot	2.0 / 3.0	90	6- 92
Escape from Jail	2.0 / 3.0	85	12- 163
Circular Draw Shot	2.0 / 3.0	70	10- 139
Cue Is Quicker than the Eye	2.5 / 3.0	90	1- 5
Straight and Narrow Three Ball Shot	2.5 / 3.0	90	2- 25
The Flying Three Ball Shot	2.5 / 3.0	90	3- 31
The Half Butterfly	2.5 / 3.0	90	4- 55
The Big X Shot	2.5 / 3.0	85	1- 115
Evel Knievel	2.5 / 3.0	75	12- 158
Position Wizard Shot	3.0 / 3.0	95	9- 124
Massey's Proposition Shot (#2)	3.0 / 3.0	90	1- 4
1, 2 and a 3-Ball	3.0 / 3.0	90	9- 127
The Chattanooga Choo Choo Shot	3.5 / 3.0	95	3- 42
Football Shot	4.0 / 3.0	90	4- 58
Rempe Eight Balls in One Shot	4.5 / 3.0	90	4- 52
Air Raid	4.5 / 3.0	90	4- 61
Giz and Hum Mess	5.0 / 3.0	90	14- 188

3.5's

	SUR/EXR	MM%	Ch.- Page
12 Rail Kick Shot	1.0 / 3.5	85	9- 121
The Possible Dream 8-Ball Shot	1.5 / 3.5	85	5- 76
Off the Point Three Railer (NA)	1.5 / 3.5	85	5- 79
"The Hustler" Bank Shot	1.5 / 3.5	85	11- 153
Long Distance Curve Ball	1.5 / 3.5	80	7- 98
Jack Up Spot Shot	1.5 / 3.5	50	15- 192
Tunnel Vision	2.0 / 3.5	90	10- 145
Luke's 8-Ball Shot	2.0 / 3.5	85	3- 46
The Showoff Spin Shot	2.0 / 3.5	85	10- 136
Ball Out of the Rack (1) (#1)	2.0 / 3.5	80	1- 14
Ball Out of the Rack (1) (#2)	2.0 / 3.5	80	1- 14

• **Mid Point**

	SUR/EXR	MM%	Ch.- Page
Pocket the X-Ball Three Ways (#3)	2.0 / 3.5	80	5- 80
The Magical Helper Shot	2.0 / 3.5	80	6- 91
Walking the Dog (#2)	2.0 / 3.5	80	7- 101
Mike's Jump Bank	2.0 / 3.5	80	11- 155
The Over and Under Shot	2.0 / 3.5	80	12- 166
Kiss Back Massé	2.0 / 3.5	80	13- 171
The Level Cue Massé	2.0 / 3.5	80	13- 182
Collision Drawback 9-Ball Shot	2.0 / 3.5	80	14- 185
Hit Your Hand on the Table (#2)	2.0 / 3.5	75	1- 23
The Jump Draw Shot	2.0 / 3.5	75	10- 140
On, Over and Around	2.0 / 3.5	75	12- 165
It Almost Looks Legal	2.0 / 3.5	70	6- 93
Dollar Bill 9-Railer	2.0 / 3.5	70	9- 128
No Scratch City	2.0 / 3.5	70	12- 162
"The Hustler" Massé Shot	2.0 / 3.5	70	13- 178
The Flying 8-Ball Bank Shot	2.0 / 3.5	60	12- 164
The Jerry Briesath Karate Chop	2.5 / 3.5	90	5- 82
Massey's Around, Over & Under Shot	2.5 / 3.5	90	12- 167
The Jeff Carter Showed Me (#2)	2.5 / 3.5	85	8- 108
The Ball Tray Shot	2.5 / 3.5	80	3- 40
Four Rail Chalk Shot	2.5 / 3.5	70	9- 133
Mid Air Collision Special	3.0 / 3.5	85	3- 35
The Mysterious 9-Ball Shot	3.0 / 3.5	85	6- 89
Time the 9 Shot	3.0 / 3.5	70	14- 184
Parting of the Red Sea	3.5 / 3.5	90	4- 59
Just Showing Off Shot	3.5 / 3.5	90	4- 62
The Machine Gun Shot	3.5 / 3.5	90	4- 71
Half Beijing	3.5 / 3.5	85	4- 65
Bachnine 10-Cent Special	3.5 / 3.5	80	4- 64
Through the Great Wall	3.5 / 3.5	80	7- 102
The Inquisitive 7	4.0 / 3.5	90	14- 186
Pocket Seven for the 8-Ball	4.0 / 3.5	90	14- 190
The Scatter Gun	4.0 / 3.5	70	8- 107

4.0's

	SUR/EXR	MM%	Ch.- Page
Corner Hook (#2)	1.0 / 4.0	60	5-74
The 92 Degree Cut Shot	1.0 / 4.0	60	15-195
Snake Shot	1.5 / 4.0	90	5-75
The Sweeper Draw Shot	1.5 / 4.0	70	7-99
The Follow Bender	1.5 / 4.0	70	7-103
Pitching a Curve Ball	1.5 / 4.0	50	15-193
Changing Direction	1.5 / 4.0	40	13-180
Going for the Cheese	2.0 / 4.0	85	9-122
Ultimate Trap Shot	2.0 / 4.0	80	6-88
The Pelinga Response	2.0 / 4.0	80	10-138
• Three Quarters			
Scratching with Style	2.0 / 4.0	80	13-177
Pocket the X-Ball Three Ways (#1)	2.0 / 4.0	70	5-80
A European Massé Shot	2.0 / 4.0	60	13-179
Michael Phelan's Challenge	2.0 / 4.0	50	1-10
Machine Gun Massé	2.5 / 4.0	80	13-172
The Koufax Curve Ball	2.5 / 4.0	75	7-104
The Lose Your Opponent Shot	2.5 / 4.0	75	9-123
The Rocket Masséå (#1)	2.5 / 4.0	75	13-174
An Inside Job 3-Railer	2.5 / 4.0	70	10-141
Christopher Walken Take One	2.5 / 4.0	50	1-8
A Friendly Shot	2.5 / 4.0	50	4-70
4-Balls In Rotation -Bank and Kick	3.0 / 4.0	85	3-45
Bottle Shot	3.0 / 4.0	75	3-33
Kiss Back to Win	3.0 / 4.0	75	5-85
4 Plus 4 (or 5) with Rack	3.0 / 4.0	70	8-113
Double Jump	3.0 / 4.0	70	12-160
Capelle's Rocket Launcher Shot	3.5 / 4.0	70	3-50
3-4-5 Shot	3.5 / 4.0	65	8-114
Inspired 4 Ball Shot	4.5 / 4.0	90	14-187
Titanic Shot	5.0 / 4.0	75	4-56

4.5's

	SUR/EXR	MM%	Ch.- Page
Mike's Power Draw Shot	1.5 / 4.5	90	10-142
Three Rail Long Rail Bank	1.5 / 4.5	60	11-156
Yo-Yo Massé	1.5 / 4.5	60	13-170
Speed Demon	2.0 / 4.5	70	4-60
Jump Draw Table Length	2.0 / 4.5	70	12-159
Massey's Massé 9-Ball Shot	2.0 / 4.5	50	13-173
The Traveling Music Shot	2.0 / 4.5	35	9-130
The Great Race	2.0 / 4.5	35	12-168
The Jimmy Moore Draw Shot	2.5 / 4.5	80	10-144
1-2-3 Proposition Shot	2.5 / 4.5	40	1-11
Slice N' Draw Shot	3.0 / 4.5	30	15-194
Edgar Nichol's Bottle Shot	3.0 / 4.5	70	3-32
Mike and Earl's Beijing 14-ball Shot	4.0 / 4.5	60	4-66

5.0's

	SUR/EXR	MM%	Ch.- Page
Mike's Massive Draw Shot	1.0 / 5.0	70	10- 148
Time Will Tell 9-Ball Shot	2.0 / 5.0	80	3- 38
Triple Reverse	2.0 / 5.0	50	10- 137
The Big Circle Draw Shot	2.0 / 5.0	35	10- 147
On the Rebound	2.0 / 5.0	25	5- 86
Exit Stage Right	2.0 / 5.0	25	13- 181
The Lucky Chalk Shot	2.0 / 5.0	20	9- 132
Gerni Brings Down the House	2.0 / 5.0	5-7	13- 176
The Rocket Massé (#2)	2.5 / 5.0	35	13- 175
George Middleditch Relay	2.5 / 5.0	5	9- 125
The Silver Dollar Proposition Shot	3.0 / 5.0	15	3- 48

Artistic Pool

Below is the complete list of shots used for the first five World Artistic Pool Championships as of 2003. In the future, competitions will include numerous shots not listed below. However, this list will provide aspiring trick shot artists with an excellent sampling of the program.

The list includes the difficulty rating (DR) for each shot as determined by the Artistic Pool Committee. The rating also indicates the maximum number of points you can earn for a shot. For example, if a shot is rated 7, then you would earn 7 points for making it on your first attempt. You get three attempts on all shots except Rapid Fire Wing Shots. If a shot is worth 7 points for making it on the first attempt, then 6 points would go for a successful second attempt, and 5 points for a third. The scoring declines from the maximum in one point increments for all shots except Rapid Fire Wing Shots and The Traveling Music Shot, which have their own method of scoring (see below).

A perfect score for this program is 333 points. I scored 230 points in the 2003 WPA Artistic Pool Championships, which is the record to date. This is 69.1% of the total possible points.

Discipline #1   Trick & Fancy

	SUR/EXR	DR	MM%	Ch.- Page
Three and Three Shot	1.5 / 2.0	6	95	9- 126
The Big X Shot	2.5 / 3.0	7	85	1- 115
1, 2 and a 3-Ball	3.0 / 3.0	8	90	9- 127
Four Rail Chalk Shot	2.5 / 3.5	9	70	9- 133
The 92 Degree Cut Shot	1.0 / 4.0	10	60	15- 195

Discipline #2   Prop/Novelty and Special Arts

	SUR/EXR	DR	MM%	Ch.- Page
Rapid Fire Wing Shots	NA/4.0	12*	60	15- 196
Massey's Over, Around & Under	2.5 / 3.5	7	90	12- 167
Jack Up Spot Shot	1.5 / 3.5	8	50	15- 192
The Over and Under Shot	2.0 / 3.5	9	80	12- 166
The Traveling Music Shot	2.0 / 4.5	12**	35	9- 130

Discipline #3 - Draw

Draw Back 4-Ball Shot	2.5 / 2.5	5	90	10-146
Pitching a Curve Ball	1.5 / 4.0	7	50	15-193
Slice N' Draw Shot	3.0 / 4.5	9	25	15-194
Mike's Power Draw Shot	1.5 / 4.5	10	90	10-142
The Jimmy Moore Draw Shot	2.5 / 4.5	11	80	10-144

Discipline #4 - Follow

Topspin Curveball	1.0 / 3.0	6	75	7-100
Inside Spinner	2.0 – 3.0-4.5	7	30-80	15-198
Walking the Dog (Shot #1)	2.0 / 2.5	7	80	7-101
Through the Great Wall	3.5 / 3.5	8	80	7-102
The Machine Gun Shot	3.5 / 3.5	9	90	4-71

Discipline #5 - Bank/Kick

The Triple Reverse Bank	1.0 / 3.0	6	85	11-152
Magical Four-Rail Kick	1.5 / 3.0	7	90	5-78
"The Hustler" Bank Shot	1.5 / 3.5	7	85	11-153
Michael Phelan's Challenge	2.0 / 4.0	9	50	1-10
On the Rebound	2.0 / 5.0	10	25	5-86

Discipline #6 - Stroke

Circular Draw Shot	2.0 / 3.0	7	70	10-139
The Jump Draw Shot	2.0 / 3.5	7	75	10-140
Dollar Bill 9-Railer	2.0 / 3.5	8	70	9-128
The Lucky Chalk Shot	2.0 / 5.0	9	20	9-132
An Inside Job 3-Railer	2.5 / 4.0	10	70	10-141

Discipline #7 - Jump

Escape from Jail	2.0 / 3.0	6	85	12-163
The Flying 8-Ball Bank Shot	2.0 / 3.5	7	60	12-164
Off the Point Three Railer (NA)	1.5 / 3.5	7	85	5-79
On, Over and Around	2.0 / 3.5	9	75	12-165
The Great Race	2.0 / 4.5	11	35	12-168

Discipline #8 - Massé

Scratching with Style	2.0 / 4.0	8	80	13-177
"The Hustler" Massé Shot	2.0 / 3.5	8	70	13-178
A European Massé Shot	2.0 / 4.0	9	60	13-179
Changing Direction	1.5 / 4.0	10	40	13-180
Exit Stage Right	2.0 / 5.0	11	25	13-181

Special Scoring

*Rapid Fire Wing Shots
Degree of Difficulty: unassigned

Contestants shoot seven consecutive Wing Shots in rapid succession. Each player shoots only one series of shots.

Scoring:

Make 7 = 12 points

Make 6 = 11 points

Make 5 = 9 points

Make 4 = 7 points

Make 3 = 5 points

Make 2 = 3 points

Make 1 = 1 Point

**The Traveling Music Shot
Degree of Difficulty: 9

Each contestant gets three tries at this series of shots. The shot consists of a 3-rail, 4-rail, and 5-rail kick shots. Your score is based on your best attempt.

Scoring:

The maximum score is 12 points.

5 points for the five rail shot.

4 points for the four rail shot.

3 points for the three rail shot.

Discipline	Points
#1 – Trick and/or Fancy	40
#2 – Prop/Novelty & Special Arts	48
#3 – Draw	42
#4 – Follow	37
#5 – Bank/Kick	39
#6 – Stroke	41
#7 – Jump	40
#8 – Massé	46
Total	**333**

19 *Mike's Poolography*

Although this book is intended to be an instructional book on trick and artistic shots, I thought you might be interested to learn more about the character that's been teaching you all of these awesome and crazy shots. I came up with a new word for this short biography. I call it a poolography because it is mostly about pool related incidents in my life.

I lived the life of a hustler up until I was about 25 years old, but I'm not going to dwell on that part of my life at this time. When I was a youngster the hustler's lifestyle seemed like fun. Some of the things that happened during that period contributed in a positive way in helping me become the person I am today. Nevertheless, I don't by any means endorse that life style.

When I talk about hustling, I'm not talking about matching up in an honest game for money. There may not be anything wrong with that. I won't be the final judge on that subject. But deceiving people and hustling them out of their money is, in my mind, completely wrong and I don't encourage it.

Some day I plan to write my memoirs because I've experienced so many things in my life that I would love to write about. At that time I'll reveal everything. In this poolography, I'm going to touch on some of the highlights of my life in pool. So lets get started at the beginning in the small towns where I grew up in Tennessee.

The Early Days in Tennessee

I come from Loudon, Tennessee. It's a small town about 25 miles south of Knoxville. About a mile outside of Loudon is a little tavern called Wickers. I first picked up a cue stick in Wickers almost 50 years ago. I was only eight years old, but it seems like only yesterday.

My mother, father and I were at Wickers one Sunday afternoon when I spied this little bumper table in the corner. I'll briefly describe the game for those of you who are not familiar with bumper pool. The table is considerably smaller than a bar table as it measures about 2' x 4'. It has two holes, which are centered at opposite ends of the table. The table has bumpers in the middle and on each side of the holes. I shot some balls at the holes and so began my career in pool.

While I was immersed in the game, my father was craving the hard stuff and Wickers only sold beer. He decided to go get some moonshine while my mother and I remained at the tavern. About 40 minutes later we heard this loud crash right in front of the tavern. We all ran outside to see what happened. My father's blue panel truck was in the middle of the road upside down. My dad was lying in the road and he was so drunk that he was mumbling something about being in a plane crash. He was taken to the hospital and, amazingly enough, escaped without any serious injuries.

Many years later I was on the *700 Club* TV program telling the story to Pat Robinson, the host. I discovered later that at that exact moment Jimmy Wicker was flipping through the channels back at Wickers Tavern without knowing the show was in progress when he saw me telling the story. The odds on that must be astronomical.

I took up pool in earnest when I was 13. Again, it seems like only yesterday. We had moved to Lenoir City from Loudon, which is about six miles north. Dick Rule, a friend from school, asked me if I wanted to accompany him to the poolroom to play some 8-Ball. To play pool you had to be 18 years old or have a permit from your parents. That was no problem. I was afraid my mom would say no so I wrote my own permit and forged my parent's signatures.

Back then pool was a four-letter word. You would never see a female in a poolroom. Occasionally a woman would come to the door looking for her husband, but they would never cross the threshold.

Dick told me the rules and we started to play. It was amazing. Although I had never played pool before, I had an understanding and a feel for the game.

The poolrooms in Loudon and Lenoir were small with only five and eight tables respectively. Each room had spittoons down one side of the wall spaced about 10 feet apart. It seemed like everyone smoked, chewed tobacco, or dipped snuff. The poolroom owners would clean the floor with sawdust. They would sprinkle it all over the place, and then sweep it up. I guess the sawdust absorbed the dirt and grim.

There were two rooms in Lenoir City. The Capital on Main Street, which was also the main highway to Knoxville, and the Smoke House on B Street. The Smoke House served the tastiest chili and hot dogs. Two chilidogs and a coke cost only 35 cents. Back then the smell of those hot dogs, spittoons, and sawdust floors was the sweetest smell on Earth.

Hustling Pool in My Hometown

We lived about six blocks from the Smoke House. I remember walking to the poolroom. The closer I got the faster I would walk. When I was about a block away and I could hear the pool balls clicking, it was like music to my ears. I would speed up even more until I was almost running by the time I entered the room.

I would take every nickel I could lay my hands on and spend it at the poolroom. At first the better players would hustle me out of my lunch money. After six months I was one of the best players in Loudon and Lenoir City. By the time I was 15 years old I was the best player and I could no longer get a game for money. To get action I would hitchhike to neighboring towns like Maryville, Sweetwater, Cleavland, Oakridge and Knoxville.

There were only two players that could beat me in those places. In Maryville it was Lefty Bennet, and in Oakridge it was Palo. The best player from the area was Eddie Taylor, the Knoxville Bear, but he was always on the road playing in tournaments. People would talk about him and tell me how great he was. I wanted to meet him and watch him play, but that didn't happen until eight years later.

Eddie Taylor was one of the greatest all around players in pool and from what everyone says that saw him play, was the greatest bank pool player ever. Eddie and I are friends now. I only wish I could have seen him play in his prime. Even now in his eighties Eddie looks like he was born to play pool when stroking a cue. Eddie was inducted into the BCA Hall of Fame so I see him at least once a year at the BCA Trade Show where we play challengers at a charity event. He's a perennial crowd favorite and is one of the nicest and friendliest people you'll ever meet.

My family later moved back to Loudon and I started playing at Charlie and Henry's Poolroom. Back then you could play for a nickel a rack. Most of the money games were for 25 cents a man check or pill pool. Each player would draw two pills with numbers that corresponded to the balls on the table. When someone made one of your numbers, you would check. The first one to have both of his balls pocketed would win the game.

On the weekends after most of the players had collected their pay the stakes would often jump to a whopping 50 cents. The only time you would see the stakes go any higher was when someone got drunk and the others wanted to take advantage of him. The action was richer in Knoxville. At Coumers or McDonalds on Gay Street you could get a game for a dollar or more.

By this time I had quit school. I occasionally worked hauling hay, cutting and hauling tobacco, and doing masonry. Those jobs paid about 25 to 40 cents an hour. I remember when I made my first big score at McDonalds. I beat a player named Weasel for $400. That was a small fortune for a 15-year-old poor boy from Loudon back in 1962. To make $400 I would have had to work about 1,200 hours. That's 30 weeks at 40 hours per week. Which route do you think I decided to follow after making that kind of bankroll?

After a while I couldn't get a game unless I gave up a big handicap. Danny Scot was my friend and first road partner. We used to hitchhike to the towns around Loudon for action, but even that action quickly dried up. My brother and mother tried to keep me from gambling, but that's a whole other story.

In the Army

My brother Larry had spent two years in the Army and he seemed to like it so I decided to join. As soon as I turned 17 I got my parents to sign for me to enlist. I took basic training at Fort Polk, Louisiana and my job training at Fort Gordon, Georgia. During basic I played very little pool.

After my training was complete I was sent to Boblingen, Germany. I was trained to be a switchboard and telephone repairman, but I ended up as the battalion's artist after I arrived in Germany. I had a knack for painting and drawing. When the sergeant found out, he had me paint signs and murals on the walls of the mess hall. I worked with Ed Row, who was a fine artist. After Ed was discharged and came back to America, he opened a poolroom in Florida. He was the artist who did a painting called *Ride the Nine*, which is probably the most famous pool related painting. I've seen it myself in poolrooms all over the world.

I learned to play Straight Pool while I was in the military and won a few tournaments including every Post Championship and the Regional tournament as well. In the tournament that covered all of Europe my best was 5th place

The most important pool related thing that happened in the military was meeting Bill "Weenie Beanie" Staton during my last month in the service. The nickname Weenie Beanie was given to him because of the chain of hot dog stands he owned around Virginia. Bill was giving exhibitions and it was very different seeing someone play with so much charisma and class. I had always loved pool but where I came from pool had a bad image. On top of this my self-image wasn't very good when I was at the pool table. Bill was the first professional I had ever seen and he turned out to be a big influence in my life, both then and later on.

Several years after I got out of the military I met Bill and we became good friends. Today Bill, his wife Norma, my wife Francine and I are the best of friends.

Bill appeared on the *Johnny Carson Show* and *I've Got a Secret* where he made a 16 ball version of the Titanic Shot, which is normally comprised of "only" 14 balls. Bill is the person who gave Rudolf Wanderone the idea to change his name to Minnesota Fats after the movie *The Hustler* came out. As you may recall, Jackie Gleason turned Minnesota Fats into a household name after playing his role.

My First Big Road Trip

After I was discharged from the military, I returned home to Loudon for about six months. Sherman Akins, my best friend at the time, was going to Little Rock, Arkansas to try to get a job painting or roofing. I decided to go with him. We hitchhiked since neither of us owned a car.

We were almost broke when we pulled into town so we rented a room under someone's staircase for $5 a week. I've seen walk in closets that were larger. The third day in town I was in a bar playing pool for a beer a game. I was having a ball. I was in dead stroke and was running out almost every time I stepped to the table. I noticed this guy named Bob Graves kept watching me from the bar. He eventually approached me and ushered me over to the side. He told me I was a fool to be showing my best game for beers. He said he knew a lot of places he could take me and make some money. I moved in with him Bob and his wife Linda and he became one of my best friends.

For the next six months the action was pretty good. We made several scores and lost a few times as well. After a while I couldn't get a game without giving up a spot (handicap) just like in Loudon. So Calvin Harcrow, a good player, and I decided to go to California. We split up in Texas and Calvin continued on to California.

Life in the Fast Lane

For the next three years I ventured from one town to another while practically living in the bars and poolrooms. I started drinking more and more and I took uppers to keep me going.

The lifestyle I was living then dictated that I might have thousands in my pocket one day and be broke the next. I would then have to hustle for $2 to make my motel money. It was amazing. I played some of my best pool for thousands and three days later I'd be dogging my brains trying to win the rent for a sleazy dive.

Small tables are called bar tables by most people. But I called them coin-operated tables because it made me look even more like a sucker. When I first arrived in Detroit Richie Ambrose started calling me "Coin Operator." That was 35 years ago and yet a few people still remember my old nickname and will call me Coin Operator when I'm in the Detroit area for an exhibition.

While I was at a tournament in Texas I met a player named Jody Hall from San Angelo. He was with Bates and his cousin Tony. Jody was a good player, probably about the 7-ball under me. He told me he knew a lot of places he could take me where no one knew me. Jody and I had a lot in common. He was a sharp dresser and he liked to party with the ladies.

Jody became one of my favorite road partners cause he made it a point of treating me right. Jody, Bates, Joey Torman and I were on the road together. Joey had just made a big score of $2,400 in Austin, Texas playing Bumper Pool, if you can imagine that. That same night we narrowly avoided a disaster. A small private plane missed the bar we were playing in by about 20 feet. The plane crashed a block away, killing everyone aboard. I remember driving by and seeing all of the fire engines and smelling burning flesh.

We all decided to go to Denver. Joey said he knew some spots where there was some good action. I had never been to Denver but Joey was well known there, so the smart move was to send me in alone. If he had accompanied me to the action spots, they would have no doubt figured I was a pretty good player.

I was in a money game when someone drugged my drink with a heavy dosage of LSD. I ended up in a hospital for a few weeks. My weight dropped down to about 150 pounds even though I am 6' 4". It took me years to fully recover and get back to some semblance of normality. For a long time I suffered from flashbacks, but through God and the help and prayers and the love of friends and family I was finally able to overcome that horrific episode.

For the last 30 years I've played pool in a more positive manner. During the first 10 years of that period I occasionally gambled with fellow professionals, but I never went back to hustling those with far lesser ability. It's been 20 years now since I've gambled with anyone at pool. During this time I've had so much more fun teaching, giving exhibitions, and competing in tournaments.

Mike the Firefighter

After I quit the life of a road player I got married and became a brick mason and a firefighter. We had a pool table at the fire hall and I installed one at home. My life started to improve. I became strong and healthy as my weight climbed to over 200 pounds. I was running and acquired a lot of other positive habits that replaced smoking, drinking and the nightlife. I started writing poems, inspirational songs and country and western tunes. Carol, my first wife, and I had our first child. Anna was a beautiful little bald headed blue-eyed girl. It's amazing how she still looks much like she did when she was a baby only now she's got blonde hair and is six feet tall.

I enjoyed being a fireman. I felt like I was doing something purposeful with my life, and I liked working with the other fireman. While working 24 hour shifts they became like family to me.

I started practicing and rediscovered my love for the game. I also began shooting trick and artistic shots. At times I would be standing near the table when I would receive a vision about a shot. I created shots that at first seemed to be impossible. Pool was transforming into an art form. I enjoyed the beauty of making a shot and controlling the cue ball. Amazingly enough the game was now even more fun than when I first started playing.

I began to give trick shot shows at senior citizen halls, detention homes, prisons and at churches to witness to people and give my testimony.

My Reunion With My Fellow Pros

I heard about a tournament in Birmingham, Alabama and I decided to check it out. I wasn't planning on playing, but I wanted to see some of my pool playing friends that I'd missed over the last three to four years. When I arrived no one recognized me at first because my appearance had changed so much. Top players like Steve Mizerak, Buddy Hall, Larry Hubbart, Wade Crane, Louie Roberts, Steve Cook and many more were entered. Don Willis, the master of the wing shot, was giving an exhibition. Don was quite an entertainer and he told some great stories about his prime as a money player. Luther Lassiter once said that if he had to choose one person to make the 9-ball for his life, Don would get the nod.

I drifted over to the practice table and executed some stroke shots. A few of the top players gathered around the table. They couldn't believe their eyes. I was playing some of the shots I'd been working on at home. These included power draws, jump draw shots, and force follow shots. Now these were not set up shots. I was playing shots that required expert technique and a powerful stroke. Most of the pros are not too impressed with set up shots, but if it's a shot that requires a difficult stroke, massé, or is a shot they can use in a game, you will definitely get their attention.

Within a year I was in demand for exhibitions at numerous professional tournaments. I remember doing my first show with Minnesota Fats in St. Joseph, Tennessee. Although it is a small town, the place was packed. Fat's shows normally consisted of about four trick shots. His show was always dominated by story telling. He was very funny, and even more so if you were familiar with the pool players he talked about. He was always boasting about being the greatest. He would say things like, "When I played Cannon Ball (Johnny Chapman) I beat him so bad they nicknamed him BB after I got done with him." Here's another: "After I beat Corn Bread Red (Billy Burgess) so bad they changed his name to No Bread Red."

Fats loved to run down Willie Mosconi. He would say, "Moscoooni, why he's the biggest nit on earth. He wouldn't bet a match if he owned a lumber company." I considered Fats to be a stand up comic more than a pool player. At one time he was a good player, but he did not play like a top professional. In fact, he was probably the most overrated and underrated player ever. He was overrated by the people that didn't know anything about pool. And he was underrated by a lot of the good players. Fats was a great game maker and he didn't dog it when the bet was high.

Over the years we did a lot of shows together. When Fats was preparing to film his trick shot video he hired me to design, set up, and teach him the shots. You should have seen him play the shots. He was like a kid with a new toy, making shots he'd never pocketed before. It was a thrill to see his eyes light up when he made the Titanic Shot on his first try!

My New Career Takes Hold

It was easy to trade days off with the other fireman so I was able to go to tournaments. I usually went to events that would hire me to give an exhibition. I loved performing and entertaining for the spectators. I continued to develop new shots and I also incorporated card tricks, feats of strength and singing into my shows. One of my favorite pool card tricks requires two decks of cards. I spread one deck all over the table face up. Then I rack six balls (the 1-ball through 6-ball) at one end of the table. I lay the other deck on the rail of the pool table with the cards still in the box. I tell everyone, "In that deck there's a card turned upside down." I then have someone pick a ball in their head and shoot into the balls with a hard stroke. The ball the person is thinking of will land on or next to the same card that is upside down in the deck in the box. I'm sorry but I can't reveal the secret in this book as I could wind up in danger with a fellow magician for revealing the secret.

Occasionally I would pull out my guitar and sing a new song I had just written. At times I would perform feats of strength. I would bet a grape juice, my all time favorite drink, that I could do more one armed extended pushups than anyone else could do with two arms. Extended pushups are much more difficult than regular pushups because you must stretch your arms straight out in front of you. I would guess that only about one person in 10,000 can do even one this way with both arms.

People would get a kick out of this whenever some real athletic looking guy challenged me. The challenger would take off his shoes and stretch across the pool table. Now technique is a big part of extended push ups just like in arm wrestling and finger pool. As a result, most of the real muscular guys could only do about 10. Once this muscular and coordinated gymnast in Clinton, Iowa put me to the test. He knocked out 63, which was the most I'd ever seen done before. But I jumped on the table and countered with 64 using only one arm. I don't think I had one more left in me if my life had depended on it.

I began to play in tournaments, which were confined to 9-Ball, Straight Pool and One-Pocket. There were no competitions for trick shot artists. It was difficult at first to perform well. Often I would have to play a match immediately after giving a 30 or 40-minute show. This made it difficult to be tournament tough. Although at first I wasn't winning any tournaments, I was becoming a popular trick shot artist.

Almost everywhere I performed the local TV station would do a piece on the tournament and have me do some shots. My first national TV exposure occurred at an exhibition for Terry Stonier in Sacramento, California. *Real People*, a popular TV show, was being filmed at a local bar. They were doing a show on a six-year-old kid named Aaron who was a very good player for his age. His father owned the bar. They asked if I would come over and do some trick shots. Later the *Real People* crew came to Chattanooga to film me for one of their programs.

Chuck Milheim, former president of Valley Manufacturing, a maker of cues and pool tables, turned out to be a major influence in my life. My first trip to Germany was after Chuck asked me to accompany him to Frankfurt to perform at their booth at the IMA Show. Some of my favorite memories are of our travels to Germany to give shows. He and his dealers would always take me to the best restaurants for dinner. Since his dealers were German, they knew the best local places, which were normally 20 to 30 minutes outside the city. I would take my cards and guitar along and entertain them. Sometimes dinner would last up to three to four hours.

At the time pool wasn't very big in Germany. In fact I doubt if there were a 100 tables in the whole country not counting the American Military bases. Today pool is very popular in Germany, which has produced several top players including Oliver Ortmann and Ralf Souquet, Thorsten Hohmann, all winners of world titles. In addition, Francisco Bustamante now makes his home in Germany.

Chuck also brought Paul Gerni to Germany a few times. I believe his efforts in promoting the sport in a positive way with our shows helped American pool take off in Germany.

Mike the Poolroom Owner

After about five more years of working as a firefighter, a friend of mine named Phil Windham and I decided to open a poolroom in Chattanooga. It became so successful that I quit the fire department and a year later opened a second room. We took in two more partners, Wimpy Henry, my father in law, and Dewey Boyd, a friend who worked for Delta Airlines.

I was in Saudi Arabia for some exhibitions while they were getting the second room ready to be opened. When I returned and saw it for the first time, I could scarcely believe my eyes. Beautiful wall-to-wall carpeting covered the floors. Why there was even carpet on the walls themselves. Plants were everywhere and the place smelled so nice and clean. The room housed 18 tables and 20 arcade games.

We were the first ones to open an upscale room in Chattanooga and now we had two gorgeous rooms. Both places were called Mike Massey's. The second room was in the middle of Brainard Shopping Center. We had to get permission from the Mayor because the city had some old laws that only allowed poolrooms in certain parts of the city. We were given the green light because of our good reputation. We didn't allow cursing or gambling. As a matter of fact, our reputation was so clean mothers would drop their kids off at our rooms while they went shopping.

Hustling Jimmy White

Although we didn't allow gambling in our poolrooms, I had taken it up again. I wasn't hustling. I only matched up against good players. I was informed there was some pool action in London, so on the way back from Saudi Arabia I stopped off in England. When I arrived I discovered the English had their version of pool. The game was played on what looked like a miniature snooker table. The pockets were rounded and shaped very different from ours and the balls were very small.

I arrived at this huge snooker club with about 30 6' x 12' snooker tables and one little pool table off to the side. I asked the manager if anyone gambled at pool and he advised me to hang around. An opponent would show up soon enough. About 30 minutes later Jimmy White came bee bopping into the place. Jimmy is one of the most famous sports personalities in Great Britain. Why he's as famous there as his good friend Ron Woods with the Rolling Stones. At the time he was the youngest player and the first lefthander to ever win the World Amateur Snooker title. At 18 years of age, Jimmy was just getting started as a pro.

Jimmy came up to me with his charming personality and asked me if I'd like to play some snooker for 10 or 20 pounds a game. A pound was worth about $2.00. I'm no dummy and I was pretty certain the houseman had called him in to snap me off (win my money). So I told Jimmy I would play him some pool. He said, "Pool, there's no pool tables here." I then pointed at the one in the back. He agreed to play.

We started off gambling at 9-Ball, which was almost never played in England at that time. I beat him. Then I spotted him the last two, which is not a very large spot when given to a good player although it seems to be for a person who doesn't understand the handicap. If a good player makes the ball before the 9-ball, they will usually make the 9-ball as well. I also beat him this way. He quit and said he would play only if I gave him 2-1 on the money. Now that is a big spot. I told him that I would play one handed if he gave me 2 to 1. He thought about it a few seconds and said no. So I countered with an offer to play him 8-Ball. I would play him one handed if he gave me 8-5 on the money. I won a few games that way and he quit again. Jimmy was a good loser.

Tennessee Tarzan vs. The Great Wally

Jimmy asked me to accompany him to a snooker hall owned by Henry West, who was an agent for wrestlers and snooker players. After we arrived I performed some trick shots and finger pool. Everyone was having a ball, laughing and carrying on. I felt like the Pied Piper.

Henry's brother Wally, who was a real character, decided to get into the act. He ripped a London phone book in half, then took one of the halves and ripped it into quarters. Then he tore one of the quarters into two eighths! All of a sudden things turned into a circus. I said let me see you do this and I dropped down on the floor and knocked out 30 extended one-arm pushups.

Wally said he couldn't do that, but he offered to arm wrestle me. Arm wrestling used to be one of my hustles when I couldn't get a pool game while I was on the road. I was a lot smaller at the time but I had very strong arms and excellent technique. One of the secrets to arm wrestling is that the person with the shorter arms has an advantage. Shorter arms provide better leverage because the arm is straight up and down. Meanwhile, the person with the longer arm is at an angle in the starting position.

Wally was very short and stocky so I was leery of his challenge to arm wrestle. He looked kind of like Ed Asner, but a lot more muscular. I knew Wally was very strong because of what he'd just done to a three-inch thick phone book. The book had looked like it had been put through a shredder. Everyone was looking at me with grins on their faces like they'd seen Wally arm wrestle before. They were wondering if I'd be fool enough to accept his offer. I did accept, but on one condition. Wally had to put his elbow on top of a book so our arms would be the same height. Some one brought another phone book and we got started.

Arm wrestling Wally was like grabbing hold of one of those arm wrestling machines that's been set at the highest level. I tried to put him down and quickly discovered it was no use. I then let up, which is another secret of arm wrestling. If you can't put them down, let them have a go at it. The idea is to hold on while they use up a lot of their energy. Then it's time to make a second attempt at putting them down. Everyone was naturally rooting for the local. All I could hear was, "Come on Wally, put him down." I thought we were going to destroy the table. We locked horns for about 15 minutes before calling it a draw.

The next day I went with Jimmy to North Hampton to play some snooker for 20 pounds a game. Did I say earlier I was no dummy? Well I retract that statement. Here I was gambling with a great snooker player on one of those huge tables that I'd only played on twice before. He beat me three or four frames (games in Snooker) and I realized I had no chance. I returned home the next day.

The next time I saw Jimmy White he had become one of the best snooker pros and was even more famous. This was about 11 years later at the World Snooker Masters.

It might interest you to know I got the nickname Tennessee Tarzan when I was 20 while Bob Graves and I were hustling pool in bars, and arm wrestling as well. Bob was a good arm wrestler and he looked stronger than I did, which made it hard for him to get a bet. At the time I had shoulder length hair and looked a little like a young Johnny Weismuller. I beat a guy arm wrestling and someone called me Tennessee Tarzan and the nickname has stuck with me ever since.

I quit arm wrestling several years later after my match with a guy that weighed about 300 pounds got very upset when he couldn't put me down. My wife

Francine influenced my decision. She told me it was foolish to risk an injury to my arms, which were my livelihood.

The Night the Lights Went Out in Georgia

Ron Maxwell asked me to do a trick shot in a movie he was directing in Chattanooga. The film was called *The Night the Lights Went Out in Georgia* and it starred Dennis Quaid, Kristy McNichol, and Mark Hamel. This was my first time to be in a movie. Since then I've been in four more.

I was in a fight scene and I did Steve Mizerak's Just Showing Off Shot for Miller Lite. Instead of hoisting a beer up off the table, I picked up a person. Someone hit him and he landed face down on top of the table. I shot, making the five balls near the side pocket. When the cue ball came around three cushions to pocket the ball in the corner, I picked him up off the table with my right arm so the cue ball could go under him to pocket the last ball. It was really neat working on the movie set and getting to meet everyone involved. I went to Kristy's 18th birthday party. While there I gave her a Meucci cue that I was endorsing at the time. I spent a lot of time watching the cast and crew shoot the movie. I was amazed at what went into a two to three minute scene.

Poolathons

My first three poolathons were for Jerry's Kids at a bowling alley with pool tables. At one event I broke the Guinness World Record for most balls pocketed in 24 hours. I participated in a 24-hour poolathon at our new poolroom as a promotional stunt and to help raise money for charity. Later I broke my own record at our first poolroom. The last time I did a poolathon I pocketed 11,230 balls at the Senator Hotel in Sacramento.

While playing on the road one of my hustles was to play one handed jacked up. I put this skill to good use when I pocketed 8,090 balls in 24 hours at yet another poolathon.

The Mike Massey Open

Our business promoted a couple of major 9-Ball tournaments. They were called the Mike Massey U.S. Open and were held in 1979 and 1981. Both took place at the Sheraton Hotel in Chattanooga. The first year we called it the Mike Massey U.S. Open because Barry Behrmann didn't hold his U.S. Open that year. David "The Giant Killer" Howard won the first event. Louie Roberts captured our second Tournament. Louie lost his first match and then reeled off 11 straight including the finals over Willie Munson. We also held a women's event the second time, which was taken by Lori Shampoo.

Steve Lillis, who I had met recently, was our tournament director. Today Steve is the chairman for Artistic Pool. Steve also runs the Gospel Trick Shot Ministries where he and other Christian poolplayers perform and witness to people about Jesus. Robin Dodson, Loree Jon Jones, Jim Rempe, Bob Meucci, Tom Rossman, Tommy Kennedy, Lou Sardo, Steve Geller, Nick Mannino and I are some of the people who have performed trick shots, sang, or just gave testimony.

During our second tournament Jimmy Mataya decided to celebrate his birthday in a big way. One night after play ended he held his own tournament, the Mataya Champagne Open. He ordered five cases of champagne, which he placed next to the podium. Then he was carried in by several players while seated in a comfortable chair. He then announced his rules for the event. Single elimination, race to one 9-ball until the finals, which were a race to three. There was no entry fee and anyone could enter until the field was filled at 64 players. You could shark your opponent and do anything to distract him except for physical contact. And each time before you shot at the 9-ball you had to drink a glass of champagne. First prize was 10 crisp hundred dollar bills, which he held up for all to see.

David Howard and Gary (The Bush Wacker) Nolan, made it to the finals. Gary wasn't much of a drinker but he was playing some fantastic pool. He beat David the first two games and only needed one more to capture the grand and bragging rights for winning the Mataya Champagne Open. He ran out to the 9-ball and was faced with a fairly easy shot. He bent over to shoot and boom, the booze finally hit him. He was so drunk he could hardly see, much less walk. David won that game and the next two to steal the crown.

Johnny Cash and Mike in the Movies

I was at a tournament in Nashville, Tennessee when I met Paul Richey and Roy Acuff. Paul said CBS was interested in making a movie based on Johnny Cash's hit song, *The Baron,* which Paul had published. After witnessing one of my exhibitions, he asked me if I'd like to help with the movie. He gave me Bill Stratton's phone number, who was the screenwriter for the movie. The film was called *The Baron and the Kid,* starring Johnny Cash. Bill hired me to be the technical advisor. I also played Burt Manning, which was a small role in the film.

The movie was shot in Atlanta, Georgia. They asked me to choose several extras for the tournament scenes from the local poolrooms. I also enlisted several of my friends from Chattanooga to be extras. My daughter Anna was in the opening scene and Jim McDermott's cue booth appeared in one of the tournament scenes. Jim made Johnny a beautiful black ebony cue that was inlaid with gold, ivory and silver.

Country is my favorite music and I had always been a fan of Johnny's, so it was hard to believe that I was going to get to work with him on a film. I doubled for Johnny in a couple of scenes and I tutored him at pool. I remember our first session. I was teaching him when his wife, June Carter, came in to see how things were going. I asked her if she would like to do a trick shot and she said, "Sure, why not." I set up the Jesse Cue Shot (page 110). At the time it was named something else as Jesse hadn't been born yet. She made the shot on her first attempt and I thought she was going to jump over the table she was so happy.

Claude Akins, Darren Mc Gavin, Greg Webb, Tracy Pollan and June Carter co-starred in the movie. Getting to meet Johnny, June and all of the other actors was a huge treat for me. I would easily rate it one of the top five highlights of my career. I was also lucky to meet Waylon Jennings, who was another of my favorite singers, when he stopped by the set to visit with his friend Johnny. Claude Akins impressed me because whenever we ate lunch, he would don an apron and help serve the food.

Bill and I got together a few times later, once at Grady Mathews Straight Pool, 9-Ball, and One-Pocket extravaganza in Florida, and another time at his home in Ojai, California. Bill was a talented writer who for eight years wrote for Hawaii Five-O. He also wrote the pilot for the Mike Hammer series and several movies of the week.

Every once in a while the movie appears on TV, so if you run across it in the listings, be sure to watch it. Hall of Fame member Dallas West told me that he thought it was the best movie on pool he had ever seen, which is pretty high praise when you consider that *The Hustler* is one of the best movies ever made

I've been a member of the Screen Actors Guild (SAG) for many years now. So when reruns of *The Baron and the Kid* are shown, I receive a royalty. It's been 20 years since the movie was made, but just last year I received a check for $8. Still, it was enough to take Francine and I out to the In-N-Out, one of our favorite burger places.

Great Friends to the Rescue

Our poolroom business was excellent for a few years. Some new rooms saturated the market and I sold my part to Phil and Dewey. Phil still operates a couple of very nice and successful rooms. Although I don't get a chance to see him very often, we're still good friends.

After 11 years together Carol and I got divorced. Our daughter Anna was 10 at the time while our son David, was 5 years old. The first couple of years after my divorce were very depressing. I was working as a house pro for Graham Earl at Buddies Billiards when Francine came in for a pool lesson. We were just friends at first, but then we fell in love and after about two more months we got married in 1986. The first few years were difficult because I was trying to make a living strictly from exhibitions and tournaments and I had been out of circulation after the divorce. Unfortunately there weren't many events and the prize money wasn't much in those I played in. In addition, there weren't many upscale poolrooms like now that were willing to foot the bill for my exhibitions. On top of that, it was expensive to travel and pay hotel bills. We were fortunate to have some very good friends that were willing to help us during this difficult period.

Stan Haines and the Birkbeck twins, Tom and Dan, were especially kind to us during this period. We stayed in Tom's condo in Florida for a while at no charge. Tom and Dan are both superb artists who specialize in watercolors. The Birkbeck's have their paintings hanging in poolrooms across America and around the world.

We also stayed with Stan off and on for a few years. His home served as our home base and he became like a brother to Francine and I. Stan was vice president of a bank in Rensselaer, Indiana. I loved staying at Stan's because I could practice pool and snooker at his house since he had a table for each.

Francine and I have made numerous friends in our travels that are very special to us. Many are poolplayers around the world but most are people who just love the game and for whom it's just a hobby.

Mr. Mike and Francine Massey

Francine and I stayed around Jackson for five months after we got married. Then we put her things in storage and hit the road in Francine's Honda Civic, which only had 100,000 miles on it. The car was packed with clothes and my pool cues and guitar. Francine owned a poodle named Harley and a cat that had just had kittens. There was no way Francine, a devoted animal lover, was going to leave the dog and cats behind. We put a box of cat litter on the floor in front and headed west. What a sight we were driving down the freeway with cats crawling all over me. They would go potty in the kitty litter and then climb up my leg, up my body, and across my arm before hopping on to the dashboard, which was their favorite spot. Our first destination was Reno, Nevada for the Sands 9-Ball tournament. The next stop was Palo Alto, California to visit her son, Wade Hennessey.

Francine eventually gave Harley to her mother who renamed him Charley. She still has the dog at age 96. Since Charlie's now about 19 years old, he has surpassed her in age since his age converts to over a 100 in human years. Granny and the dog still share a morning walk every day even though their pace has slowed a bit. Francine's mom worked as a nurse until she was 92, so now I know where

Francine gets all of her energy. It's in her mom's genes. Francine's father was a doctor in New York. He passed away at 52 while waving by to a patient.

Our childhood lives were in no way the same. But they say that opposites attract, so that must have been true in our case. Francine is educated and very literate. I also teach english even though I have a hard time spelling dog. Of course the english I teach is on the pool table. We do have one thing in common, which is our love of children. She has three wonderful children and I have two of my own. Her sons are Wade and Graeme and her daughter is named Laura Lee. None of them is into pool, at least not yet. My son David doesn't play much. On the other hand, Anna plays on a couple of teams in the APA. She and her husband just got their own pool table, which shows that they are getting serious about the game.

Since Francine and I got married, she's acquired a lot of hobbies. She's been into quilting, photography, making beaded necklaces and earrings. At present she's into making Teddy Bears.

My First 200

Around 1991 Francine and I traveled to Sweden to help Jurgen Sandman teach at his billiard training camp. I loved teaching with Jurgen, who I think has done more for the positive side of pool than anyone else I know. Jurgen is an excellent teacher and I learned a lot from his techniques while he was instructing students. I've helped him at his training camp twice. A couple of Europe's great champions learned pool there. One was Gerda Hofstatter, who I met there when she was 17. She had tremendous talent and I knew she would become a champion some day.

I enjoyed being around the young kids. As a bonus, being in such a creative and positive atmosphere helped my game tremendously. It seemed like every day I practiced I would have numerous runs over 100 balls playing Straight Pool. In one stretch I had a 107, 144 and 183. We were playing on tight Brunswick Gold Crowns but my concentration, attitude and confidence was so strong I thought I couldn't miss.

My first 200-ball run came while playing Gerda. It was a 217. the next day she posted a run of 57 against me, which was her best at the time.

330 Racks in 24 Hours

The European Junior Championships were going to be held the weekend after training camp. I was already scheduled to give an exhibition when I came up with the idea of holding a 24-hour poolathon playing 9-Ball to raise money for the juniors.

I would play 9-Ball for 24 hours. My goal was to run as many racks as possible. Combinations and 9-balls on the break would not count. If I made the 9-ball before the other balls had been pocketed, the 9-ball would be respotted and only complete runouts would count. If I missed any ball, that was simply a wasted rack. In essence, the rules were the same as if I was playing the ghost. After the break I would get cue ball in hand.

I practiced for this marathon with a few sessions at the training camp. I discovered I could average about 26 runouts an hour. This led me to believe that I could average about 20 an hour over a 24-hour period. I would be playing speed pool in rotation, which required much more accuracy than my other poolathons where I was not penalized for missing (except that I wouldn't get credit for making a ball). I set my goal at 500 racks.

Jurgen contacted the President of the Pool Billiard Federation in Austria. He talked the major TV station in Innsbruck to have a pool table set up in their studio. After training concluded, Jurgen, Gerda, Francine and I piled into Jurgen's Volvo station wagon and drove straight through from the middle of Sweden to Austria. We stopped only to eat and get refreshed. Every 300-400 kilometers (185-250) miles) Jurgen would stop at a rest area to stretch his back and close his eyes for about 10 minutes. Then he'd jump back in the car, all fresh and ready to go. There's no speed limit on the autobahn and Jurgen definitely took advantage of that by driving 200 kilometers an hour (about 125 MPH). Even at that speed, cars would come up behind us flashing their headlights. They wanted us to move over to the right lane. Drivers who get caught passing on the right side face a stiff fine.

After we arrived and rested, we headed to the TV studio for the poolathon. I did my previous poolathons as promotions or to raise money for charity. This time, however, we decided to contact the people at Guinness World Records to get the rules for establishing a record. I don't remember exactly what the rules were. I think I could take a five-minute break every six hours and I had to have a certain number of witnesses sign a statement. Heck, I figured I was going to have at least a million watching on TV and a live audience of 50-60 people.

The TV station ran their regular programs, but they would break away every 2-3 hours to check on my progress. I also had four people volunteer to rack the balls including Jurgen, who was kind enough to offer his services. At the time Francine was into quilting, so she sat about 10 feet from the table and quilted for 24 hours straight. The equipment was first class: a Brunswick table and Centennial balls.

The balls were racked, the clock began to run, and I broke the balls, starting my poolathon. After the third rack, I missed a shot I thought should have gone. That's when I noticed they forgot to trim the pocket inserts. This can cause a perfectly hit shot that would go on a normal table to be spit out like a bad tasting black spot of avocado. Since there was no table mechanic handy and the poolathon had commenced, there was no turning back. I would have to try to run racks for 24 hours on brutal equipment in front of a huge TV audience.

I managed to get off to a pretty good start by running 25-30 racks per hour for the first couple of hours, about what I had expected despite the tight pockets. But then my count per hour started to drop considerably. After about 10 hours of running racks my back and wrist both began to hurt. The concrete tile floor did not help my condition. I felt like quitting, but kept going. I was 44 years old at the time and in good shape, but had obviously not prepared myself fully for this marathon. Meanwhile, Francine was in dead stroke, having not missed a stitch.

While I was shooting a number of the juniors came by to watch. I fed off their energy and enthusiasm because I got my second wind just like I used to after running 8-10 miles. But after 22 hours I was totally exhausted. Over the last two hours my average dropped to 7-8 racks an hour as I hung on while eagerly awaiting the finish line. I ended up running 330 racks in 24 hours. That felt like quite an accomplishment considering the conditions. Francine finished her quilt and we were a dead tired but happy family. Jurgen gathered up the papers with 60 or more signatures as proof for the people at Guinness but later lost them. Maybe someday i'll contact the TV station, get some footage and send it to Guinness.

My Youngest and Best Fan

We then arrived at the venue for the tournament. Now guess what? After 24 hours of non-stop pool, I was scheduled to give an exhibition in a few hours for the kids. I knew better than to lay down because I wouldn't have been able to get up. I loved the way they awarded bronze, silver, and gold medals at the competition, just like at the Olympics.

After my exhibition I had something happen to me that I'll never forget. We were standing outside while getting ready to leave. I was signing autographs in a hurry because I was very tired and hungry as well. When I sign I usually put "Jesus loves us, Mike Massey", but since I was in a hurry to leave I just started signing my name. All of a sudden I felt someone tugging on my pants leg. I looked down and saw this little boy, about seven years old. He was holding my photo up towards me, which I had signed with just my name. He spoke in English but with a German accent when he asked me to put "Jesus loves me" on his photo.

This little fan made my exhausting efforts worth all the pain in my wrist and feet. He also made up for my hunger, which was so intense I felt like my stomach was saying, "Thank you" every time I swallowed.

I was proud of my poolathons impact on pool. So many people saw it on TV that a few months later pool was recognized as a sport in Austria. Billiards had been previously recognized, and most of the money provided by the government went for caroms. Now the money was split with the Pool Federation. The President of the Austrian Pool Federation made me an honorary member. I received a pin and he said what I did on TV was one of the reasons pool was now recognized as a sport.

Mike Massey Open - Swiss Version

Francine and I returned many times to teach pool at the Lan Haus Hotel near St. Gertraudi near Innsbruck. The owners Jacob and Manfred Larch and their families became like family to us. Even Jesse Cue and Star (two of our dogs) became friends with their giant German Shepard. They've since sold the place so we haven't been back for a few years. However, we have many wonderful memories walking, mountain climbing and visiting with our friends. Austria and Switzerland are unbelievably beautiful and so I urge you visit these places if you've never been there and get a chance.

After I signed as a representative with Cue-Tech we started going to Switzerland quite often, over 20 times now. Hans Peter Schild was Cue-Tech's distributor in Europe. Hans Peter, his wife Roxanne, and son Jeffrey also became some our best friends and we usually stayed with them. I gave exhibitions, taught, and played in tournaments. For the last seven years I've gone over for the Mike Massey Open, a 9-Ball tournament they named in my honor. I give a show and compete in the event. The tournament draws some pretty tough players from Switzerland, Germany, and Italy. The best I've done in my own tournament is second. I've also finished third a couple of times. Ralf Souquet played in it as a warm up for the 2001 World 9-Ball Championships in Cardif, Wales. I knocked him out on my way to a 5th place finish. My tournament must have warmed him up pretty good because Ralf came in second the following week to Mika Immonen, winning $30,000.

Mike Defends His Dog Star

One night Francine and I were asleep with our dogs Jesse Cue and Star, who were in bed with us. The bed was against a concrete wall and I was sleeping on that side. About 2am I had one of those dreams that seems so completely real. A big rabbit was chasing Star, who only weighs seven pounds. Star is normally not afraid of anything, but this was one scary looking rabbit. When Star and the Rabbit ran in front of me I gave the rabbit a hard kick. Man did it hurt when my toe hit the wall. I jumped out of bed while holding my right foot, moaning in pain. Francine thought I'd had a heart attack. I looked at Star she appeared to be smiling at me. Maybe she had the same dream. For the next two weeks I limped around the pool table while performing my exhibitions. After that episode, Francine and I switched sides.

The Great Pool vs. Snooker Challenge

Thomas Ramsayer, a poolroom owner and friend in Switzerland was curious as to who would win if poolplayers and snooker players competed against one another. So he held an event with two poolplayers against two snooker players. Each team had a male and female player. He chose Ewa Laurance and me for the pool team. Thomas contacted Barry Hearn, a top promoter in pool and snooker. Hearn sent over Allison Fisher and Ronnie O'Sullivan. Now this took place before Allison had ever come to America. Ronnie, who was only 17 at the time, would later become the number one snooker player in the world.

Before our matches began, we traveled throughout Switzerland giving exhibitions and clinics. Ronnie's game was incredible. Most snooker players use very little english (or side as they say in Great Britain). Ronnie was an exception as he was drawing and spinning the cue ball all over the place like he was shooting on a pool table. The match went as expected. Allison and Ronnie beat Eva and I at snooker and we bested them at pool.

The money for men's snooker is huge. In 2003 Ronnie won $250,000 for a maximum break of 147 points in the World Championships and yet he didn't even win his match! In 1995 Steven Hendry earned more prize money than Greg Norman, the #1 golfer that year. On the other hand, Allison, who won practically every Women's World Snooker Championship, was making a small fraction of what the men made. Allison won 11 world titles, including her wins at doubles, but had little to show for her efforts. Every time Francine and I saw Allison after that we asked her when she was coming to America to play on the women's tour.

I remember spending some time with Allison at the pool table, showing her how to play position on certain shots. I was surprised at how little she knew about pool. Obviously she caught on super fast as she won her second event after landing in America. The way she pocketed balls and played snooker I predicted she'd be #1 in pool within a year.

Several year back when I first started traveling to Austria I met another prodigy, a little girl who was only about seven at the time. She had a beautiful stroke and could run a rack occasionally. Her name is Jasmin Ouschan. She is 17 as this is being written and has finished as high as 7-8 in a WPBA event at the 2002 WPBA Nationals. When she comes to America to play full time I will bet a RC Cola and a Moonpie that she makes it into the top three within a year. Any takers?

The Applause Meter Tells All

A couple of years after I met Ronnie in Switzerland we spent Christmas with him and his family, which was a real treat. While there I practiced on his snooker table in preparation for the Second Annual World Snooker Trick Shot Championship. This event is nothing like ESPN's Trick Shot Magic or the World Championship of Artistic Pool. In those competitions, the shots determine the winner. The World Snooker Trick Shot Championship, in contrast, is based more on entertainment. Although I might have more skillful shots than the snooker players, when it comes to telling jokes, they've got me beat by miles.

Dennis Taylor, John Virgo, Steve Davis, Willie Thorne and several others are extremely funny and entertaining. Any of them could easily make a living as a stand up comic. Dennis gives speeches at men's clubs, so he is unbelievably smooth at delivering a punch line. John was a co-host for nine years for a popular TV quiz program called *Big Break*. I was a guest a few years ago on the show along with Sam Torrance, the 2002 Ryder Cup Captain. I had a great time that day meeting him and his wife Susan. I even received a golf tip from Sam on my grip. Sam happens to also be a good snooker player.

The first year I competed in the event, I came in second to Terry Griffith, a former World Snooker Champion. Terry, Francisco from South Africa and I had tied for first. We had a shoot off to determine the winner. We had to execute the Speed Demon shot, which is the one where you shoot a ball softly toward the corner pocket. Before it arrives you've got to fire in seven balls off the rail into the same pocket. Terry captured the title.

The year I stayed with Ronnie I won the title. Since the event is decided by an applause meter, I don't consider it a true world championship. Nevertheless, it is an entertaining event and is very popular on TV, which has broadcast it all over the world. As a result, I have gotten some great exposure from it, especially across Europe. The competition has also given me a chance to travel to Sun City, South Africa, a place I would not normally have been able to visit. The event has been held there three times.

Golfing with the Baboons

Even though the competition only lasted for a day, Francine and I spent a week there. I played two golf courses designed by Hall of Fame golfer Gary Player of South Africa. These are the courses where they hold an annual tournament with a two million dollar first prize.

Although the two courses are only about a mile apart, they couldn't be any more different. One is like a high desert course with very few trees. The other is very lush with tons of trees and greenery. The 13th hole on the upper course has a very elevated tee. The green far below has a pit beside it that is home to 35 big crocodiles that crawl around in it. Golfers have no problem with this hazard as they get a free drop if their ball lands in the pit.

You've got to be very careful when playing the lower course as deadly snakes reside in the bushes. And you don't want to mess with the cute little baboons should one cross your path. My group was waiting to tee off when at least 50 baboons crossed the fairway. When the coast looked clear we hit our tee shots and walked down the fairway to play our second shots. We got to our balls when all of a sudden we saw this huge female baboon not far from the fairway. She was staring at us and throwing a fit. At first we thought she was going to attack us. Then we noticed that her little baby baboon was still on the other side of the fairway. We picked up our balls and hurried toward the green and a moment later she crossed the fairway to get her baby.

The people at the hotel said we were given the same room Nick Faldo had stayed in a week before. Nick had won the event, which at that time "only" paid a million dollars to the winner.

I only got to compete in two of the three events in South Africa. The year of the third one the American government shut down and I didn't have enough time on my passport to go. Francine missed the second trip because she got very sick while flying in a small plane from upstate New York to Kennedy Airport. I continued on to Johannesburg while she took a taxi back to Woodstock, New York.

I've played in the World Snooker Trick Shot Championships seven times and won it twice while finishing second on three other occasions.

Mike Massey and Steve Davis - The Amazing Duo

Steve Davis and I made a video together called The Amazing Duo. It was produced by Matchroom Sports. We did a trick shot show in front of a small invited audience of around 70 people. This was great fun as I got to see a whole other side of Steve I'd never seen before. Steve has always been very friendly and a complete gentleman, but I had no idea that he could be so funny and entertaining. Steve gives a very entertaining show, as he is very witty and good at improvising. He used these talents to good effect for our show because we were without a script or story board. We just winged it from start to finish. The host, Jeremy Beatle, had had his own TV show for about seven years running at the time. They taped our show, which was to be sold on video, but it also ended up being shown on TV in a few countries.

At the end of the program they showed some bloopers. The two funniest are the introduction and a shot in which Francine miscued on the first take. She and I were getting ready to shoot a double version of the Just Showing Off Shot (Steve Mizerak's shot). This required a different variation as we were on a 6' x 12' snooker table. On her first attempt she said, "Oh shoot" when she miscued. It sounded like something else (your guess) on the tape.

Jeremy's introduction for Steve was perfect. He said, "Ladies and Gentleman, we have one of the greatest snooker players of all-time here tonight to entertain you, six time World Champion Steve Davis." When Steve came out it sounded like 400, not 70, people were applauding, no doubt because Steve is one of the most popular sports personalities in Great Britain.

When Jeremy introduced me, he said, "When it comes to trick shots, one name stands out above everyone else and he's not even a poolplayer, he's an American pool table, ladies and gentleman, Mike Massey!" I came out to a nice round of applause while someone went to Jeremy and informed him of his colossal blooper. He couldn't believe his mistake, but it was hilarious. I love the English people because they really know how to have fun and enjoy themselves.

Since we were taping a video, we could do as many takes as necessary, within reason, of course. When Steve was playing the Mysterious Flying 8-Ball Shot he was having a little trouble. The ball kept jumping too far. It must have landed on the floor at least six times. The video turned out better this way because Steve kept coming up with funny lines, which made for more great stuff for the blooper section.

Steve is also very skillful at trick shots on a snooker table. I especially like his one handed screw (draw) shot into the side pocket. He places the blue ball (the 5-ball in snooker) on the center spot with the cue ball about a foot away and straight in the side pocket. Then he pots (pockets) the blue ball into the side while drawing the cue ball into the other side pocket. He holds the cue like a dart and spears it in and he seldom misses this shot.

I've traveled to many competitions with Steve in different parts of the world and its always a delight to see him. Since our video was filmed, Barry Hearn and his staff, especially Sharon Tokley, have done so much to promote 9-Ball. In the process Steve has become a very good 9-Ball player. Barry has promoted the World 9-Ball Championships for the last five years as well as the Mosconi Cup. I only wish we had more promoters like him throughout the world because that would make the sport even more popular than it is today.

Karen Corr won the Women's World Snooker Championship, which had concluded the day before the taping. We used the same table they had used for the championship and after our video was complete, they gave me the cloth. I had everyone sign it. Hopefully I can retrieve it from storage some day, as it is one of my most prized possessions.

In Australia with Steady Eddie

One of my favorite snooker and pool players is Eddie Charlton from Sidney, Australia. Eddie, who's been a great player for 50 years, was chosen to carry the flag for Australia at the Olympics once and was recently inducted into the Australian Sports Hall of Fame. I've known Eddie for 14 years now, and I enjoy every chance I get to perform with him and to compete against him.

If you've never seen Eddie or watched him play, just think of what golfer Gary Player would look like as a poolplayer. Eddie's the consummate professional, a snappy dresser, and a complete gentleman. He's also a former boxer and one tough competitor.

Eddie and I gave several exhibitions together in Australia at community clubs. I watched his game very closely and was amazed at how well he played by cuing almost exclusively on the center axis. Most poolplayers believe that you must use lots of english. Eddie disproves this theory as he is able to play world-class snooker and pool while almost never using english. Since Eddie almost never had to allow for deflection, his game was very consistent for a long time, which helped him to earn his nickname of Steady Eddie.

Earl's Chinese Machine Gun

I have been to Mainland China four or five times and have had some strange and wonderful experiences in the land of a billion people. The first time in China I was endorsing Cue Tech Cues. James Chang, the owner of Cue Tech, organized a 9-Ball tournament in Beijing that featured about a dozen Cue Tech player representatives. An exhibition was also part of the program. The American players were Earl Strickland, Joanne Mason and myself. Luc Salvas from Canada, Allison Fisher from England, and Toda from Japan were some of the other competitors along with some players from China whom I was not familiar. The men and women played separate round robins. I had the best record in the men's division with only one loss, which was to Toda. There was no prize money but I did win bragging rights. Joanne Mason won the women's event.

The exhibition took place after the tournament on New Years Day in China, which is on a different date from ours. We had a live audience of around 400 people. Many in attendance were from the Olympic Committee, the government, and the media. The exhibition was also televised live on CCTV Sports, one of China's two channels, both of which are controlled by the government.

Earl and I did the show together. Most pool fans know that Earl is a great 9-Ball player. What they may not realize is that Earl is also very good at artistic trick shots. With his great stroke and creativity he would definitely be one of the favorites to win any artistic event. So Earl, I hope you keep playing in 9-Ball tournaments until I retire in another 20 years. Do we have a deal?

Earl and I had a ball doing the show. I think we nailed every shot on the first attempt. His shows are a lot like mine. He doesn't just want to do the set up shots. He likes to perform the shots that require a good stroke. Earl also loves to execute Wing Shots in which you must pocket a ball while it's rolling down the table. Earl will roll the ball fast down one side of the table and when the ball is about a foot from the end rail he will slice it in the opposite corner about 90 miles an hour. I know the cue ball doesn't go nearly that fast but it sure seems like it does. Earl even shoots Wing Shots with accuracy behind his back. As a matter of fact, I've even seen him make them with his eyes closed! Indeed, when Earl gets in the zone on these shots, he produces a truly mind boggling spectacle for any audience.

When Earl gave his version of the Machine Gun he tried to explain to the interpreter what he was going to do. The interpreter didn't understand what Earl was saying so Earl held his cue like Elliott Ness of *The Untouchables* and aimed it at the audience. Then made he made this sound like a machine gun, rattling off a volley of shots while he waved it from side to side. If it had been a real machine gun, I guarantee you we wouldn't have had an audience when Earl was done. You should have seen the looks on the faces of the guys in those brown uniforms that the high ranking military wear. They weren't smiling. After Earl made the shot and got back in his routine, they began laughing again.

Mike's Surprise Delicacy

After our exhibition we attended a banquet at the People's Hall, which is China's answer to our White House. Earl and Francine are very particular about what they eat, so the first thing Earl does when he arrives in a foreign land is to locate the nearest McDonalds. He doesn't like taking chances with the food in foreign countries until he finds out for sure what he's eating. Francine is much the same way only she is more into health food. Whenever we are in China together and are at a banquet, they always bring out the peanuts first. As soon as the peanuts arrived, Earl and Francine would reach out and get a handful. I guess they figured they couldn't go wrong with peanuts.

I'm the polar opposite of those two. I'll eat anything. I haven't found a food yet that I don't like as long as it has been cooked, and I also like sushi and raw fish. But I draw the line at eating something that is still moving around like some of the "delicacies" they serve in Snake Alley in Taipei, Taiwan

There was a tremendous variety of food at the banquet at the People's Hall. I was chewing on something quite tasty, although I had no idea what it was. Francine asked one of the members of the Olympic Committee to name my treat. Turns out it was something kind of like a snake with legs that lives both in the water and on the ground. After that I told Francine not to inquire about the food. I figured what I didn't know wouldn't hurt me.

New Years is a big holiday in China and yet the streets were nearly vacant as most people were home watching TV. Families that don't have TV's will get together with those who do. While driving around town it's not uncommon to see 20 to 30 people gathered around a little TV set outside a small hut. We discovered later that 400 million people saw our show on TV.

A few days later when we went to the airport people would recognize us and try to imitate our actions with a cue. When they saw Earl they acted like they had a machine gun. When they saw me they would pantomime my finger pool, which was a funny sight to see.

Bigfoot Invades China

During another trip to China I was performing exhibitions all around the North Eastern part of the country with a company called Olio. They make pool tables in Taiwan. We traveled by van and visited two cites per day. It was great to ride through the small villages you'd never get to see while in the air. There were eight of us packed into the van, but only Alice Hong, the worldwide representative for Olio, could understand English. Even my interpreter didn't even know English, but she was very pretty. She was a popular TV personality in China who I'll refer to as Miss China because I can't recall her name.

Whenever I described my shots, Alice would pass the explanation on to Miss China. She would then relay the description to the live and TV audiences. Under normal conditions my hour-long shows consist of 25-30 shots. Because they needed to take time to interpret the shots, we were limited to about 10 shots per show.

We followed the same routine twice every day. We would arrive in a city, meet the governor or some other official, have a great dinner and then give a show. One day we arrived in a small city (by their standards) of only 3-4 million people. They had 30 armed guards escort me to the poolroom to meet some high-ranking official. When I arrived there was a big banner with a huge photo of myself draped on the side of the building, which was two stories high. The banner was easily 40 feet wide. Man was my ego puffed up. Then I looked across the street at a snooker hall that was covered with a banner of Steve Davis that was eight stories high. I know because I counted the floors. I was immediately humbled from that experience.

The next morning we embarked on a three-hour drive to the next city. In route all I could see was an endless sea of watermelons. For 150 miles it was nothing but watermelons on both sides of the road. Vendors were selling them for a nickel each, so we stopped a couple of times to buy some. Man were they were delicious, but they were also filled with water. In China you will not encounter restrooms at rest stops or restaurants like at home. I didn't see a single one for the whole trip, but I was certainly in need of one for two very good reasons. Need I say more?

I realized I wasn't going to make it to our destination, not with a half hour left to go. I got the driver to stop by a patch of woods and then I headed into the jungle dressed in my vest, tuxedo pants, in short, my complete getup. I came to a field with a few workers down on their knees. One of them looked up at me and, by his expression, must have thought a flying saucer had landed. His eyes bulged to the size of silver dollars. Here I was, all 6' 4" and 250 pounds of me and dressed to the max in a place where the average person stands 5' 6". I retreated back into the woods to take care of business. I could envision the headline the next day: Big Foot Spotted in Northern China. Sub head: Wearing Shiny Armor and a Big Frown.

I flew home a few days later after purchasing some Beanie Babies for Francine, as they were much cheaper in China.

A Near Brush with Death

Francine and I experienced a couple of scary incidents on one of our trips to Poland. We had just finished a show in the southern part of the country and we were headed north to Warsaw to give another. The place I was going to give the exhibition was also hosting a tournament for Polish players. My chauffeur was scheduled to play at 6:00, it was already 4:00, and we had 200 miles to go.

We were riding in a new Mercedes. The roads in Poland are not nearly as good as the Autobahn in Germany where people routinely drive at speeds unheard of in the U.S. I was sitting in the front with the driver while Francine was seated in the back with the organizer of my tour. We were barreling up the highway in the left lane at over 200 kilometers an hour (over 130 MPH) for about 60 minutes when I started to get nervous.

I noticed there was a long line of cars and trucks almost bumper to bumper in the right lane when a thought went through my head. I wondered what if someone decided to pass up ahead. The instant I thought that a little truck darted out in front of us. There was no way we could stop in time so the driver jerked the car to the left onto a grassy medium. Thank God for disc brakes. If the car had not been equipped with them, I'd be masséing my cue ball at my mansion in the sky and Francine would be making Teddy Bears with golden wings. Our driver hit the brakes a few times, and then shot right back up on the highway. He couldn't understand English, but I'm sure he now knows what SLOWDOWN means.

The Mafia Cab Drivers

While in Warsaw on another trip to Poland, Francine and I went shopping for souvenirs. We bought a few things and then caught a cab for the ride back to the hotel. After the taxi had gone a block we came across two giants who were standing in the road blocking our passage. They were both wearing leather jackets and leather gloves. I thought this was rather strange because of the warm weather.

The taxi stopped and the driver locked the doors. One of them leaned over the hood and ordered the cab driver to get out. Meanwhile, Francine and I were trying to figure out if they were robbers or what. The cab driver pulled out, almost running over one of the giants. The other big fellow smashed his fist hard into the top of the cab and onto the back window. I know now why they were wearing the leathers. According to our driver, they were Mafia cab drivers and he was on their turf.

The Russians Do Love Vodka

I really enjoyed my two trips to Moscow. The first time I gave a demonstration for the Olympic Committee. Jurgen Sandman, who arranged everything, wanted me to give my show at the same time as the Junior Olympics. I was astounded at the number of people that were at the Coliseum for the opening of the event. Simply amazing. The President of Russia was there, so security was very tight. There must have been at least a 1,000 troops checking people out and searching them for weapons.

The Coliseum, which seats over 100,000 people, was packed. And there were another 30,000 athletes and members of the parade. What a show.

The following day we were scheduled to give our demonstrations of the cue sports for the Olympic Committee. They included snooker, carom, three cushion, pyramids, which is Russian billiards, and American pool. On hand were snooker players from England, Russian billiard professionals, and myself. We were all standing at our tables ready to go when Juan Antonio Samaranch, the President of the Olympics, made a grand entrance with an entourage of about 20 people. He is extremely popular in Russia and with sports people around the world. You would have thought the Pope had arrived.

Jurgen, Mr. Samaranch and the various heads of the federations held a short meeting. Then Mr. Samaranch checked out the various cue disciplines by playing a few shots at each one. He started with pyramids, then proceeded to snooker where I was helping out with the demonstration. Next up was billiards, followed by pool. I played a short set of 9-Ball with a Russian player, then demonstrated some trick shots, which have universal appeal and are seemingly loved by all. After executing a couple myself, I set up the Jesse Cue Shot for Mr. Samaranch. You should have seen the look of glee in his eyes when he made the shot. Somehow he managed to avoid jumping up and down as June Carter had when she made the same shot.

The Russians love of vodka was definitely confirmed at the banquet. I was seated with one of the board members of the pyramid committee. He was also the host of a popular TV program, a Russian version of the *Wheel of Fortune*. After traveling throughout the world, I have come to believe that every country has adopted our mania for game shows. He said, "I know you're a world champion but I'll play you for money if you match me shot for shot of vodka." I told him my counter offer was to play him one handed if he would do 20 pushups every time I did. He gave me a strange look, and our match never came to pass.

The table for Russian Billiards is 6' x 12', the same as in snooker. But shot-making is much more difficult because Russian billiard balls are much bigger than American pool balls. In addition, their pockets are only an eighth of an inch wider than the balls! The Russians take a lot of pride in their game of Russian Billiards.

I was in Germany for the World Artistic Championships in 2002 when I was extended an invitation to compete in the Russian Pyramids World Tournament. Two weeks before the event I was in Kasikstan for a show. While I was there I practiced Russian Billiards for a week. I love playing the various cue sports, so I guess my enthusiasm for a new game helped my frame of mind and my perform-ance. I surprised everyone with a 5th place finish. After the tournament I was told that I was now considered a Master of Russian Billiards. However, I'm sure there are hundreds of players in Russia and the adjoining countries that could beat me at the game.

Pool is surely one of the most loved sports worldwide so the thing I enjoy most about traveling to foreign lands is seeing the enthusiasm of the young players. You might also be surprised to know that some of the nicest rooms I've seen are in Moscow.

Mike Meets the New Mike Massey

The second time I traveled to Moscow I went to several more locations. By that time American pool had grown considerably. One room was a sports bar with 10 pool tables that featured American style food. The room was designed with an American theme. Why it even had a painting of Uncle Sam on the wall. One night while I was giving an exhibition, a Russian player approached me who wanted to show me some trick shots. He had a good stroke and loved playing massé shots. The Russian could hardly speak English, so when he told me his name, I thought my ears were playing tricks on me, I was certain he was asking me a question because his name is so similar to mine. Turns out he is named Mike Mossin, but his nick-name is Mike Massey. I'm certain this is the first time I've ever run across any-one who was named after me.

Mike is a professional photographer by trade. He took some great shots at the 2003 World Artistic Championships, which were held in Kiev, Ukraine. He com-peted in the event and he also participated in the Trick Shot Magic competition later in 2003. If he and I had both made it through the first round, he would have been on TV in America. That would have been something if we had both appeared in the finals and they introduced us by our nicknames. Mike Massey Versus Tennessee Tarzan. Now that would be really confusing. I wouldn't have know if I was coming or going.

I Win the 9-Ball Masters

When I turned 50 I decided to play in one of Steve Mizerak's Senior 9-Ball events. I missed the first one because I was in Europe for an exhibition. The next event was to be held in Nashville at JOB Billiards. I wanted to play there because Jim Blaylock, the owner, is a good friend who has done a lot to promote pool. In addi-tion, I had just written a new song called *I Hope My Trip to Heaven Won't Send My Soul to Hell* that I wanted to pitch to Tanya Tucker. I knew that Paul Davis fre-quented JOB's, and that he had written four number one songs for Tanya. I also had a couple of other friends in Nashville that I thought could get the song to her. My plan was to go present the song to them if I got knocked out of the tournament.

Before the tournament I stopped in Memphis to practice with Herb Wilmott at Bartlette Billiards for a couple of days. The last day I forgot my pool cue when I left the poolroom and returned to our motor home, which was parked in a RV park. That night at 1am I heard someone knock on my door. I went and opened the door and Herb handed me my cue and said, "If you're going to win the tournament, you might need this." I amazed that he found us.

I arrived in Nashville the next day and performed a few trick shots at JOB's for TV to promote the tournament. While in their wonderful tournament room, I noticed that they had woodcarvings of all of the players who had won there. The wood carvings were in picture form and were hanging on three walls. They looked to be about 3 feet x 5 feet. I got really inspired when Jim said, "Mike, win this tournament and you'll be the next one up there."

The field of 83 players was one of the tour's strongest yet. This was the last tournament of the season and the top 10 point earners would receive bonus money. The field included such big names as Steve Mizerak, Grady Mathews, Claude Bernatchez, Mike LeBron, Buddy Hall, Dallas West and many others. About the only top senior who was absent was Bob Vanover, who had a previous commitment.

I was scheduled to give an exhibition, as I am at so many events that I attend. Splitting my time between playing and my shows always reduces my odds of winning. Nevertheless, I started strong by winning my first four matches pretty easily. I don't think any of my opponents got past four games in the races to 11. I then pulled out a double hill match against David Bollman, a very good player from Virginia. I then beat Grady "The Professor" Mathews for the hot seat. Claude Bernatchez sent Grady home with a 3rd place finish so it was down to Claude and I for the title. Claude, who was ranked first on the tour, had been playing great pool all year long. Since Claude had locked up the tour points title for the year by reaching the finals, he was in a real positive frame of mind.

The finals were a race to 13. Now if you are not breaking well in 9-Ball, it doesn't matter how well you are running balls because you're not going to win against an opponent who is breaking well. He will simply string (run) more racks than you. After 11 games I was trailing 2-9 when I won a game and got my break working. Every time I broke I would look up at the wall and think of that woodcarving. I think the final score was about 13-11. Claude congratulated me and said, "I guess you wanted it more than I did."

One of the lessons I've learned from competition is that you've got to believe you can win, but you've also got to want to win. Belief and desire can truly move mountains. I had a lot of desire and motivation to win because of the prize money, but I also wanted a woodcarving of myself on the wall.

As Paul Harvey would say, "I've got to tell the rest of the story." After the tournament, Francine and I left for Woodstock, New York to visit her aunt, who was 100 at the time. After we arrived I played my song for her next-door neighbor and then told him I wanted to pitch it to Tanya Tucker. He said that in two days she would be giving a concert 15 minutes from there. I couldn't believe it. I thought this has got to be fate, that this song was meant for her. I called John Stacey, one of my best friends in Nashville. John, who used to be Mel Tillis, drummer, is now a producer who knows practically everyone that's in the music business in Nashville. His wife Margie is a superb vocalist and violinist. John had helped me before on a few of my songs, so I asked him if he knew anyone who played in Tanya's band. He replied that Wayne Massey was her drummer, but he wasn't sure if he was still with her group.

The day of the concert I arrived early. There was a man setting up musical equipment on stage and I asked him if he knew Wayne Massey. He said, "I am Wayne Massey." I told him who I was and I gave him a cassette copy of my song to give to Tanya. He said he couldn't promise if she would listen to it, but he would give it to her manager.

Well it's been six years now and I still haven't heard anything from her manager, although I did change my phone number soon after our meeting. So Tanya, I doubt if you're reading this book, but if you do you need to hear my song cause it's a guaranteed hit for you.

My World Artistic Pool Titles

The World Pool Association (WPA) and Billiard Congress of America (BCA) have been sanctioning Artistic Pool for about five years as this is being written. Artistic Pool is now recognized as a discipline that anyone from any country can participate in.

So far I've done quite well, winning five of the six events in which I've competed. My titles would include two nationals and three world events. I didn't have to compete in two of the nationals because they were qualifiers for the World Championship for which I was already qualified. The World Championships of Artistic Pool is a totally separate event from ESPN's Trick Shot Magic.

In Artistic Pool each competitor must shoot 40 shots. Contestants get three attempts on each shot. Every shot has a point value from 5 to 11, except for two shots that have special scoring. On those two shots it's possible to make 12 points. Every competition has been exciting, but the 2003 event in the Ukraine topped them all. Up until that event no competitor had scored 200 points, but at that tournament six people exceeded that figure. In addition, no one before had made all five massé shots in the programs eighth and final discipline.

I won the event with 230 points, one more than Stefano Pelinga. Stefano's turn came right after mine. On his third and final attempt at a difficult massé (Exit Stage Right, page 181) he missed by a scant half inch. If Stefano had made the shot, he would have been the new world champion. I was very fortunate he missed because he normally shoots that shot very well.

Although we had first and second locked up, four players were still fighting for third place. Andy Segal, who had never competed in the event before, made the shot to jump into third place. Then Tom Rossman made the Exit Stage Right to vault ahead of Andy and become the first person to make all five massés. The players, spectators, referee and Steve Lillis went wild. History in the making.

Charlie Darling, the 2001 World Champion was up next. He missed the shot. Ralf Eckert from Germany, who was also playing in his first event, missed as well. Sebastian Giumelli from Argentina was the last to shoot the Exit Stage Right massé. He made it on his last attempt to capture third from Tom. The excitement was electric. Giumelli fell to his knees and made a fist with both hands, looked up and shouted at the top of his voice.

In all of my years of playing I've only seen one other event that was more exciting. It was the time Warren "The Monk" Costanzo beat Mike Sigel in a big 9-Ball tournament Richie Florence promoted at the Tropicana in Las Vegas. First place paid 25 grand, which was a lot of money at the time. Mike was on the hill (he needed one game to win) while The Monk needed two games. Mike suffered an unlucky break, getting corner hooked on the 9-ball, but he managed to play a good safety. The Monk, who faced a very difficult shot, studied the table for at least 10 minutes. He then stood up and fired in a table length cut shot to send the match to double hill. Then he broke in the 9-ball to win the match. The Monk almost fainted and had to be given some oxygen. I've never seen so many people around a table before. There must have been 2,500-3,000 spectators.

I am quite optimistic about the future of Artistic Pool. More and more people are taking up the sport and it is ideally suited for TV. You don't have to know a thing about pool to enjoy ESPN's Trick Shot Magic. Ever since Matt Braun, his wife Bettiane, and Allen Hopkins have been producing the event, which has earned very good ratings. Matt and his wife also produce the men's and women's Challenge of Champions and the 7-Ball events which are also shown on ESPN. Allen is the producer and promoter for the huge Billiard Expo every March in Valley Forge, PA. He is assisted every step of the way by his wife Dawn, who is also a top player on the WBPA. The Expo is host to several amateur tournaments and pro events as well. Starting in 2004 they will also hold an Artistic Pool competition.

I've been on ESPN or ESPN2 about 70 times since they started showing Trick Shot Magic. Now it seems like I am recognized everywhere I go. When Francine, Phil Capelle and I went for In-N-Out Burgers in Las Vegas, even the guy who handed me our order knew who I was.

The competition has been very good for pool. It's drawn a lot of new fans to the game. In return, I'm sure Trick Shot Magic has also helped the billiard industry as well as myself and my fellow competitors.

I won the first two Trick Shot Magic competitions, but was shot down by Tom Rossman in the third event in the semifinals. He went on to capture the title in a close final match against Stefano Pelinga. Pelinga has two seconds and a third. Paul Gerni has finished second and third. These high finishes have given each of us lots of exposure worldwide because the program has been shown in several other countries.

Pool Hall Junkies

The cast of the movie *Pool Hall Junkies* included such big names as Mars Callahan, Chaz Palmenteri, Christopher Walken, Rod Steiger, Allison Eastwood, Michael Rosenbaum and Rick Schroeder. I was very fortunate to get a speaking role in the movie thanks to being in the right place at the right time. I was giving an exhibition at a home show in Salt Lake City where the movie was filmed. Mars and Chris Corso, the co-writer, came by and told me they wanted me for a part in the film. I said, "Great. When do I start?" Mars said I would be needed in two days. I was scheduled to leave for Switzerland in two days, but I thought I could change my flight since I didn't have to be there for a few more days. By changing my flight I would now have to do the show the same day I arrived in Switzerland. I would be suffering from jet lag, but that would be a small price to pay for being a part of the movie.

I changed my flight and picked up my sides (script). *Pool Hall Junkies* was a fictitious movie, just like *The Hustler* and *The Color of Money*, but they used some real nicknames like Jersey Red and Boston Shorty. Now the real St Louie Louie, the character I played, who is deceased, stood 5' 10" and weighed 160 pounds. The fellows who played Jersey Red and Boston Shorty, who are also deceased, were close to the same age in real life. But in the movie Jersey Red was about 75 and Boston Shorty was about 35, so the scenes in the movie weren't exactly based on real life. They wanted to use my real name but I didn't because I don't hustle any more. Furthermore, by playing someone other than myself, I was really acting. I thought that adopting the part of someone other than myself would give me a better chance for other roles.

Since the movie came out I've gotten calls for two other roles. The first was for *Push Nevada*. I didn't get the part. The other call came when I was committed to the BCA Trade Show, so I missed out on being in the movie *Starsky and Hutch*.

I really enjoyed participating in *Pool Hall Junkies*, which I think is a good movie. The film reminded me of the life I used to live and it brought back some memories. The actors did a great job and some things in the movie very accurately portrayed the life of a pool hustler. Chaz Palmenteri played the role of Joe, who reminded me of someone I knew in Dallas. Whenever the man walked into a poolroom it would get real quiet and the temperature seemed to drop about 10 degrees.

I've also known many people like Mike, the role played by Christopher Walken. People like Mike weren't good players, but they loved the action. For them it was like betting on a horse, only their mount was a poolplayer.

Ricky Schroeder reminded me of Allen Hopkins when he used to travel on the road. Allen was like an old western gunfighter going into Dodge to take on the fastest gun. Allen was known for giving up tremendous handicaps and yet he seldom booked a loser.

Mars, who has good fundamentals, looks like a player at the table and he does in fact play quite well. Mars' skill at pool made *Pool Hall Junkies* the first pool movie where the main character could actually play. In most other movies when the main characters got down to play a shot you could tell that they weren't very good at pool. I might note, however, that Jackie Gleason, who played Minnesota Fats in *The Hustler,* was a fine player.

Pool Hall Junkies was a very low budget independent movie so there was little money for promotion. The film didn't do very well on the big screen, but most of the people I talked to who saw the movie liked it a lot. On a positive note, HBO picked up the rights for distribution for Video and DVD. *Pool Hall Junkies* was also nominated for a sports movie award. A version of the movie has been produced for airlines, cruises and regular TV. If you are offended by bad language and prefer not to watch movies with cuss words, I would advise that you see the edited version.

Maestro, Billy Bob, and Bubba

Francine and I were spending a week in 2002 with Tom and Max Costello, two of our dearest friends, when I was given an opportunity to test my acting skills in a real life situation. Tom, who loves pool, has a table in his house along with every book and gadget there is for pool. I think he has also collected every *Pool & Billiard Magazine* and every *Billiards Digest* back to their very first issues.

Tom told me a friend named Lloyd Elloitt was coming over to play him who was a Maestro. The Maestro was a decent player who loved to play One-Pocket. Tom said he looked like he was leading an orchestra as he displayed all of the appropriate gestures with his cue when he played. I told Tom we should have some fun by letting my friends, the twins Billy Bob and Bubba, hustle him. No money was involved. This was to be a good-natured prank.

Billy Bob and Bubba were both roles to be played by yours truly. Tom wasn't sure if our ploy would work because Maestro had seen me on TV. Anyway, here was the plan: When Maestro showed up, Tom was going to spend 15 minutes with him to set the stage. I was to then arrive in my Bubba disguise, which included false buckteeth, overhauls and a baseball cap. I was also going limp noticeably and act like I was mentally a bit on the slow side. Tom was going to tell Maestro he had friends visiting him who were twin brothers who like to play pool. Even though they were twins, each was distinct from the other.

When it was time for me to enter, I knocked on the door and Tom said, "Hey Bubba, come in and join us in a game of pool." I limped into the house and sat for a while and watched them play. After the game Tom excused himself and asked me (Bubba) if I would like to play. I said, "I'd sure like to play a game of One-Pocket." I used an awkward bridge, stance and stroke, but still beat Maestro three games straight. Instead of stroking I was poking at the cue ball with a hard and awkward punch stroke. To the average poolplayer I would have looked helpless. I never made more than two balls in a row, but I also never left him a decent shot.

Tom returned during the first game and at times I couldn't keep from laughing. Whenever I felt the urge to laugh, I made a funny kind of sound, sort of like a nervous laugh. After the third game, I hung up the cue and told them I had to go to the store. When I left I stood outside the door and listened to Tom and Maestro for a few minutes. Tom said, "I can't believe you let Bubba beat you." I could tell Maestro was really upset because he kept insisting that I was so lucky and that I had an awful stroke.

I went to my motor home and changed into some normal clothes. I then returned as Billy Bob wearing no disguise whatsoever. I entered the house and I asked Tom if he had seen Bubba. I was worried about him because he hadn't taken his medicine. Tom told me Bubba had left 15 minutes ago before introducing me to Maestro. I started by telling Maestro that Bubba was a little different. I said that when we were young he had smoked too much wacky weed, but that he was a good old boy who wouldn't harm a fly.

I asked Tom if Bubba had played any pool and Maestro said, "Yea, he beat me at three games of One-Pocket." I said, " One-Pocket, he beat you playing that. Why Tom and I just showed him how to play it yesterday." Maestro said, "Well he beat me but he got lucky." I then asked Maestro if he wanted to play a few games of 9-Ball and he said to rackem up. I beat him three or four games. Then Tom took a photo off the wall, handed it to Maestro and asked him if he knew who it was. He said, "Sure, that's Mike Massey." Tom looked at me and smiled. Maestro, who was still holding the picture, looked at me and then the photo. You should have seen the look on his face. He was speechless. I have to say that he was a great sport about the whole charade. But I imagine he also now checks the ID's now of anyone that Tom asks him to play.

Pool School In Paradise

I've been very proud to be a part of *Pool School in Paradise*. I have three of the finest partners in Allison Fisher, Gerda Hofstatter, and Paul Potier. Allison is one of the top three women poolplayers of all time. The other two would be Jean Balukas and Karen Corr. Of course, this is just my opinion, but I don't think many would disagree. Gerda is a former World Champion and has been ranked in the top five or 10 for many years now on the WPBA. Paul is a former Canadian Champion and is one of the best teachers I know. He's excellent at communicating and teaching all aspects of the game.

Our school is in Vancouver, Canada at the Grandville Hotel. We have held eight schools as this is being written and we continue to get many returning students. Charlie Tompkins has attended five schools while Rick Rodgers, who wrote the forward to the book, has been four times. Each has shown steady improvement. Charlie was a beginner at the start and is now close to a six in the American Poolplayers Association (APA). There handicap system for 8-ball ranges from two (a beginner) to seven.

APA Tour

I do a lot if exhibitions for the APA. Every year one or more times I visit Bruce Barthelette and Bob Grudzinski. Bruce has over 900 teams in Connecticut. Bob is based in Massachusetts.

Bruce is a good player and has a lot of natural ability. He's beaten some top players in tournaments and is planning on playing in some artistic pool events. He is one of my favorite sparring partners and could have easily been a top player if he had dedicated more time to playing. But Bruce has been very successful running his league operations, which are very time consuming. Bruce's wife Ann has also played a major role in building their business.

Bruce and I love to play golf so he invited me, James Tolkan (Top Gun) and Jim Young to come play the Orchards Golf Club in Hadley, Massachusetts. The U.S. Women's Open will be held at the club in 2004. Afterwards we played pool at Bruce's house. In most movies James plays a tough guy but in real life he's one of the nicest people you would ever meet. He is also one of the best poolplayers among the actors. One night he almost ran two consecutive racks of 8-Ball but missed the 8-ball in the second rack. The runouts were by no means routine. James and I have done some charity events together and we've become close friends.

A few years ago we played in a charity golf tournament at Turning Stone Casino. Frankie Avalon and a few more celebrities gave their time for the cause. It was lots of fun and we raised quite a bit of money for charity. James is now hooked on golf and as is determined to get good at it. I just hope he keeps playing pool.

I also enjoy visiting Bob Grudzinski. The pleasure is doubled at Bob's house because he has two pool tables. I've done exhibitions at the VFW for about five straight years for him and each time it's been like walking into the *Twilight Zone*. Before arriving, I tell Bob who will be there and where they will be sitting. I can also forecast who is going to be the first one to ask me to sign a cue ball or photo. I get a kick out of performing for the seniors because the audience still loves my show even though they've seen it several times before. I always have a few new shots for them. After the show I give a little concert for some of the fans of country music. I normally have a new song as well.

Terry Justice is the largest APA league operator with about 1,500 teams comprised of more than 10,000 players. Terry is located in Baltimore, Maryland, which is where Trick Shot Magic is held at the ESPN Zone. Terry and his wife Val invite Francine and I to come stay with them so I can practice on their table for the competition and get adjusted to the time change.

I also enjoy visiting Gene Birklands in Seattle, Washington in August prior to our Pool School in Paradise. These are just a few areas I visit every year, so I hope to see you there.

3 Million Miles and Counting

I've logged to 35 countries and all 50 states thanks to the sport of pool. I've traveled over 3 million miles performing most of the shots in this book and many more that aren't. I've tried to choose my favorite shots. I can honestly say that I've enjoyed every country I've been in, but it's always good to get back to America after a long tour overseas.

I hope you've enjoyed our book. I say ours because without Phil Capelle there is no way I could have written this book. People have been asking me for 15 years now when I was going to come out with a book on trick and artistic shots. I was very fortunate that Phil wasn't engrossed in another project when I asked him to help me. And of course I'm fortunate to have my wife Francine, who kept me motivated and on track to complete the book.

There are a lot of people I would like to mention who have influenced me in a positive way, and some of my old running mates from back in my hustling days. When I started writing my poolography, I actually wrote several stories of my hustling days, but then I realized it was getting way too long, so I decided to stick with the more positive things that have happened since I quit that lifestyle. Although there are many more stories I would love to tell, I will have to save them for my biography.

I would like to close by saying that I'm very thankful for my talent, and I thank God for it. The game has been very good to me. I've gotten to travel the world, see places, and meet people that I would have never had a chance to meet if it wasn't for my gift.

I've been playing pool now for almost 44 years and I never get bored with the game. As Gerda Hofstatter would say, "It's a beautiful thing."

Appendix

Biography - Mike Massey

Mike Massey has been considered pool's best trick shot artist for almost 30 years. He was voted the best in history by *Billiards Digest*. Since the BCA and WPA began sanctioning Artistic Pool in 2000, Mike has won every event in which he has competed except one. His sole loss came in the 2001 World Championships when he lost to Charlie Darling by a single point. Mike has also won three of ESPN's Trick Shot Magic competitions and came in third in another.

Mike's record in other pool games is not super impressive but he has won professional events in 9-Ball, 8-Ball, One-Pocket, Straight Pool and snooker. Some of his titles came in major events.

Two of Mike's most amazing accomplishments were in two 24-hour poolathons. In one he pocketed 8,090 balls playing with one arm. In the other poolathon he ran 330 racks of 9-Ball in Austria on live TV. The following is a listing of some of Mike's tournament wins and other accomplishments.

Championships

2003 – ESPN World Invitational Trick Shot Magic Champion

2003 – World Artistic Pool Champion - Ukraine

2002 – World Artistic Pool Champion - Germany

2001 – World Artistic Pool Runner-up - Las Vegas

2000 – World Artistic Pool Champion – Las Vegas

2000 – 2001 ESPN World Invitational Trick Shot Magic Champion

2002 – National Artistic Pool Champion

2000 – National Artistic Pool Champion

> NOTE: Mike didn't compete in the 2001 and 2003 Nationals. These were qualifiers for the Worlds Championship and since Mike was the current champion he didn't have to qualify.

Matchroom's World Trick Shot Masters Champion – This is a Barry Hearn Production that was held in England.

Two Time World Snooker Trick Shot Champion – This was also a Barry Hearn production.

1996 – Senior Masters 9-Ball Champion

> Mike has played in five senior tour events: Best finishes: first, second, seventh.

Hall of Fame 9-Ball Champion

Holland National 8-Ball Champion

Miller Lite World Series of Tavern Pool 9-Ball – Pro Division

> Most of the top players competed and this was the largest bar table event in the history of the game. Mike was runner up to Dallas West.

BCA 8-Ball Nationals – Second to Nick Varner

1982 National 9-Ball Champion

1982 Tallahassee 9-Ball Champion

1970 Tulsa 9-Ball Open – This is where Mike first met Jimmy Caras, who was a positive influence on Mike's life. Mike was mostly hustling pool at the time, but he won this event. Mr. Caras told him he had a lot of talent and should be playing in tournaments.

High Runs

High run in 9-Ball tournament play: 9 racks

High run in a 9-Ball challenge match (money): 13 racks

High run in a Straight Pool exhibition match: 224 balls

High run in a Straight Pool money match: 163 balls and out against Richie Ambrose in a game to 200.

High run in 9-Ball one handed jacked up: 4 racks on a bar table.

Mike in the Movies

The Night the Lights Went Out in Georgia – Starring Dennis Quaid, Kristy McNichol, Mark Hamel and Don Stroud.

The Baron and the Kid – Starring Johnny Cash, June Carter, Darren McGavin, Claude Akins and Track Pollan. Mike played the role of Burt Manning, helped write the script, and was a technical advisor.

Justice – A film made in Switzerland starring Maximilian Schell. Mike designed some snooker trick shots for the movie and taught Max how to make them.

Chalk – A low budget independent film by Rob Nielsen. It was shot in San Francisco and it featured a few other pool players. Mike did a trick shot and had a couple of lines.

Pool Hall Junkies – Starring Mars Callahan, Chaz Palmenteri, Rod Steiger, Rick Schroeder, Allison Eastwood, Christopher Walken and Michael Rosenbaum. Robert Leblanc was the technical advisor. Mike was a supporting actor in the role of St. Louie Louie.

The International Celebrity Traveler

Mike has been filmed for TV in virtually every country he's been to. Some of these were TV specials and some were for sports. Below is a partial listing of the many countries Mike has visited.

Mike feels that the game has been very good to him as he has gotten to travel the world and make many new friends. He has visited 35 countries and all 50 states while traveling an estimated 3 million miles. Mike feels at home anywhere, but is always glad to return to America.

Australia	Holland	Saudi Arabia
Austria	Italy	Scotland
Belgium	Japan	Spain
Canada	Kazakhstan	Sweden
China	New Zealand	Switzerland
Czechoslovakia	Norway	Taipei
England	Philippines	Ukraine
Finland	Poland	Wales
Germany	Russia	

Mike on the Tube and More

Mike has appeared on too many TV programs in America to mention them all. However, some of them include: *700 Club, PTL Club, Real People, PM Magazine, Crook and Chase, National Geographic,*

Best Damn Sports Show and about 70-80 times on *ESPN's Trick Shot Magic* (including reruns).

Mike was hired to set up and teach Minnesota Fats the trick shots for his video on trick shots.

Mike did the voice over commentary on the DVD of the movie *The Hustler*. He also recreated the difficult shots performed in the movie and is in the documentary.

Mike and the Celebrities

Below is a list of some of the celebrities, sports people, movie stars and TV personalities Mike has taught, played, or set up trick shot for.

Tom Arnold	Sugar Ray Leonard	Maximilian Schell
David Arquette	Dan Majerle	Paul Sorvino
Mars Callahan	Jerry Orbach	Jennifer Tilly
June Carter	Chaz Palmenteri	Billy Bob Thornton
Johnny Cash	Ron Perlman	James Tolkan
Gary Coleman	Lou Diamond Phillips	James Woods
Alex Corretja	Tracy Pollan	
Ice Cube	Pat Robinson	
Jason Gedrick	Michael Rosenbaum	
Michael Irvin	Juan Antonio Samaranch	

Mike's Other Interests

Mike second favorite sport is golf. He loves working out with weights since he has resumed his training regimen. He enjoys writing and singing country and country gospel songs and is on three albums. On one he recorded 20 years ago (Saved By the Bell) he was a guest singer on Jimmy Raschel's *Winners Heart*, Mike has four songs on the album. *The Other Side* is a collaboration with six people who are each involved in pool. They include Dawn Hopkins, Lou and Carmen Sardo, Buddy Sardo and Jerry McWorter.

Mike has four videos. Pat Fleming of Accu-Stats Video Productions produced two instructional videos of Mike's trick shots. Another video called *Massey Shots* presents one of his shows. A video called *The Amazing Duo* features Mike and Steve Davis performing trick shots on a snooker table.

Mike has been a firefighter, brick mason, painter, carpenter, roofer, switchboard telephone repairman and artist.

The People in Massey's World

I have been very fortunate to meet so many wonderful people in my travels throughout the world. Below is an index of the people who are mentioned in the book. My apologizes to the many fine people who I may have overlooked while writing the book.

Trick Shot Glossary

The glossary below is for trick shots only. Certain definitions will apply to all pool games and to pool in general while others only relate to trick shots.

A

Action   When you've secured a wager on a shot or a game.

Aim   The process of determining the direction you wish to shoot the cue ball.

Aiming Line   The direction in which you intend to send the cue ball.

Air Bridge   Playing a shot with your bridge hand held above the table.

Angle   Any shot that is not straight in has a cut angle.

Artistic   Something that is done skillfully and tastefully and is a thing of beauty.

Artistic Pool   A discipline in pool which consists of a series of trick shots and skill shots. It is also a series of tournaments.

B

Backspin   Spin on the cue ball imparted by draw which makes it reverse its initial direction after contacting the object ball.

Balance Point   The point where the cue is in balance, which is the point where 50% of the weight is in front and behind.

Ball Tray   A plastic accessory that holds all 16 balls when they are not in use.

Ball's Width   2.25". A useful measurement for setting up the balls.

Ball in Hand   A rule that allows a player to place the cue ball anywhere on the table (in 8-Ball or 9-Ball) after his opponent has scratched or committed a foul.

Bank Shot   A shot in which the object ball contacts one or more cushions before going into a pocket.

Bar Box   Tavern sized tables. They are normally 3 1/2' x 7'. Coin operated.

Barking   Using loud and/or abusive language in order to rouse a potential opponent's manly instincts so they will wager on a trick shot.

Bed   The playing surface of the table.

Behind the Line   Any ball that's between the head string and the head rail.

Bend the Cue Ball   When the cue ball curves as it rolls across the table.

Big Table   A 4 1/2' x 9' table. Used for professional tournaments.

Billiard   A shot in which the cue ball glances off one object ball before hitting another ball into the pocket.

Bite   1) How well the cue ball takes english off the cushions. The better it takes english, the better the bite. 2) When someone asks to borrow money.

Blockers   Balls that prevent the cue ball from taking a specific path across the table

Break Speed   The speed you use when hitting the cue ball on the initial shot of a game of 8-Ball or 9-Ball.

Bridge   Using the front hand to support the shaft of the cue.

Bridge Hand   For a righthanded player it's their left hand. Vive versa for lefties.

Butt   The back end of the cue stick.

C

Call   The act of designating a specific pocket for a shot.

Called Ball   The designated shot.

Called Pocket   The designated pocket for a shot.

Carom   A shot in which the object ball glances off another ball on its way to the pocket.

Centerball   Hitting the cue ball in the dead center with a level stroke.

Chalk   A small cube with a tacky substance that is applied regularly to the cue tip to help prevent miscues.

Cheating the Pocket   Shooting the object ball into either side of the pocket.

Cheese (The)   A money ball in 9-Ball.

Chirping   When a player converses with the crowd in an animated manner.

Choke Up   Holding the cue well forward of your normal position. The choke up grip is used for special shots.

Cling   The momentary contact of the cue ball and the object ball. It can vary slightly depending on the condition of the balls. Also called a skid or, in England, a kick.

Clock   A tool for referencing the correct spot to hit the cue ball. For example, 6:00 refers to center draw. 12:00 is center follow.

Close the Angle   When the cue ball rebounds off the cushion at a lesser angle than the angle of approach.

Closed Bridge   A bridge with a loop for the cue, formed by connecting the tips of the thumb and index finger to the middle finger.

Cloth   The material that covers the slate and cushions.

Cluster   A group of object balls that are touching or are very close together.

Combination   A shot that involves two or

more object balls. Two ball combinations in which the first ball drives the second into the pocket are the most common.

Combo   Short for combinations. (See combination).

Coin Wrapper Shot   A shot in which a coin wrapper is uses as a prop.

Compress the Cushion   The extent to which the cushion sinks in when struck by a ball.

Conditions   How a table is playing. Refers to pocket opening, speed, cushions, and other factors, including the cleanliness of the balls.

Contact Point   The spot on the object ball that the cue ball must hit to make the shot. The contact point is always the farthest point on the object ball.

Corner Hooked   When the cue ball is deep in the jaws and the edge of the pocket blocks the cue ball's path to the object ball.

Cross-Corner   A bank shot into the opposite corner pocket when the cue ball crosses the intended path.

Cross-Side   A bank shot into the opposite side pocket where the cue ball crosses the intended path of the object ball.

Crowd Pleaser   A trick shot that generates substantial applause from onlookers.

Crutch   (See mechanical bridge).

Cue   The stick with which you shoot.

Cue Ball   The all white ball which you shoot with the cue.

Cue Ball Speed   The rate at which the cue ball is traveling across the table.

Curve   What happens when you hit down on the cue ball with english.

cushion.

Cushion   The raised surface that surrounds the edge of the playing surface. It is made of rubber and covered with cloth.

Cut Shot   Any shot that has an angle to it.

Cut Angle   The angle, often expressed in degrees, of any non straight in shot.

D

Dead Center Hit   See centerball.

Dead Combination   A combination shot that's lined up to the pocket which virtually can't be missed as long as it is struck close enough to the perfect point of contact.

Dead Shot   A shot that's lined up to the pocket. A shot that can't be missed.

Deflection   Hitting the cue ball with english that causes it to take off to the opposite side of the english. Also known as squirt or push off (an English term).

Diamonds   Markings along the top of the rails that are useful in calculating bank shots and kick shots and as targets for position routes.

Dirty Balls   Balls that have chalk and other contaminants on their surface. They react differently than balls with a clean and slick surface.

Double Hit   Hitting the cue ball two or more times in succession. It's a foul.

Double Kiss   When the cue ball strikes an object ball two times in one shot.

Double Jump Shot   A jump shot in which the cue ball flies over a blocker, and then bounces over a second one.

Draw Shot   Hitting the cue ball below center and applying backspin. On a straight-in shot the cue ball will come directly back towards you.

E

Eight-Ball   A game in which each player shoots either the solids or stripes. When their entire group has been pocketed the 8-ball is the gamewinning shot.

Elevate   Shooting with the butt of your cue held above a level position. Used primarily for jump shots and masses.

Elevated Bridge   Raising the palm of the bridge hand off the table to play a shot.

End Rail   Either the head rail or the foot rail.

English   Side spin that results from stroking the cue ball on either side of its vertical axis.

European Style Massé Stroke   A technique for playing massé shots that is more like throwing a dart with an over handed action.

Execution Rating   Mike's rating for the difficulty of making a trick shot.

Extreme Draw   Hitting the cue ball as low as possible without miscuing.

Extreme English.   Hitting the cue ball as far off center as possible without miscuing.

Extreme Follow   Hitting the cue ball as high as possible without miscuing.

Extreme Spin   A tremendous amount of spin on the cue ball that results from striking it as far off center as possible.

F-G

Ferrule   The hard piece of plastic or ivory at the end of the shaft to which the tip is attached. Ferrule's are normally white, but can also be black or brown.

Follow   Top spin that causes the cue ball to roll forward after contacting the object ball.

It's applied by striking the cue ball above the horizontal axis (above center).

Follow Shot   Applying topspin to the cue ball by hitting it above it's equator.

Follow Through   The final phase of the stroke. Extending the cue tip past the cue ball's original location.

Foot of the Table   The end of the table on which the balls are racked.

Foot Rail   The rail at the end of the table where the balls are racked.

Foot Spot   The spot on the table that's on the middle of the foot string. It's where the head ball of a rack is located and where balls are spotted.

Foot String   An imaginary line that crosses the table two diamonds up from the foot rail. It goes directly over the foot spot.

Foul   Scratching or not meeting the legal requirements of a legal shot or legal safety.

Freeze   The act of placing a ball in direct contact with another ball or a cushion.

Frozen Ball   A ball that is in contact with another ball or a cushion.

Friction   A drag on the cue ball or object ball that slows it rate of progress. It results from contact with the cloth.

Full Ball   Sending the cue ball into 100% contact with the object ball.

Full Tip of English.   Cuing one tip from the exact center of the cue ball.

Gaffed Balls   A couple of balls that have been connected, usually with a screw. Also refers to balls that have indentations or that are weighed unevenly.

Ghost Ball   1) An imaginary ball that is located at the desired point of contact. 2) A ball that is momentarily placed where a ball will contact another ball. Used in setting up a shot.

Grip   How you hold you cue with your back hand.

H-I

Half Ball Hit   An aiming technique where you aim the center of the cue ball at the far edge of an object ball.

Half Diamond   A distance of 6.25" on a big table. Also a point on the cushion midway between the diamonds. It's a useful measurement for setting up shots and for aiming.

Half Tip of English   Striking the cue ball half of the diameter of the cue tip away from the center of the cue ball.

Hanger (Hanging)   A ball that's sitting in the lip of the pocket or a shot that is very easy.

Head of the Table   The end of the table from which you play the opening break shot.

Head Rail   The rail between the two corner pockets on the end of the table at which you break.

Head Spot   The exact center of the head string, midway between the two side rails.

Head String   An imaginary line that runs across the table two diamonds up from the head rail.

His Nose is Open   When a player is on a losing streak and won't quit.

Hold-up English   Spin that deadens the cue ball's rebound off the cushion. It also slows the cue ball down. Also known as reverse english. Often referred to as killing the cue ball.

Hooked   When another object ball is blocking the cue ball's direct access to the designated object ball.

Hustler   One who hustles, deceives, or cons.

Hustle   Conning an opponent into wagering on a shot or game that he has little or no chance of winning.

Illegal   A shot which, if used in competition, will result in a foul.

Inside English   Applying sidespin on the same side of the cue ball as the direction of the cut shot.

In Jail   When the cue ball is in a position where it looks like there is no way you can make the shot.

Intentional Miscue   Purposefully cuing so far off center that you are assured of a miscue. The technique is used on a few trick shots.

J-K

Jack-It-Up   The act of raising the bet on a shot.

Jacked Up   1) When you must raise your bridge to shoot over an obstructing ball. Raising the backhand and shooting a draw shot when the cue ball is near a rail. 2) Shooting with your cue in an elevated position.

Jar the Pocket   When a ball that has missed comes to rest in the jaws of the pocket. It usually results from shooting too hard.

Jaws   The area of the playing surface that is inside the edges of the pocket.

Jawed   When the object ball barely misses and comes to rest in the pocket opening.

Joint   The midsection of the cue that holds the shaft and butt together.

Jump Cue   A cue that is designed specifically for playing jump shots.

Jump Draw Shot   A shot in which the cue

ball flies over an obstructer, then reverses its direction after contacting the object ball.

Jump Shot   A downward stroke that causes the cue ball to leave the bed of the table and sail over obstructing balls. Jump shots are illegal when you hit the bottom of the cue ball and try to scoop it into the air.

Jumped Ball   An obstructing ball that's been cleared.

Jumping the Table   When a ball flies off of the playing surface.

Kick Shot   Shooting the cue ball into one or more cushions before contacting the object ball.

Kiss   When the object ball glances off another ball.

Kiss Back   When you shoot directly into a ball that is frozen or very close to the cushion and the cue ball rebounds back.

Kitchen   The area of the playing surface between the head string and the head rail. It's the area from which you break.

L

Lady's Aide   (See mechanical bridge).

Lefthanders Mirror Shot   A reference to a shot that should be set up in the exact same position only on the opposite side of the table. This is done so lefties can easily reach the shot.

Legal Shot   A shot that can be used in completion without incurring a foul.

Lengthen Out   When the cue ball or object ball rebounds off a cushion at a wider angle than normal. When the cue ball goes long.

Level Cue   Setting up for a shot with your cue as level as possible without elevating the butt.

Lineup   1) Placing two or more balls so that they point in a specific direction. 2) Eyeballing a shot before you shoot it.

Lip   The edge of the pocket.

Locked Up Tight   When the cue ball is behind one or more obstructers that make it impossible or appear to be impossible to play a successful shot.

Long   When a bank shot misses to the far side of the pocket. Also when a player runs the cue ball past the ideal position zone.

Long Rail Bank   A table length bank shot.

Long String   An imaginary line that runs down the middle of the table. Balls are spotted along the long string, starting at the foot spot.

M

Machine Gun Massé   A shot in which sev-eral object balls placed near a rail are each struck in succession by using a massé stroke.

Massé   A shot in which the cue ball curves radically as a result of a nearly vertical stroke on the side of the cue ball.

Massé Cue   A short and heavy cue that's ideally suited for playing masse shots.

Massé Stroke   A unique type of stroke in which you hold the cue in a very elevated position and strike down sharply on the cue ball.

Maximum Draw   Hitting the cue ball as low as possible without miscuing.

Maximum English. Hitting the cue ball as far off center as possible without miscuing.

Maximum Follow   Hitting the cue ball as high as possible without miscuing.

Mechanical Bridge   A long handled imple-ment with an attachment that has several ridges in which the cue is placed. It is used for shots that can't otherwise be reached.

Mike's Success Ratio   The percentage that Mike expects to make a trick shot.

Miscue   What occurs when the tip fails to stick properly on the cue ball at impact.

Mushroom   When a tip spreads out and become wider than it's original shape.

N-O

Nap   The degree to which parts of the cloth rise above the rest of the playing surface.

Natural Angle   The angle the cue ball or object ball takes into the rail equals the angle at which it rebounds from the cush-ion.

Natural English   English that adds speed to the cue ball as it rebounds from a rail. Right english when cutting to the left, and vice versa. Running english is another term for natural english. Outside english is natural when kicking or shooting into a cushion.

Natural Spin   See natural english.

Nine-Ball   A pool game played in rotation with balls 1-9. The first player to sink the 9-ball wins. You can win by running out or by making the 9-ball as long as you hit the low-est numbered ball first.

Object Ball   The ball which you intend to pocket on a trick shot.

One Handed Jacked Up   Shooting with your cue held above the table and without a bridge.

Open Bridge   A bridge formed by laying the hand flat on the table and placing the cue in a vee formed by the thumb and index finger.

Open the Angle   English that causes the cue

ball to rebound from the cushion at less of an angle than the angle of approach.

Outside English Applying sidespin on the opposite side of the cue ball when cutting an object ball. Right english when cutting to the left, and vice versa.

P-Q

Pocket Billiards The formal name for pool.

Pocket Speed Hitting a shot with just enough force so that the object ball drops with a few inches to spare. Pocketing balls at a slow speed.

Point (the) The sharp edge where the pocket ends and the rail begins.

Point of Aim Where you want the cue ball to be when it makes contact with an object ball or cushion.

Pool Games that are played on a rectangular table with six pockets, a cue ball and several colored balls.

Poolography – The story of a poolplayer's life and times as they pertain to the game of pool.

Position Where the cue ball is located in relation to the next shot.

Proposition Shot Offering a wager on an unusual and/or very difficult shot that the person offering the wager knows very well.

Punch Stroke A type of stroke that resemble a short, quick jab.

Pure Stroke A very fine stroking action where the tip makes perfect contact with the cue ball.

Push Shot An illegal shot in which the cue maintains contact with the cue ball for a fraction of a second longer than on a normal shot. This results in multiple hits on the cue ball. Push shots usually occur when the cue ball is very close to or frozen with an object ball.

Quick Jab A short, punch like stroke.

R

Rack 1) A triangular shaped object that is normally used to put the balls in place at the start of a game. 2) A device that is used to help in the set up of certain trick shots or as a prop during the shot.

Rail The raised surface that surrounds the playing surface. It includes the cushions.

Rail Bridge A bridge that's formed by placing the bridge hand on the rail. The cue is normally under the hand between the index finger and middle finger.

Rail Shot When the cue ball is frozen to the cushion or is very close to it.

Rake (See mechanical bridge).

Regulation Sized Table A 4 1/2' x 9' sized table. This is a professional size. Any table in which the playing surface is twice as long as it is wide is also considered regulation.

Reverse English Sidespin that causes the cue ball to rebound off the cushion at a sharper angle than the approach angle.

Reversing Direction Spin on the cue ball that alters the cue ball's path.

Riding the Cheese A forceful shot at a money ball that is largely dependent on luck to be successful. This is commonly use is Nine Ball.

Rock Slang for the cue ball.

Rocket Massé A type of massé shot in which the cue ball travels a long distance at a high rate of speed.

Roll Off When an irregularity in the table or a not perfectly level playing surface causes a slow moving object ball to roll off line.

Rotation 1) Spin on the cue ball. 2) When the ball are pocketed in numerical order.

Running English English that opens up the rebound angle.

S

Scratch When the cue ball disappears into any of the six pockets.

Scratch Shot A shot in which a scratch is very likely or is unavoidable.

Set Up Rating Mike's rating for the difficulty of setting up a trick shot.

Setup Shot – A trick shot in which success or failure depends primarily on placing the balls in the correct positions on the table.

Sideboards When a ball that is near a pocket makes a shot play much easier.

Side Rail The rails that run along the length of the table.

Sidespin A clockwise or counterclockwise spin on that cue ball that results from applying english.

Shape (See position).

Short A bank shot that misses on the near side of the pocket. When the cue ball fails to reach the intended location for good position.

Slate The hard playing surface that rests under the cloth.

Slip Stroke A uncommon gripping technique in which the player, during their final stroke, slides their grip hand back on the cue and regrips it several inches back of its original position. This normally comes from a very loose grip and it is a natural occurrence.

Snatch See draw shot.

Snooker 1) When the cue ball is behind a blocker. 2) A game similar to pool only played on a table with smaller pockets and smaller balls. Snooker tables are usually 5' x 10' or 6' x 12'.

Snookered When the cue ball rests behind a ball which blocks a direct hit on the designated ball.

Stance The position that you take for a shot.

Straight In Refers to a shot where the cue ball and object ball are lined up directly at the pocket.

Snow Slang for the cue ball.

Solids Balls numbered one through seven.

Speed The force with which a shot has been played.

Speed Control The ability to control the cue ball's rolling distance. Good speed control is essential for playing good position.

Speed of Stroke The speed that you apply to the cue ball with your cue.

Spin Your Rock Applying English to the cue ball.

Spot A location on the table. The foot spot and the head spot.

Spot Up Placing a ball on the foot spot. Usually it occurs after a money ball has been pocketed and a foul had been committed.

Squirt (See deflection).

Stick It Stopping the cue ball dead in its tracks upon contact with the object ball.

Stone Slang for the cue ball.

Stop Shot (See stick it).

Stripes Balls numbered nine through fifteen.

Stroke The swing of the arm, wrist and hand that propels the cue through the cue ball.

Sweat Watching a trick shot artist play their trade, or someone play a shot in any game. A player might say, "Sweat this shot."

Sweater A person who is watching a pool game.

T

Table Roll (See roll off).

Takes Well When english applied to the cue ball is creating the desired effect when the cue ball strikes the rail.

Tangent Line A line that runs at a 90-degree angle and through the center of two balls that are either frozen or extremely close to each other.

Target Zone An area where you would like the cue ball to come to rest.

Thin Hit A shot in which very little of the cue ball contacts the object ball.

Throw Friction between the object ball and cue ball that changes the path of the object ball. English can cause throw, as can contact.

Time Shot 1) A lucky shot in which the balls roll around the table in a series of collisions before the object ball is pocketed. 2) A skillful shot that requires perfect timing.

Tip The small round leather item that is attached to the ferrule. Also refers to how much English is used on a particular shot.

Topspin Spin on the cue ball that results from striking it above center. It can also arise due to friction even though the cue ball has been hit in the center or even, at times, below center.

Toy Slang for the cue ball.

Trap When the cue ball is in such a position that it looks like a successful shot is all but impossible.

Trick Shot A shot that is not normally encountered in regular pool games, but that has great entertainment value.

Trick Shot Artist A person who is especially adept at making trick and fancy shots.

Triangle Another term for the device used to rack the ball. The area in which the balls are racked.

Two Piece Cue A cue that has a joint in the middle and that comes apart.

V-W-Y

Vertical Massé Stroke Playing a massé shot with the cue at a 90 degree angle to the table.

Warm Up Strokes A series of movements of the arm, hand and wrist that prepares the shooter for the final stroke. Like a waggle in golf.

Whitey Slang for the cue ball.

Window A gap between two closely spaced balls which exposes the object ball to a direct hit

Wooden Rack The device used for racking the balls. Also used as a prop in trick shots.

Woofing See barking.

Yo-Yo Massé A massé shot in which the cue ball travels some distance down the table before reversing its direction and coming straight back

How to Hire Mike

Exhibitions and Clinics

I regularly travel throughout the world giving exhibitions and clinics to all levels of players. If you would like to arrange for an exhibition and/or clinic, please e-mail me at francinemassey@aol.com or write: **www.billiardspress.com**.

Pool School In Paradise

Every year I conduct a pool school along with Allison Fisher, Gerda Hofstatter, and Paul Potier. The five-day school is held in Vancouver, British Columbia. It is usually conducted in August or September and lasts for five days. During that time we almost live with our students. If you are interested in attending, visit our web site at: **www.poolschoolinparadise.com**

APA Tour

The American Poolplayers Associaton (APA) is now the largest pool league with over 200,000 members nationwide. I have done a lot of exhibitions for the APA. So if you want to see my show live, you can contact the APA league operator in your area to see when I might be coming there. The best time to catch me in either Boston or Connecticut is around the middle of December.
www.poolplayers.com.

Mike's Trick Shot Videos

These videos are the perfect companions to this book. All 57 shots in the two videos also appear in the book.

Trick Shots Volume One – 26 shots – App. 1 hour
Instructional On Set Up Trick Shots
Trick Shots Volume Two – 31 shots – App. 1 hour
Instructional For Artistic Shots, Finger Pool and More

Artistic Pool

Although trick shots and Artistic Pool have been thought by many to be one in the same, Artistic Pool really should be considered to be a distant cousin to trick shots. There are no automatic set up shots in Artistic Pool. The majority of shots played in Artistic Pool demand at least a moderate to high level of skill. In short, most of them take hours of practice before a player can achieve even a modest degree of consistency. What trick shots and Artistic Pool share in common is that each offers some completely gorgeous and outrageous shots, the kind that leave spectators' jaws dropping, and the kind that are virtually never seen in regular pool games. For a complete listing of the Artistic Pool shots in this book, see pages 250-252.

There are more opportunities for those seeking to compete in Artistic Pool than ever before. A world championship has been contested since 2000 and there are numerous other events as well. To learn more about artistic pool visit:

www.artisticpool.org
www.mikemassey.com
www.billiardspress.com/trickshots.html

Books and Tapes on Trick Shots

There are numerous other fine books and videos on trick shots and artistic pool. Below is a partial listing of some that I feel I well worth your attention.

Books

Byrne's Treasury of Trick Shots in Pool and Billiards - Robert Byrne
0- 15-614973-7 293 pages - Harcourt Brace Jovanovich – 1982 -

The Pool Hustler's Handbook - Chef Anton
ISBN – 0-9716026-0-3 $14.95 128 pages - Tricks of the Trade, Inc.

Tricks and Games on the Pool Table - Fred Hermann
ISBN – 0-486-21814-7 95 pages - Dover

Willie Jopling's Book on Pocket Billiards - Willie Jopling

Winning Pool and Trick Shots - Nick Varner   - 141 pages

Videos & CD-ROM

Byrne's Standard Videos of Trick Shots – Robert Byrne - 2 videos

Magical Menu of Pool Ball Wizardry – Chef Anton
Accu-Stats Video Productions - 50 Minutes

Artistic Pool Manual - Rick Malm - A CR-ROM on artistic shots.

Mind-Boggling Trick Shots – Yoshikazu Kimura   45 minutes

Billiardspress.com

Billiardspress.com is the companion web site to Billiards Press. The site is packed with features that should be of interest to the pool enthusiast. Below is a partial listing of what you can find at the site.

Home Page – Late breaking stories and polls.

Books – Compete information on instructional books by Phil Capelle. Includes testimonials, book briefs, and complete table of contents.

Instruction – Feature articles, A Mind For Pool, recommended instructors.

Video + Book – Information on *Capelle on 9-Ball, Archer vs. Reyes.*

Massey's World – Information on Mike Massey's World of Trick Shot, Artistic Pool and much more.

The Pool Room – Discussions on League Pool, Tournament Pool, etiquette, and the rules.

New & Views – Stories on poolplayers and opinions and discussions on matters of importance regarding the sport.

Pro Report – Post tournament coverage of selected events.

Research – Included are The 500 Game Study, current feature, Archer vs. Reyes, and Capelle's Discoveries.

About Us – Profile of Phil Capelle, Billiards Press, and why I love pool.

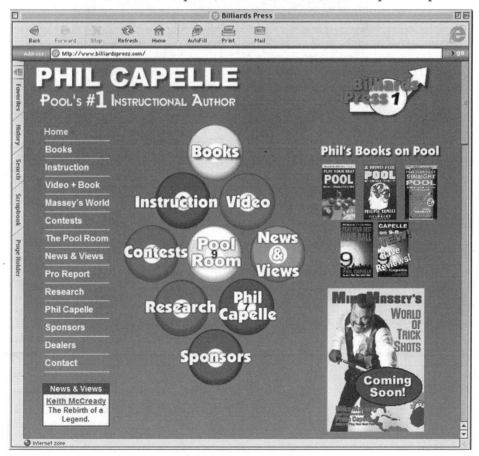

Instructional Books by Philip Capelle

Photo by Lara Rossignol

Author of 6 Instructional Books on Pool
Columnist for *Pool & Billiard Magazine*

Phil Capelle

I've been continuously involved in pool in several capacities since I took up the game in early 1969. In 1995 I founded Billiards Press with the goal of providing students of the game with the finest instructional books on pool. *Play Your Best Pool* was published in late 1995. Since then I have written five more books and other projects are in the planning stages. I enjoyed working with Mike Massey on *Mike Massey's World of Trick Shots* and truly hope that the book will go a long ways towards promoting our great sport.

I continue to learn new things every day about this fascinating and challenging game of pool. In the years ahead, I look forward to sharing my findings with you, and I hope they help you to enjoy pool even more.

Play Your Best Pool

Your Complete Textbook on Pool
0-9649204-0-9

$29.95 U.S. - **464** pages
For Players of All Levels
Contents:
- Fundamentals • Shotmaking
- How to Use English
- Position Play • Eight Ball • Nine Ball
- The Mental Game • Competitive Play
- How to Improve • Practicing Pool
- How to Buy Equipment • Appendix

Over 400 Illustrations

A Mind For Pool

How To Master the Mental Game
0-9649204-1-7

$19.95 U.S. - 320 pages
Contents:
Part One: Your Game
Part Two: Competition
Part Three: The Journey
- 120 lessons on the mental game
- 80 lists for evaluating your game
- 295 Laws for Pool
- Over 500 great quotes
- Appendix

Play Your Best Straight Pool

A Complete Course on 14.1
Features a New Player's Guide
0-9649204-2-5

$24.95 U.S. - 416 pages
Contents:
- Position Play • Pattern Play • Secondary
Break Shots • Cluster Management • Break Shots
- How to Run a Rack • Safety Play • Strategy
- Shotmaking • Learning to Play Straight Pool
- All About High Runs • Appendix

355 Illustrations

Play Your Best Nine Ball

Your Complete Guide to Nine Ball

0-9649204-3-3

$29.95 U.S. 480 Pages

Contents:

- Shotmaking
- The Break
- Position Routes
- Fine Points of Position
- Principles of Position
- Pattern Play
- How to Run Out
- Cluster Management
- Reading the Table
- Push Out Strategy
- Safety Play
- Kick Shots
- The ABC's of
- Strategy
- Competitive Nine Ball
- Practicing Nine Ball
- Appendix

470 Illustrations

Capelle on 9-Ball - Archer vs. Reyes

A companion guide to the video of a pro match.
A landmark study on pro pool.

0-9649204-4-1 200 Pages 2 Hours 15 Minutes

Book/VHS $43.95 U.S.

Book/DVD $49.95 U.S.

The Book

Part I – The Match

Capelle takes you shot-by-shot through the match.
Key shot are diagrammed – all perfectly to scale.
100+ lessons for your game

Part II – The Pro Method

Discover how the professionals use their time.
Archer and Reyes: a contrast in styles.

The Video

Part I – The Match

Archer and Reyes fight for survival at the Sands 23.
Over a dozen superb runouts.
Learn from Bill Incardona's commentary.

Part II – Lessons from the Pros

25 shots analyzed in detail by Phil Capelle.
Extensive use of special effects.
Alternative shot selection for amateurs.

To order direct, call 888-295-7665 or 714-894-1157

Visit us on the web at billiardspress.com

Dealer Inquires Welcomed